A Devil's Vaudeville

Northwestern University Press
Studies in Russian Literature and Theory

Series Editors
Robert Belknap
Caryl Emerson
Gary Saul Morson
William Mills Todd III
Andrew Wachtel

A Devil's Vaudeville

THE DEMONIC IN DOSTOEVSKY'S MAJOR FICTION

W. J. Leatherbarrow

NORTHWESTERN UNIVERSITY PRESS / EVANSTON, ILLINOIS

Northwestern University Press
Evanston, Illinois 60208-4170

Printed in the United States of America

10 9 8 7 6 5 4 3 2 1

ISBN 0-8101-2049-6

Library of Congress Cataloging-in-Publication Data

Leatherbarrow, William J.
A devil's vaudeville : the demonic in Dostoevsky's major fiction / W. J.
Leatherbarrow.
    p.   cm. — (Studies in Russian literature and theory)
  Includes bibliographical references and index.
  ISBN 0-8101-2049-6 (cloth : alk. paper)
  1. Dostoyevsky, Fyodor, 1821–1881—Criticism and interpretation.   2. Devil in
literature.   3. Demonology in literature.   I. Title.   II. Series.
PG3328.Z7D485 2005
891.73'3—dc22   2004029865

In memory of
Leslie Walter Burton
(1922–2001)

Contents

Acknowledgments

This monograph began life in 1996 as an invitation to contribute an essay on Dostoevsky to a proposed volume on demonism in Russian literature. The invitation and the proposal came from Dr. Pamela Davidson, of the University of London, and I am extremely grateful to her for pointing me in the direction of a topic that has engaged my interest ever since. The volume she had in mind has recently been published, under Dr. Davidson's editorship, as *Russian Literature and Its Demons* (New York and Oxford: Berghahn Books, 2000), and my contribution to it forms the basis of Chapter 4 of the present volume.

My further work on this volume was made possible by the understanding of my colleagues in the Department of Russian and Slavonic Studies at the University of Sheffield, England, and I am grateful to them not only for that, but also for the unfailingly stimulating intellectual environment they have provided to me over many years.

The timely completion of the work was made possible by a research leave granted by the University of Sheffield. I would also like to acknowledge the vital support of the Arts and Humanities Research Board, which granted me an award under the research leave scheme in the spring semester of 2001, one that allowed me to work uninterrupted on the final stages of the book.

Note on Transliteration and Sources

Transliteration of Russian in the main body of the present volume follows a modified Library of Congress system designed to make the text more readable to a general audience. In particular, first and last names ending in -*ii* have been changed to -*y*, and awkward -*iia* endings have been changed to -*ia*. Also, the letters *Ia*- and *Iu*- at the beginning of names have been changed to *Ya*- and *Yu*-, respectively. Where a standard English form for a name exists, this has been retained. Bibliographical references retain the transliteration system used in the titles cited, and Russian names and titles in the notes and bibliography are transliterated according to the unmodified Library of Congress system, but without diacritics.

References to Dostoevsky's works throughout this book appear in parentheses in the text and are by volume and page number (e.g. XIV, 255) to F. M. Dostoevskii, *Polnoe sobranie sochinenii v tridtsati tomakh* (Leningrad: Nauka, 1972–90), often referred to as the Academy edition. Where the publishers have divided a volume into two separately bound parts, an additional number appears after the volume number (e.g. XXIX/1, 375). Unless otherwise stated all translations from the Russian are by the author.

A Devil's Vaudeville

Sourcing the Demonic

IN DOSTOEVSKY'S FIRST work of fiction, the novel in letters *Poor Folk* (1846), there is a passage where the middle-aged hero, Makar Devushkin, describes the reaction of neighbors to his sentimental friendship with the much younger heroine, Varvara Dobroselova. The passage is from Devushkin's letter to Varvara, dated August 1: "Everyone in our lodging house knows every last detail and they point their fingers at your window; I know that they point. And when I went to have dinner with you yesterday, they all shoved their heads out the windows, and the landlady told me people are saying that the devil [*chert*] has taken up with an infant, and then she called you by an indecent name" (I, 70). Devushkin's besotted enchantment with the rather self-seeking and far from innocent Varvara leads him to assume that it is he who is seen as the predator, and this blinds him to the delicious irony of the landlady's remark; but the implicit frame of this apparently "frameless" exchange of letters allows the author and reader to collude behind the hero's back and to wonder who indeed the devil is and who the infant, particularly given the virginal implications of Devushkin's name (*devushka:* maiden) and the way Varvara subsequently exploits his devotion.[1]

This is arguably the first significant mention of the devil in Dostoevsky's fiction, and it is entirely appropriate that it should occur in a context where it serves a highly suggestive, ironic, and above all ambiguous function. The inscription of the demonic in Dostoevsky's fiction from this point on is a complex phenomenon, rarely straightforward, and most often designed to establish and exploit uncertainty and ambiguity, both in what might simplistically be called narrative *content* (for example, plot development, characterization, and ideological meaning) and in narrative *form* (for example, the nature of the relationship between the narrator and his narrative and the trustworthiness of his stance). Such ambiguity in the appropriation of demonic motifs no doubt partly reflects the nature of the "Father of Lies" himself and his traditional role as dissembler, deceiver, and tempter, but it is also a reflection of the diversity of cultural sources from which Dostoevsky derived both his understanding of what the demonic means (his demonology) and the physical forms or phenomena in which devils are depicted and through which the presence of the demonic may be mediated (and here one might coin the matching term "demonography"). This introductory chapter seeks to explore in general terms how the demonic was depicted, how its presence was signaled, and what that presence suggested in the three major sources from which Dostoevsky appears to have drawn material for the inscription of the demonic into his own art: first, the Russian folk tradition; second, Christian, in particular Russian Orthodox, "demonology"; and, third, the appropriation of the demon figure by European Romanticism and its reconfiguration in Russian literature during the first few decades of the nineteenth century. This introduction also explores the significance of the demonic for Dostoevsky's aesthetic views and practices: first as a consequence of his elaboration of an aesthetic system in which the aesthetic and ethical categories were not clearly separable, so that concepts of good and evil were contaminated by those of beauty and ugliness; and second by his apparent acknowledgment of the widespread view in Christian culture that secular art itself might be demonic. Subsequent chapters trace in detail how the demonologies and demonographies thus sourced fed into Dostoevsky's own use of the demonic and how his views of the relationship between art and demonism helped determine the narrative strategies employed in the production of his major fiction.

THE DEVIL IN RUSSIAN FOLKLORE

Several scholars, both Russian and Western, have made clear to what extent Dostoevsky was aware of and affected by the traditions, beliefs, practices, and language of the ordinary Russian folk (the *narod*).[2] As a child he listened to fairy tales told by his nanny Alena Frolovna, whom he remembered fondly in his later years; his brother Andrei Mikhailovich recalled how the Dostoevsky children delighted in folk tales recounted by former wet nurses on later visits to the household[3]; family members took the children to popular entertainments,[4] and Dostoevsky himself later recalled the impact on him of the Russian puppet theater (XXII, 180). The Dostoevsky family's relatively low social standing, when compared with that of other Russian writers such as Tolstoi and Turgenev, also increased their familiarity with ordinary Russians, and in "The Peasant Marei," an episode recounted in his *Diary of a Writer* for 1876, Dostoevsky recalls the help of a peasant who consoled him when he was frightened in the woods as a child. Such childhood familiarity with the world of the Russian peasant was, of course, greatly amplified during Dostoevsky's years of Siberian imprisonment and penal servitude. His fictionalized account of those years in *Notes from the House of the Dead* (1860–62) makes clear not only the extent to which the outlook of the Russian *narod* substantiated his own emerging views on the sanctity of native Russian culture, but also the extent to which popular imagery and culture entered his own discourse (to the extent, for example, that he kept a "Siberian Notebook" of popular sayings [IV, 235–48]). In arguing that as a result of such encounters with native Russian folk tradition Dostoevsky's subsequent work was "profoundly folklorized," Faith Wigzell draws attention to the fact that the production of his major novels coincided with a period when Russian oral culture was appearing in print in large quantities.[5] This is true, and no doubt the profusion of such material fed into Dostoevsky's fiction, but we need to recognize that this material, including folk beliefs about the devil, was systematically collected by *educated* Russians, and it is difficult to assess the extent to which this process of mediation might have contaminated original belief. The same is true of the undoubted influence that the works of Nikolai Gogol had on Dostoevsky and his own approach to art. Gogol's early Ukrainian tales in the collections *Evenings on a Farm Near Dikanka* (1831–32) and *Mirgorod* (1835) were constructed out of Ukrainian folk belief, and they contain many references to demons and supernatural evil. Again, we need to bear in mind, when we consider the appropriation of folk belief in Dostoevsky's own fictional inscriptions of the demonic, the extent to which such beliefs might have entered his fiction not directly, but as mediated through Gogol's work, where they were no doubt contaminated by other traditions of depicting the demonic. But this is a problem affecting mainly Dostoevsky's early "Gogolian" works and as such is largely beyond the remit of the present study.[6]

Apart from the difficulty of accessing unmediated folk beliefs held in Dostoevsky's time, the problem of establishing a secure "demonography" of the Russian folk devil is further compounded by regional variation in his popular representation, as well as by the fact that in Russian folk belief as a whole the devil is only one among a gallery of figures who embody aspects of what Russians call the "unclean force" (*nechistaia sila*), the supernatural "other world" (*tot mir*) of evil forces hostile to the world of man. In a recent essay on the Russian folk devil, Wigzell further argues that, apart from regional variations, popular beliefs and representations of the devil were also subject to evolution over time and the tendency to vary according to the oral genre in which they occurred, producing, for example, a prankster in a humorous folk tale, but a much more terrifying figure in a popular ghost story (*bylichka*).[7] Moreover, the emergence of the devil as a part of Russian folk belief in the "unclean force" was in itself a form of contamination, a consequence of the Christianization of Russia, and his appearance in popular culture represented, as Simon Franklin puts it, "a kind of colonization of paganisms by Christian discourse."[8] The devil in Russian folklore was, therefore, essentially a Christianized cuckoo in a pagan nest, and he lacked the prominence, the proud individuality, the majesty and the philosophical significance of the ironic fallen angel at odds with the divine order associated with the post-Miltonian Western European typology of Satan. As Linda J. Ivanits observes, Russian folk culture "lacked demonological notions," in the sense of a "highly developed [. . .] system of beliefs based on a philosophical understanding of the devil's role," well into the nineteenth century.[9] As a consequence, Russian folk tradition favors the typology of the "petty demon" (*melkii bes*): "Popular imagination distinguished between *the* devil, or Satan, and the hosts of minor demons serving him. It is the latter that appear in countless tales, legends, fabulates, and memorates relating to the devil's activities in the everyday life of the peasant. Here Satan appears only occasionally and dimly."[10] This typology feeds into Russian literature of the nineteenth century via the work of Gogol, who favored a view of the devil as a shabby manipulator ensnaring human souls not through promises and pacts of Promethean grandeur, but through the mire of pettiness (*poshlost'*) that distracted man's gaze from all that was worthwhile in life and all that rendered him human. It subsequently culminated in Fedor Sologub's novel *The Petty Demon* (1907), where evil loses all pretensions to transcendence, while the image of a shabby, largely inert, and distinctly second-rate devil emerges most memorably in Dostoevsky's fiction in the figure of Ivan Karamazov's devil.

Despite this tendency to assume the guise of a sort of supernatural used car dealer, the devil in Russian folklore possesses a capacity for evil that the peasant did not underestimate, and that we should not either. The "unclean force" of which this devil was a part, and the "other world" he inhabited, represented an objectively existing reality that was opposed to man's in the cosmology of the Russian *narod;* they were not merely outward projections of a psychological evil existing subjectively in human nature, a function that the devil later assumed in Russian Romantic literature. The Russian semioticians Yuri Lotman and Boris Uspensky suggest an explanation for this dualistic cosmology in what they consider to be the historical tendency of Russian culture to organize itself in binary oppositions: "The basic cultural values (ideological, political, religious) in the system of medieval Russia are arranged in a bipolar value field divided by a sharp line and without any neutral axiological zone."[11] Such absence of a neutral value field between opposing extremes, if true, would indeed encourage the view that what is not of this world and created by God must therefore be the "other world" and be the domain of evil spirits. Moreover, in pre-Christian belief, that "other world" was an inversion or mirror image of this world, where "right," in both its directional and moral connotations (a double meaning also embraced by the Russian word *pravyi*), becomes left or "sinister." The importance of inversion is reflected widely in Russian folk belief, where mirrors were potential gateways into (and from) the "other world,"[12] where the left was the devil's side,[13] and where one way to detect the devil was to look at the world upside down and through one's legs.[14]

As we have seen, the "unclean force" embraced not only the devil, but various other spirits. The most commonly encountered of these in folk literature are the *leshii* (wood demon), the *bannik* (bathhouse spirit), the *vodianoi chert* (water demon), the *rusalka* (mermaid, or water maid), and the *domovoi* (house sprite), although there are many others.[15] What they have in common is their association with a particular place, although individual characteristics vary from spirit to spirit. The *leshii* inhabits woods and forests, where he carries off young girls, whom he sometimes marries, and lures unwary travelers into ravines. He is sometimes identifiable by the fact that he wears his kaftan buttoned the wrong way (left over right) and has his shoes on the wrong feet—again attesting to the importance of inversions in popular belief. Similarly, the *vodianoi chert* inhabited stretches of water and lured people to their deaths by drowning. Indeed, drowned corpses and places where drownings had occurred were regarded as "unclean" in popular lore. The *rusalka* herself was held to be the soul of a drowned maiden or child, determined to lure men to their deaths. Particularly interesting and malign was the *bannik*, the spirit of the bathhouse, which was held to be a place where the peasant was exceptionally vulnerable to evil forces because in it he removed his cross and belt, both regarded as protection against the unclean force. Lotman and Uspensky suggest that the persistence of the view that the bathhouse is a sinister, unholy place might derive from the fact that in pre-Christian times such places, along with barns and forges, often served as clan or family temples and thus possessed a sacred pagan significance.[16] Moreover, a predilection for the bathhouse in preference to attending church was popularly seen as a sign that a person was a sorcerer (*koldun*), and it was precisely such behavior that "revealed" the tsar-pretender Grishka Otrepev as antichrist during the Russian dynastic crisis of the seventeenth century.[17] Superstition held that the soft touch of the *bannik* foretold good fortune, while his cold, prickly touch betokened misfortune (despite all this, the bathhouse [*bania*] was traditionally a favorite place for peasant women to give birth, provided that precautions were taken to protect the soul of the newborn child). Although these spirits were generally malign and had to be avoided or placated, the *domovoi* was a generally benevolent spirit-protector of the household, usually held to be the soul of a dead ancestor or former head of the family. Ivanits, however, points out that by the end of the nineteenth century the *domovoi* was increasingly held to be unclean and associated with the devil.[18]

In popular belief, devils were distinct from these nature spirits in two main ways. First, rather than being attached to specific places in the peasant's world, they were from hell, from which base they launched their malignant assaults on the unlucky inhabitants of this world. We shall discuss in due course the mechanisms by which such movements between the nether and upper worlds became possible. Second, whereas the relationship of man to malign nature spirits retained some element of ambiguity, in that such spirits could be placated, even harnessed to the peasant's own designs, no such ambiguity attached to the devil and his behavior. As Ivanits succinctly suggests, "The devil's most outstanding characteristic was his total hostility toward man. The devil existed for the sole purpose of inflicting harm and prompting evil deeds."[19] Duplicity, deceit, and ambiguity were the devil's key weapons, and his general evasiveness is reflected in the many terms by which he was known in Russian folklore, the most common of which included *chert, bes, d'iavol, demon,* and *satana.* Attempts have been made to assign some sort of hierarchy to these terms, and such a hierarchy arguably emerges in later literary depictions of the devil, but it is probably right to say that in common usage the terms were often interchangeable.[20] It was considered unsafe to mention the devil by name, for fear that this would summon his presence. As a result, what Wigzell calls "taboo names," such as "he" (*on*) or "that one" (*tot*), were used to refer obliquely to devils (and indeed to other manifestations of the unclean force).[21] The implication was that words have the incantatory power to make evil manifest, and this will be significant for our later discussion of the relationship between the demonic and secular narrative. This implication is relevant as well to those occasions in Dostoevsky's fiction when characters employ such apparently innocent verbal formulae as "The devil take it!" (*Chert voz'mi!*) or "Go to the devil!" (*K chertu!*). Conversely, a measure of protection from evil was afforded by making the sign of the cross, popularly believed to immobilize devils and clearly drawn from Christian tradition, or by drawing a circle. Felix J. Oinas has highlighted the importance of the magic circle in folk belief about the devil. He argues that *chert,* the most commonly used term to denote the devil in Russian, is derived from the word family that includes *cherta* ("line" or "limit"), as well as the verb *chertit'* ("to draw"), and that this denotes an origin in the pagan ritual of drawing a circle to protect oneself from demonic forces: "Once the magic circle has been drawn, anybody inside it will supposedly be unable to get out and anyone outside will be unable to get in."[22]

Having outlined in this way the main typological characteristics of the devil and other malign spirits within the unclean force as conceived by the Russian peasant, let us now try to identify a *semiotics* of evil within that same belief system, that is, the signs through which that unclean force and its agents manifest their presence. Popular belief throws up a rich array of such semiotic markers that we need to acknowledge, for many of them find their way more or less unchanged into the world of Dostoevsky's fiction, where they vie, in their role of signaling the agency of the demonic, with markers derived from other belief systems or cultural models. The most obvious of these markers are to be found in the guises traditionally assumed by the devil in Russian folk belief, in addition to his conventional "uniform" of horns, tail, cloven feet, and abundant bodily hair. The most common of such forms are animate creatures, and the devil may appear to the unwary in the guise of black cats, dogs, wolves, pigs, snakes, magpies, flies. and even such apparently benign forms as horses, hares, squirrels, mice, and so on. However, the inanimate world cannot be trusted either, and objects such as balls of thread, stones, heaps of straw; places such as swamps, pools or lakes, or where treasure was buried; as well as natural phenomena such as snowstorms and windstorms also betrayed the presence of the unclean force.[23] The belief that the devil was from another world translated easily into his identity as a foreigner, with the result that he was often referred to as a "guest" or "visitor." Moreover, reflecting no doubt the influence of Byzantine Orthodoxy, where the devil was often an Ethiopian, Arab, or Turk, he was often presented in Russian popular belief as black, and the word *murin* (moor) became a euphemistic or taboo name for the devil.[24]

By far the richest source of demonic pickings in popular belief is to be found in places, times, or situations that can broadly be described as being "threshold" or "liminal" (Latin *limen,* "threshold"), an area that impacts deeply the way Dostoevsky conjures the demonic in his fiction. As an embodiment of the concept of transition from one space, state, or time to another, the "threshold" in whatever form was seen as an ideal conduit that allowed devils to pass from the "other world" into this one and as such represented a particularly dangerous concentration of the unclean force. Holes in the earth were particularly obvious liminal phenomena, but in popular lore the concept was extended to include other apertures, such as open doors and even open mouths, so that yawning became an activity fraught with the danger that the devil might seize the opportunity thus presented to enter one's soul. As might be expected, the actual threshold of a building was seen as a place where the unclean force might be strong, and even today Russians hold it to be unlucky to extend a greeting or accept anything over the threshold, or to stand in a doorway.[25] Other examples of liminal spaces where it was dangerous to loiter included crossroads, ravines, roadsides, edges of fields, village–country boundaries, and cemeteries (the last offering the particularly fearful combination of holes in the earth and connotations of transition from this world to another). Mirrors also possessed liminal significance in that they represented a potentially demonic boundary between this world and a "sinister" world of inverted reflections. Liminal states included birth and death, moving house, and marriage, and it was considered a wise precaution to invite known sorcerers to a place of honor at the wedding table in order to placate the unclean force at a particularly vulnerable moment.[26] Danger was also great at liminal times such as mid-summer, midwinter, the equinoxes, dawn, midday, and midnight.[27] My analysis of Dostoevsky's works below will reveal the extent to which he exploited the demonic potential of the threshold motif, but we might recall for the moment the entrance of Svidrigailov in *Crime and Punishment,* when he "steps across" the threshold of Raskolnikov's room and thereafter assumes the role of his demonic alter ego; or the events that befall Ordynov in *The Landlady* when he decides to move house and subsequently falls under the spell of the "sorcerer" Ilia Murin (note the name!) and the enchantress Katerina; or Goliadkin's preoccupation with his reflection in the mirror at the start of *The Double,* shortly before the appearance of his malevolent double.

What he terms the "chronotope" of the threshold is an important component of Mikhail Bakhtin's analysis of dialogism and carnivalization in the novel, an analysis with profound impact on our understanding of Dostoevsky's novels. Bakhtin coined the term "chronotope" to denote a definitive point in a narrative, when its temporal and spatial dimensions intersect and fuse, emphasizing their mutual interdependence and producing a "moment" that transcends normal "biographical" time. Chronotopes are thus "the organizing centers for the fundamental narrative events of the novel. The chronotope is the place where the knots of narrative are tied and untied. It can be said without qualification that to them belongs the meaning that shapes narrative."[28] The "polyphonic" novel, as practiced by Dostoevsky, which refuses to privilege the author's voice and where all discourse is thus dialogized and unfinalized, narrates a world that is forever in process, forever on the "threshold" of transition to some other stage, and Bakhtin demonstrates how the Dostoevskian novel is structured on threshold situations that form "the fundamental 'points' of action in the novel," usually instantiating crises and breaks in a life.[29] Later in this book we use an analysis of *Crime and Punishment* in particular to show how the threshold chronotope in Dostoevsky is infused with folkloric significance, in order to signal not only crises, but demonic eruptions.

Bakhtin's careful demonstration of the function within Dostoevsky's works of forms drawn from popular carnival and carnivalized literature is also highly significant for our purposes, for carnival by its very nature exploits to the full the possibilities of liminality. Not only does carnival time represent a transition from one set of hierarchies and rules to another, where the fool can masquerade as king, where normal social relationships and behavior are suspended or inverted, and where moral and social principles are relativized and subjected to destruction and renewal, but the very *form* of carnival exploits and renders ambiguous the threshold between spectacle and audience. Carnival, argues Bakhtin:

> does not, generally speaking, belong to the sphere of art. It belongs to the borderline between art and life. [. . .] In fact, carnival does not know footlights, in the sense that it does not acknowledge any distinction between actors and spectators. Footlights would destroy a carnival, as the absence of footlights would destroy a theatrical performance. Carnival is not a spectacle seen by the people; they live in it, and everyone participates because its very idea embraces all the people. While carnival lasts, there is no other life outside it.[30]

We shall defer further discussion of carnival and its demonic potential until our analysis of *The Devils*, perhaps the most obviously carnivalized of all Dostoevsky's works. But before moving on we should consider Bakhtin's views on two essential aspects of carnival—the wearing of masks and the function of laughter—and compare those views to those held in Russian folk tradition, where they carry a powerfully demonic semiotic charge. In its very essence, of course, the mask is charged with liminal significance, irrespective of its function in any given circumstance, in that it represents the threshold between two identities. Bakhtin draws a distinction between the mask in its popular function within folk culture and the mask as it was appropriated by Romantic art. Arguing that the theme of the mask is "the most complex theme of folk culture," he goes on to define its function thus:

> The mask is connected with the joy of change and reincarnation, with gay relativity and with the merry negation of uniformity and similarity; it rejects conformity to oneself. The mask is related to transition, metamorphoses, the violation of natural boundaries, to mockery and familiar nicknames. It contains the playful element of life; it is based on a peculiar interrelation of reality and image, characteristic of the most ancient rituals and spectacles.

Moreover, in this popular, carnival form the mask gives rise to more complex and grotesque derivations, such as parody, caricature, the grimace, eccentric postures, and comic gestures. In its Romantic form, however, the mask acquired a wholly new function and meaning "alien to its primitive nature": "now the mask hides something, keeps a secret, deceives. [. . .] The romantic mask loses almost entirely its regenerating and renewing element and acquires a somber hue. A terrible vacuum, a nothingness lurks behind it."[31] We shall see later the extent to which Dostoevsky avails himself of the symbolism of the mask, particularly in its Romantic form, but we should note for now that Bakhtin's awareness of a disjunction between its popular and Romantic forms is founded on his assumption that carnival is essentially a renewing and regenerating phenomenon, characterized above all by a "gay relativity" (*veselaia otnositel'nost'*). It was precisely this positive element in carnival that encouraged authorities to license it as a form of public safety valve that allowed the people to let off steam and thus discharge harmlessly in role-play and laughter any desires to overturn the existing order. Such a view, however, seriously under-emphasizes the darker, demonic significance attached in Russian folk tradition to masks, and for that matter to role-play and laughter. As W. F. Ryan claims, "to Russians masks were associated primarily with pagan, usually midwinter, rituals which were regularly condemned by the Russian Church as satanic,"[32] and it is easy to see how in folk belief the liminal properties of the mask, along with its function to confuse, would fit well with the deceitful role of the "Father of Lies." The same holds for the practice of role-play, for in Russian popular belief the "pretender" acquired distinctly unholy significance, largely as a consequence of events in Russian cultural and historical tradition. This is an idea to which we shall return when considering the function of role-play and imposture in *The Devils*, where it contributes significantly to that novel's demonic semiotics.

For Bakhtin the ritual laughter that attended carnival was liberating and, like carnival itself, gave expression to "a mighty life-creating and transforming power, an indestructible vitality."[33] It debunked established institutions and released the participant from the pressures of normal hierarchical structures. Lotman and Uspensky, however, have pointed out that in medieval Russia laughter possessed a demonic and blasphemous significance that went beyond a merely liberating function. In their essay "New Aspects in the Study of Early Russian Culture" they write:

> Russian medieval Orthodox culture is organized around the opposition holiness vs. Satanism. Holiness excludes laughter (cf.: "Christ never laughed"—[a saying from Saint John Chrysostom]). [. . .] Thus holiness allows both ascetic severity and a pious smile, but it excludes laughter. [. . .] The Devil (and the whole demonic world) is held to possess the features of "holiness inside out" and belongs to the inverted, "left-hand" (that is, "sinister") world. Therefore this world is blasphemous in its very essence, that is, it is not serious. This is a world that guffaws; it is no accident that the Devil may be called the "jester" (*shut*) in Russian. The kingdom of Satan is the place where sinners groan and gnash their teeth while the devils laugh.[34]

Lotman and Uspensky refer here specifically to medieval *Orthodox* culture but, as we shall see, the absorption of folk belief about the devil into Russian Orthodox demonology (and vice versa) means that it is neither possible nor desirable to seek a clear division of the two. In each, laughter is both liberating and dangerous, and the clearest external sign of the latter, impious form—according to Lotman and Uspensky—is that it is not contagious: "For those who are not in league with Satan, it is terrifying rather than comical." Such noncontagious laughter is endemic in *The Devils*, in particular, where it contributes a distinctly hysterical dimension to the novel's mood; but we shall also explore the role of destructive laughter as a demonic marker in several of Dostoevsky's other works.

If such laughter was held to be symptomatic of demonic possession, or of "spoiling" by the "evil eye" (*porcha; isportit' glazom*), as such effects were known, then so were other outward manifestations of what might be construed as hysteria. These included the phenomenon of "shrieking" (*klikushestvo*), a condition that affected women in particular and that took the form of dramatic and uncontrolled howling when confronted with events or objects of religious significance. *Klikushestvo* was a widespread phenomenon with perhaps tens of thousands of cases in Russia by the end of the nineteenth century, when it was first subjected to medical study.[35] Other nervous disorders, including epilepsy—a condition suffered by Dostoevsky himself— were also popularly attributed to demonic intervention or possession, as were forms of obsessive behavior, such as drunkenness and gambling. Readers of Dostoevsky's novels will have already recognized here several important semiotic markers that indicate demonic influence in a number of Dostoevsky's works. The phenomenon of *klikushestvo* appears in *The Brothers Karamazov;* epilepsy afflicts several of Dostoevsky's most significant characters, including Myshkin (*The Idiot*), Kirillov (*The Devils*), and Smerdiakov (*The Brothers Karamazov*); an early draft of what became *Crime and Punishment* was to address the problems of urban drunkenness, which theme survives in the final novel in the subplot of Marmeladov; and gambling is invested with transcendental significance in *The Gambler,* where the town of Roulettenberg becomes a sort of hell hole, sucking in the souls of Russian aristocratic gamblers who have lost touch with their native Russian values.

Certain physical defects were also associated in popular belief with the devil. The most widely acknowledged of these was lameness, a characteristic popularly attributed to Satan himself, the apparent consequence of his rather heavy fall from grace. The motif of lameness is frequently encountered in Dostoevsky's writings and is semiotically complex. Linda Ivanits has drawn attention to its association with the Russian folk devil in *The Brothers Karamazov*,[36] but the motif occurs in other novels, as well as in Dostoevsky's notebooks and newspaper articles, where it assumes a rich additional meaning through its oblique association with Romantic, as well as folk, demonology. The process of association pivots on the figure of Byron, whose works perhaps contributed more than any other literary model to establishing the typology of the demon in Russian Romantic literature. The cult of Byron that possessed Russian literature in the 1820s and 1830s was seen by Dostoevsky as symptomatic of the Russian educated public's alienation from true Orthodox Russian values, in favor of a demonic infatuation with Western European civilization, a civilization erected on false material values that were inimical to the genuine spirit of Russia. Byron and Byronism, preoccupied with disillusion and despair, were for Dostoevsky entirely natural manifestations of Western European cultural decline. As he wrote in his *Diary of a Writer* for December 1877, "Byronism, though a momentary phenomenon, was a great, sacred and necessary one in the life of European man" (XXVI, 113), one that gave voice to "the dreadful anguish, disillusionment and despair" that accompanied European cultural collapse in the age of revolution. European man, deceived by the bankruptcy of revolutionary idealism, slumped into despair and a destructive individualism, to which Byron's heroes gave expression:

> The old idols lay shattered. And it was at this very moment that a great and mighty genius appeared, a passionate poet. In his melodies there resounded the anguish of mankind in those days and its gloomy disillusionment with its mission and with the ideals by which it had been deceived. This was a new and hitherto unheard-of muse of vengeance and sorrow, of cursing and despair. The spirit of Byronism suddenly seemed to possess the whole of humanity, everything responded to it. (XXVI, 114)

Not even Russia could avoid this response, if only out of compassion for what Europe was passing through. But, according to Dostoevsky, Pushkin—whose temperament and writings outgrew the effects of Byron—had demonstrated that Byronism was essentially alien to Russian nature, the true reflection of which was to be found not among the Westernized elite, but in the ordinary Russian people:

> The greatness of Pushkin, as a presiding genius, consisted precisely in the fact that, despite being surrounded by people who almost completely failed to understand him, he so soon discovered a firm path, a *great and longed-for way out for us Russians, and he pointed it out.* This way out was the people, *worship of the truth of the Russian people.* (XXVI, 114)

The Russian educated public's worship of Byron, its assumption of his "values," and the incarnation of those values in the figure of the Romantic demon were thus essentially blasphemous. The demonic significance of Byron in his Russian context is signaled, perhaps unwittingly, by Dostoevsky in his repeated preoccupation with the fact that Byron was *lame.* In his working drafts for the *Diary of a Writer* for February 1876 he observed: "I am convinced (well, at least to a small extent) that had Byron not been lame, then perhaps he would not have written his *Cain* or *Childe Harold,* or rather he would have written them differently" (XXII, 184). The same observation, in more or less the same form and emphasizing the link between Byron's lameness and the nature of his art, is repeated throughout Dostoevsky's notebooks, on no fewer than five occasions.[37] The attribution of the mark of the devil to Byron thus encourages a thought-provoking link between the typology of the Russian folk devil and the demonology of Russian Romanticism, the significance of which for Dostoevsky's depiction of the demonic we examine later in this chapter.

Meanwhile, we must return to the Russian folk devil in order to identify one final aspect of his typology, one that possesses great resonance in Dostoevsky's art: the association of suicide with the activities of the unclean force. Suicide is a reasonably common motif in Dostoevsky's novels, where it is usually committed by characters associated in one way or another with moral bankruptcy, such as the sensual monster Svidrigailov (*Crime and Punishment*), the hopelessly westernized and nationally alienated Kirillov (*The Devils*), the languidly empty Byronist Stavrogin (*The Devils*), and the lackey-murderer Smerdiakov (*The Brothers Karamazov*). Dostoevsky's drafts for the denouement of *Crime and Punishment* entertain two possible resolutions of Raskolnikov's dilemma: to follow Svidrigailov down the road of self-destruction, or to accept the humility and faith of Sonia and find salvation in Christ. This stark choice between suicide and God, and the wholly negative charge thereby attached to the taking of one's own life, reflect the view held in the Christian church that suicide is a sign of ultimate ingratitude and a sin against God. But they also reflect how suicide was regarded in popular belief, where the devil was traditionally held responsible for the act and where suicides were often depicted as the devil's sheep, or as horses drawing the devil's cart. A failed suicide attempt would elicit the judgment that "the devil would not take" the victim.[38] Folk belief thus assigned suicides to the category of "unclean dead" or *zalozhnye pokoiniki,* a category that also included victims of drowning, premature deaths, sorcerers, witches, and other violent deaths. (The etymology and literal meaning of the term *zalozhnye pokoiniki* is not clear to me, although the adjective—usually meaning "pledged"—was also used to designate land laid aside as fallow. It could thus refer to the state of limbo occupied by such unclean dead.) It was believed that the earth would not accommodate such people, that they would rise from the grave or their bodies fail to decompose. In any case, they could not be buried in consecrated ground. The failure of a body to decompose was also popularly held to be a sign of heresy, although in Orthodox belief it suggested sanctity, an ambiguity that, as we shall see, Dostoevsky exploits after the death of Zosima in *The Brothers Karamazov.*[39]

THE DEVIL IN RUSSIAN ORTHODOX BELIEF

Those scholars who have compared the treatment of the devil in both folk and Orthodox demonology have generally argued against the desirability or, indeed, the possibility of disentangling the typology of the devil in the two traditions. W. F. Ryan, for example, writes: "the Devil, or devils, of the Bible and Christian literature, as visualized by medieval Christian writers and artists, were regularly identified with the spirits of Slavonic folklore."[40] Such syncretism, achieved by the absorption and toleration of paganism in the popular belief system of Christianized Russia, accounts for what is commonly referred to as the *dvoeverie,* or "dual belief," of the Russian peasant who is prepared to accommodate apparently heretical pagan values, such as belief in the redemptive power of "mother earth," within his view of himself as "Christian,"[41] and who, while praying to his Christian God for comfort, support, and salvation, is not averse to keeping up the payments on his pagan insurance policy by seeking to placate the spirits of the "unclean force." Such apparent duplicity is in fact explicable in terms of the binary model of Russian culture, constructed by Lotman and Uspensky and referred to earlier, according to which cultural change in Russia involves not only the acceptance of a new system of values, but also the need to inscribe the old values into the new, but now "with a negative sign."[42] This process of "turning the old culture inside out" resulted in the transmutation of pagan gods into Orthodox demons after the Christianization of Russia, so that "the everyday practice of Christianity is an invaluable source for the reconstruction of East Slavonic pagan culture."[43]

It is clear then that our discussion of Orthodox demonography must focus on areas where it differs from, rather than absorbs or replicates, the typology of the Russian folk demon, and it will therefore occupy a relatively brief space here, though this be out of all proportion to the importance of Orthodox views of evil in Dostoevsky's work. Moreover, as Simon Franklin points out, there is no such thing as a specifically "Orthodox" tradition of demonism as distinct from broader Christian traditions.[44] In turning to hagiographic texts, where devils were shown attempting to corrupt or beguile holy men, Franklin produces a typology of the "Orthodox" devil that, although sharing with folk belief an insistence upon his objective reality and lack of moral ambiguity, presents him as inhabiting a cosmology that is monistic rather than dualistic. Rather than a major player in a world of evil that coexists with God's world, the devil is presented in Orthodox belief as a subordinate figure in a singular universe where God reigns supreme, a further stimulus to the Russian literary tradition of depicting "petty" demons:

"When all is said and done, or tried and tempted, the Devil is a loser. He has no hold over the future; he can act only where God permits and where man loses vigilance; he can be resisted and expelled."[45] Partly as a consequence of this subordinate role, and partly due to the lack of canonical teachings on or descriptions of him, the Orthodox devil is "very hard to pin down." His image in Orthodox writings and iconography was not created whole, but accumulated over time from fragments of diverse traditions and texts: "The Devil is an extrapolation, a field of possibilities, a set of interwoven traditions."[46] His genealogical imprecision translates into a typological vagueness where his only constant characteristics are those of inconstancy, adaptability, flexibility, lack of clear focus, and deceptiveness (characteristics that can lead to a perceived, but *only* perceived, moral ambiguity in that he can make himself attractive or appear as a friend). His physical features can include wings and a tail (although horns and cloven hoofs appeared only later), a slight or "weedy" appearance, and hair that stands on end. Like the folk devil, he can appear as a foreigner and is a master of disguise, able to assume the form of animals. His multiplicity of identities is matched, again like that of the folk devil, in the variety of names by which he is known, including "taboo" terms, such as *vrag* (enemy), *lukavyi* (the cunning, crafty, or sly one), or *nepriiazn'* (a term suggesting "hostility").

Franklin concludes his authoritative, but lightly written typology with an interesting comment on the failure of the Orthodox devil to make a convincing transition from hagiographical text to the literary genres that emerged in the nineteenth century, particularly the novel, where the emphasis shifted to naturalism and the devil found himself "stranded in the wrong aesthetic."[47] This is a helpful contribution to the direction of our present argument, for it points up how secular literature in the nineteenth century was forced to embrace typologies of the devil other than those afforded by Orthodox hagiography, typologies where the emphasis was more frequently on figurative demon*ism* (that is, the demonic as a mode of behavior) and less on demons in a truly literal form.

THE ROMANTIC LITERARY DEMON

Franklin makes the point that in Orthodox representation, as in folk tradition, the emphasis was usually on *devils*, small letter and plural, rather than on *the* Devil—"Neither in Byzantium nor in Russia was there much emphasis on a towering figure of Satan in splendor"[48]—with the result that the figure of the devil never transcended his pedestrian nastiness to become anything other than a symbol of malignant, but essentially banal, evil.

Although we may seek to attach high allegorical or metaphorical significance to him, we could only do so on the basis of our own "cultural modeling," and not as a product of Orthodox demonology, where devils remain essentially minor in nature:

> They are not tragic or avuncular or nobly doomed free spirits. They are not Miltonic or Byronic. They can of course make themselves appear attractive, even affable and charming, but in no sense can they be presented as admirable, or as pitiable, or as providers of legitimate aesthetic interest and pleasure. Their essence is thoroughly nasty.[49]

It took Romanticism to provide Russian culture with a model of the devil that ascribed to him a grandeur, a profound philosophical significance and ambiguity, and a rich complexity to which the malicious imps of folk and Orthodox tradition could never aspire. Moreover, as we shall see, such qualities also had the effect of rendering the figure of the devil, or demon, acceptable and assimilable to the artistic criteria and forms of the age. No longer was the devil adrift in the world of nineteenth-century literature and "stranded in the wrong aesthetic"; instead he embodied qualities that allowed him to stand as a representation of the human condition, as modern literature sought to identify and depict it. With the rise of a secularized intellectual class in the wake of Westernization, Russian literary representation of the devil lost what Valentin Boss calls the "rustic accent and monkish manner," which it had derived from folk and Orthodox images.[50] The previous clear separation of devil and man, which had seen the latter as the victim of the former's attempts at "spoiling" or temptation, became blurred. The devil surrendered his former palpable objectivity, he acquired human characteristics, he even attracted human sympathy, and eventually he became a potent symbol of late-Romantic man's alienation from the existing order, both worldly and metaphysical, of his disillusionment with life, his willful rebelliousness, and his Promethean, but destructive, individual potential. Bakhtin goes further, arguing that Romanticism invested the devil with a high seriousness and philosophical gravitas in excess of anything he had previously possessed:

> The Romantic treatment of the devil is also completely different from that of popular grotesque. In the diableries of the medieval mysteries, in the parodical legends and the *fabliaux,* the devil is the gay ambivalent figure expressing the unofficial point of view, the material bodily stratum. There is nothing terrifying or alien in him. In Rabelais' description of Epistemon's ghostly vision, the devils are excellent and jovial fellows. At times the devils and hell itself appear as comic monsters, whereas the Romanticists present

the devil as terrifying, melancholy, and tragic, and infernal laughter as somber and sarcastic.[51]

It seems to me that Bakhtin, in his preoccupation with the liberating qualities of carnival, has got it wrong in his emphasis on the "gay," "jovial," and "comic" qualities of the medieval devil, at the expense of the undoubted and objective cosmic evil and hostility he also represented in both the Russian folk and Orthodox traditions. But Bakhtin is right to signal in such dramatic terms the sea change in perception of the devil that accompanied the Romantic movement, a change that saw him become, in Boss's words, "an individualist devil freed of his traditional attachment to the Bible."[52] The process of ascribing to the Romantic devil a melancholic, tragic, and rebellious individualism also made possible his appropriation for the purpose of giving expression to political and social dissent. The proud rebel against the cosmic order is easily remodeled as an individual at odds with the current social order, in which role he can be enlisted in the service of sundry political and ideological causes. The prototype of the Romantic demon, Milton's Satan, was, for example, admired by the Decembrist revolutionary Kiukhelbeker as a figure of real philosophical interest, rather than merely the "disgusting monster" of the devil's earlier incarnations. The Marxist Lunacharsky followed the lead of many others and saw the Satan of *Paradise Lost* as a revolutionary, although he had little time for his Russian equivalent, Lermontov's Demon, whom he dismissed as little more than a self-obsessed tempter with no worthy agenda.[53] An inevitable consequence of remodeling the devil as revolutionary freethinker and a product of social disorder is the concomitant *domestication* of evil. No longer an absolute condition possessing a metaphysical reality, evil is relativized and brought within the finite parameters of man's political and social preferences. Thus, although Romantic *demonography* does wonders for the aggrandizement of the devil's image, Romantic *demonology* humanizes, and therefore diminishes the stature of, his cause.

The typography of the demon figure in European Romantic literature had its origins, as remarked earlier, in Milton's *Paradise Lost,* where the figure of Satan was freed from the "stereotyped devils of Dante and Tasso" as they were derived from medieval superstition that was fed by popular lore and ecclesiastical imagery.[54] Milton's work was known to Russians, via French translations, from as early as the 1730s. But, as Adam Weiner points out, Milton's Satan was not assimilated directly into the demonography of Russian literature, which on the whole has tended to prefer images owing more to the sly and subordinate Mephistopheles in Goethe's *Faust,* a work more in accord with the Russian preference for the shabby, down-at-heel devil, and with which the Russian educated public became familiar only in the 1820s and 1830s. Milton's view of the devil as a Puritan revolutionary entered Russian Romantic literature only indirectly and in ironized form through Byron's works and the Russian imitations these spawned.[55]

The archetype of the demon in this particular Russian incarnation is provided by Mikhail Lermontov's narrative poem *The Demon* (1839), although Pushkin had suggested the type earlier in his lyric "The Demon" (1823), where the "malignant spirit" (*zlobnyi genii*) is possessed of a seductively rebellious and corrosive irony. This spirit visits the poet during the latter's moments of youthful intoxication with love, life, and "elevated feelings," moments when he is charged with joy, hopes, and poetic inspiration. With his "poisonous discourse" he pours cold water on the poet's idealism and instills a "cold venom" in his soul. This spirit thus fits the job description of the Romantic demon, embodying the qualities of Romantic agony and disillusion, although the most outstanding thing about his typography is that he has none. In Pushkin's lyric, the demon has become demon*ism*, to borrow Simon Franklin's distinction: what was literal has become metaphorical, and a traditional symbol of objectively existing, transcendent evil has been internalized and pressed into service as a poetic means of giving expression to what is essentially a human psychological and existential malaise.

Lermontov's demon at least looks like the real thing, as he flies over the mountains and gorges of the Caucasus, and does demonic things such as causing the death of his rival for Tamara's affections. But he, too, works better as a metaphor than he does as a devil, giving extraordinarily potent expression to the tragedy of Romantic despair and alienation. He is the "spirit of exile" (*dukh izgnaniia*), possessed of an ironic despondency; excluded from paradise by his pride, "he sowed evil without enjoyment"; he smolders with the desire for reconciliation, but on his own terms; he is "a tsar of knowledge and freedom," though this brings him nothing but an all-consuming boredom, his soul an "indestructible mausoleum of hopes and passions that have perished." He also possesses the sensuality that, so Boss argues, formed part of the baggage that the devil acquired in the process of humanization he underwent in Romantic demonography.[56] Because the demon thus depicted was a projection of essentially human qualities and of a contemporary human malaise, he ceased to be a "supernatural" figure, one lacking credibility and artistic verisimilitude, and instead he became a candidate for inclusion, with only minor amendments, in the portrait gallery of the modern social and psychological novel. Lermontov was thus able to extend, almost unchanged, the typology of his Demon into Pechorin, the central figure of his highly influential novel *A Hero of Our Time* (1840). We shall see in due course the extent to which Dostoevsky appropriated the model offered by Pechorin in order to expose the demonism of several of his own characters, most notably Svidrigailov (*Crime and Punishment*) and Stavrogin (*The Devils*).[57]

BEAUTY AND THE BEAST

In Lermontov's poem the destructive, malignant evil of the Demon, his moral ugliness, is strangely offset by his physical grandeur, dramatic appeal, and formal beauty, aspects perfectly captured by Mikhail Vrubel's (1856–1910) well-known illustrations to the poem. Lermontov—who was temperamentally attracted to evil and prone to dramatize himself as a malevolent and demonic soul in open revolt against the cosmic order—depicted his Demon, to whose refinement he devoted most of his creative life, as "shining with an unearthly beauty" (*krasoi blistaia nezemnoi*). The same conviction that evil may assume pleasant aesthetic form reappears in more earthly guise in the elegant and stylish figure of Pechorin, of whom his one-time lover Vera says: "In no one else is evil so attractive."[58] Interestingly, Lermontov was to turn his back on this notion of an aesthetically attractive evil in his poem "A Fairy-Tale for Children" ("Skazka dlia detei"), which although it appeared in 1840, only one year after the completion of *The Demon*, is in conception a much later work. Here Lermontov offers a much debased and trivialized account of the demon figure, one that owes more to Mephistopheles than to the Miltonic/Byronic devil. He apologizes for his earlier apotheosis of evil, saying that "it was mad, passionate, childish delirium" (*to byl bezumnyi, strastnyi, detskii bred*), and continuing:

> But I did not always thus imagine the enemy of pure and holy motives. My young mind was perturbed by a mighty image; among other visions he shone like a king, still and proud, with such a bewitchingly sweet beauty that it was frightening. [. . .] And my heart was seized with longing. And this wild delirium pursued my reason for many years. But as I parted with other dreams, so I divorced myself from him too—in verse! ("A Fairy Tale for Children," Stanza 6)

If, for Lermontov, the contamination of beauty by the demonic was a consequence of wild, Romantic longing from which he claimed to have recovered, then, for Dostoevsky, it was an illusion and a symptom of moral decline, to which he never succumbed. As Robert Louis Jackson puts it, in his classic study of Dostoevsky's aesthetic views: "The concept of the unity of moral and aesthetic categories, of the good and the beautiful, is posited by Dostoevsky in all periods of his creative life."[59] At the heart of his aesthetic system is the notion of ideal beauty as described by Plato and constructed on the inseparability of aesthetic and moral categories. For Plato, true beauty combined aesthetic perfection with moral perfection, purity of form with purity of purpose; and man is attracted to such beauty precisely because it represents for him an ideal combining harmony, perfection, and pure fusion of form and content, toward which he—imperfect, discordant, and impure—can strive. Ideal beauty is thus *iconic* (the Russian word *obraz* denotes both "form" and "icon") and possessed of a truly religious significance in that it produces a morally and spiritually transfiguring effect in those receptive to it. This notion passed into the mainstream of European aesthetic thought via medieval Christian aesthetics and came to dominate German idealist aesthetics through the works of Schiller, Schelling, and Hegel; through the latter it came to "structure and dominate Dostoevsky's entire world outlook: it is the controlling center of his views about art."[60] As such it finds emphatic expression in what is perhaps the most complete statement Dostoevsky made of his aesthetic views, the essay "Mr. -bov and the Question of Art" (1861), where he defends the concept of ideal beauty from the twin threats posed by Byronic sensuality and utilitarianism. In a passage of central importance, he writes:

> Art is just as much a necessity for man as eating and drinking. The need for beauty and the creation that embodies it is inseparable from man, and without it perhaps man would not wish to live on earth. Man thirsts for beauty, finds it and accepts it *without any conditions* and just because it is beauty; and he bows before it in reverence, without asking what use it is or what you can buy with it. And perhaps precisely in this lies the greatest secret of artistic creation: that the image of beauty it creates immediately becomes an idol *without any conditions.* But why does it become an idol? Because the need for beauty develops most when man is in discord with reality, in a state of disharmony, at odds with it, that is to say when *he is most alive,* for man is most alive precisely at those times when he is seeking something and striving; at such times he manifests within himself a most natural desire for everything harmonious, for calm, and in beauty there is both harmony and calm. [. . .] And therefore beauty is immanent in everything healthy, that is, in what is most alive, and it is a necessary requirement of the human organism. It is harmony; it contains the pledge of tranquility; it embodies the ideals of man and mankind. (XVIII, 94)

On the basis of such conviction, summarized in Keats's "'Beauty is truth, truth beauty,'—that is all/Ye know on earth, and all ye need to know" ("Ode on a Grecian Urn"), Dostoevsky never succumbed to the illusion of an aesthetically attractive evil. Indeed, the idea that demonic or even amoral qualities could combine with external attractiveness to produce a satisfying aesthetic experience was one to which he remained opposed throughout his life. In the figure of the Byronic hero, whether demon or human, such qualities had appeared to assume a kind of "beauty" (*krasoi blistaia nezemnoi*), but for Dostoevsky—if not for some of his characters—such "beauty" was a sterile deceit, for it lacked a moral ideal. In "Mr. -bov and the Question of Art" he dismisses the Romantic quest for demonic beauty as an aesthetic aberration, a result of self-indulgence, satiation, and moral indifference:

> We have seen examples where man, having achieved the ideal of his desires and not knowing what else to aim for, being totally satiated, has fallen into a kind of anguish, has even exacerbated this anguish within himself, has sought out another ideal in life and, out of extreme surfeit, has not only ceased to value that which he enjoys, but has even consciously turned away from the straight path, and has fomented within himself strange, unhealthy, sharp, inharmonious, sometimes even monstrous tastes, losing all measure and aesthetic feeling for healthy beauty and demanding instead of it exceptions. (XVIII, 94)

We see this aesthetic confusion in the figure of Svidrigailov, where it takes the form of an implacable sensuality, and in Stavrogin, himself a demonic Byronic figure who deliberately marries a cripple in order to revive his perverted but flagging aesthetic sense. It is significant that, as Richard Peace points out, Stavrogin's wife is a deformed echo of that ideal of classical beauty, the Madonna.[61] The same confusion leads Dmitry Karamazov to the conclusion that there must be two kinds of beauty—ideal beauty (the beauty of the Madonna) and unhealthy beauty (the beauty of Sodom). The terms in which Dmitry expresses to Alesha what he has to say are of great value in allowing us to understand the relationship of "beauty" and the demonic in Dostoevsky:

> Beauty is a terrible and terrifying thing. Terrible because it's indefinable, and it's impossible to define because God presents nothing but enigmas. Here the shores meet, here all contradictions live together. Brother, I'm very uneducated, but I've thought about this a great deal. There are terribly many mysteries! Too many enigmas oppress man on earth. Make what you can of them and try to keep your nose clean. Beauty! Besides I cannot bear it that a man, even though noble of soul and with a fine mind, should start from the ideal of the Madonna and end with the ideal of Sodom. It's even more terrible when a man with the ideal of Sodom already in his heart does not renounce the ideal of the Madonna, and his heart is ablaze with it, truly, truly ablaze, just as in his years of youthful innocence. No, man is broad in his nature, even too

broad, I would narrow him down. The devil [*chert*] only knows what he is, that's the trouble! What appears shameful to the mind is sheer beauty to the heart. Is there beauty in Sodom? Believe me, for the vast majority of people it is indeed in Sodom—didn't you know that? It is terrifying that beauty is not only a terrible, but also a mysterious thing. Here the devil [*d'iavol*] struggles with God, and the battlefield is the hearts of men. (XIV, 100)

The beauty of the Madonna described by Dmitry is clearly that iconic ideal beauty that brings man to aesthetic and moral completeness, but the beauty of Sodom is a seductive, and destructive, lure that promises sensual gratification, yet only at the cost of the loss of all sense of a moral and aesthetic ideal, *bezobrazie* (chaos, formlessness) rather than *obraz*. One comes from God and offers the hope of salvation ("Beauty will save the world," says Prince Myshkin in *The Idiot*); the other comes from the Devil and offers only damnation. Dmitry's problem is that both appear to him as beauty, and he is simultaneously drawn to both:

If I am to fly into the abyss [of debauchery] then I shall do so precipitously, headlong, and I shall even be pleased to find myself in such a degrading situation, I shall consider it beautiful as far as I am concerned. But in the very depths of that shame I shall suddenly begin a hymn. Let me be cursed, let me be low and base, but let me also kiss the hem of that garment in which my God is cloaked; even if I'm chasing after the devil at that very moment, I am still Thy son, O Lord, and I love Thee, and I feel that joy without which the world could not be. (XIV, 99)

In his confusion Dmitry attributes this aesthetic duality to beauty itself, but as Jackson notes in a comment that is central to a proper understanding of Dostoevsky's aesthetic views: "*it is not beauty which is ambivalent, but man who experiences two kinds of beauty*" (italic in original).[62] Dostoevsky's friend, Nikolai Strakhov, recalls him saying: "Only that is moral which coincides with your feeling of beauty,"[63] and in a well-known letter to N. D. Fonvizina in 1854 Dostoevsky cites Christ as the image of perfect beauty precisely because in the classical manner Christ embodies an ethical ideal in perfect physical form, he is the Word made flesh. What is more, in the same letter he suggests that man's aesthetic sense, as manifested in love for the beauty of Christ, provides an ethical guide superior to reason's conception of what is right and wrong: "Moreover, if it were proved to me by somebody that Christ lay outside the truth and that the truth actually lay other than in Christ, then I would rather remain with Christ than with the truth" (XXVIII/1, 176). The theme of beauty thus joins the other semiotic markers identified in this introduction in its ability to signal the nature of a

22

character's stance in relation to Christ or the devil. We shall later explore in particular its role in *Crime and Punishment,* where Raskolnikov's infatuation with the "beauty" of Napoleon demonizes his theoretical stance on crime, but where his revulsion from the moral ugliness of the "superman" Svidrigailov anticipates, and gives legitimacy to, his moral rebirth in the novel's epilogue.

NARRATIVE AND THE DEMONIC

"My friend, real truth is never true-to-life, did you know that? In order to make the truth true-to-life you really have to stir a bit of falsehood into it" (X, 172). Stepan Trofimovich's comment in *The Devils,* made (significantly, as we shall see) to the narrator Anton Lavrentevich G-v, has clear implications for narrative art that aspires to verisimilitude. Such implications are recognized by the narrator of *The Idiot* in a digression at the start of part 4, when he describes how in novels and stories "writers for the most part try to take certain social types and present them vividly and skillfully—types who are very rarely encountered in precisely that form in real life, but who are nevertheless almost more real than reality itself" (VIII, 383). Remarks like these suggest two reasons why the view has persisted in Western culture that imaginative narrative might in itself be demonic. First, it involves falsehood and deception, which are of course the primary weapons of the devil in his attempts to seduce and ensnare the souls of the unwary. Narrative fiction is inspired lying: it involves presenting what has not happened as though it had, and what is not real as though it were. The narrator of such fiction uses the devices of the devil in order to "draw us into the novel's world through an entire arsenal of snares: confusion, deception, pity, connivance, temptation."[64] Second, the authors of such narratives assume creative *authority,* which should be the prerogative of God alone. The writing of narrative fiction thus travesties divine creation in that the writer creates false worlds and then peoples those worlds with men and women created not by God, but from his own imagination. Thus the traditional analogy of God-as-Creator with writer-as-creator is one that supports demonic interpretation, whereby writing, like secular artistic creation in general, represents an importunate assumption of God's role. The key word here is *secular:* both Adam Weiner and Pamela Davidson recently commented on the Christian church's traditional wariness of the arts of narrative when not employed directly in the service of God's creation, a wariness that coincides with the binary model of Russian culture discussed above, whereby in the absence of neutral ground what is not from God must inevitably be from the devil.[65] Weiner cites James Billington's view in his classic study of Russian culture, *The Icon and the*

Axe,[66] that, unlike the critical theology of the West, Russian Orthodox theology was essentially passive, emphasizing the worship of divinely received wisdom and forms, and that this encouraged a tradition whereby the role of the artist was to elaborate and praise divine creation, not to foreground his own.[67] Davidson recognizes the same distinction between art as divinely inspired *revelation* and art as demonically corrupted and idolatrous personal *creation*, but she emphasizes that the Christian church's view of secular art as intrinsically demonic is traceable back to the rise of secular culture in general and is not only a feature of the "passivity" of Russian Orthodox worship. Both Weiner and Davidson emphasize the critical role of Peter the Great, whose reign saw the acceleration of secular culture in Russia and the consequent "demonization" of the art that culture produced. Both also offer clear illustrations of the link between narrative and the demonic, in both Western and Orthodox culture: Davidson cites the fate of the lovers Paolo and Francesca in Dante's *Inferno,* whose corruption begins with the joint reading of a narrative, the romance *Lancelot du Lac*[68]; Weiner gives the example of the Russian traditional tale of two brother-monks who are attended by angels on their right shoulders as they discuss spiritual narratives. But:

> When the monks left off the spiritual narratives and began to converse on secular matters, then the angels of God would go from . . . their cell, and two demons would approach these two monks, and . . . write down their words on charters, and one devil going up to one monk, the other devil to the other monk, they would secretly whisper into their left ears, and when the devils had scrawled all over their charters, then they would begin to write on themselves what the monks were saying. And soon the demons would be so covered with writing that there would not remain a clean spot on them.

Weiner cites this text as one of the earliest Russian depictions of the association between the devil and writing, one that clearly implies that "while sacred narratives lead to divinely sanctioned discussions, impious discussions instantaneously engender demonic narratives."[69] Both Davidson and Weiner also cite the Russian church's *Stoglav* (*Book of a Hundred Chapters,* 1551), with its warning to artists "to create nothing from their own fantasy."[70]

If the writing of secular narrative is implicitly demonic in its very purpose of "creating 'paper' worlds designed, at least momentarily, to blot out the evidence of God's authorship,"[71] then the act of reading such narratives is also fraught with danger. If the writer of secular fiction invites his reader to recognize and enter a world not created by God and to prioritize that world at least temporarily through the suspension of disbelief, then the reader is implicitly demonized by consenting to that invitation. The act of reading thus becomes a form of demonic pact, a conspiracy against the primacy of divinely created reality. The terms of this pact are clearly set out in the nineteenth-century realist novel, where the writer implicitly agrees to do nothing too obvious to violate the sense of verisimilitude, in return for the reader's willingness to suspend disbelief. They are, as Weiner argues, much less clearly set out in the far more "demonic" form of the modernist narrative, where any understanding between writer and reader is underwritten by deceit and untrustworthiness on the part of the narrator. The result is an unstable text that, "by muddling the line between reliable and unreliable, attempts to scare away our wits themselves, challenging our ability ever to distinguish between evil and good, and thus to protect ourselves against the mind's invasion by the forces of darkness."[72]

Weiner argues that Dostoevsky's art, and in particular his "demonic" novel *The Devils*, "bears witness to the author's anxiety over the whole novelistic endeavor,"[73] as though he were aware of the fact that, despite his overall ideological purpose of reaffirming Russian Orthodox Christian values in the face of the contamination of the Russian upper classes by Western European moral and political nihilism, there is, in the words of Jean Racine, "no such thing as a work of art written without the collaboration of the devil."[74] Thus the construction of Dostoevsky's novels is founded upon a clash of Orthodox and novelistic sensibilities, where the desire to affirm God's creation is paradoxically achieved through the demonically incited novel form relying on narrative invention. Moreover, that very novelistic form—the form dominating Russian literary discourse in Dostoevsky's time—is itself a product of that same Western culture that has given rise to the "demonic" forces undermining Russian Orthodox culture. The repudiation of false Western values must therefore include the repudiation of the form in which that repudiation is couched. Weiner's careful analysis of *The Devils* as a novel in which the overtly demonic content contaminates the narrative and in which the implied author and narrator are implicated in the turpitude of the demonic characters is extraordinarily elegant and persuasive, and it fully merits the recapitulation given here. The analysis turns on the assertion that the whole novel dramatizes a struggle between sacred and profane narratives, and here the role of the personalized narrator Anton Lavrentevich G-v is central. Much critical attention has been devoted to G-v's apparent shortcomings as a narrator: he claims to be rendering an accurate and impartial "chronicle" of recent events in "our town," but as his account unfolds the reader is increasingly aware of his unreliability as a witness and of the lacunae and embellishments that contaminate his account.[75] In assuming the role of "chronicler" G-v is appropriating a narrative form enshrined in ecclesiastical texts such as the Lives of the Saints, where it is used to bear witness to holy events and in which the chronicler plays a wholly unassuming and self-denying role as mediator of the divine purpose. The dominant image of such an Orthodox chronicler in Russian literature is, of course, that of Pimen in Pushkin's historical drama *Boris Godunov*. But G-v's "chronicling voice" is progressively compromised by his "authorial" or novelistic voice, which prioritizes narrative invention over self-effacing description. Increasingly he insinuates opinion into his "facts," he uses unreliable sources, he imaginatively embellishes his text when facts are lacking, and like the omniscient narrator of a nineteenth-century novel, he reports the innermost workings of other characters' minds, workings to which he has no real access. In a particularly elegant argumentative flourish, Weiner suggests that he is more akin to Pimen's deceitful pupil, the pretender Grigory Otrepev, than to Pimen himself, in that he gives up the impartial recording of history in order to make it himself, and he scoffs at Liza's plans to publish an impartial chronicle of current events.[76]

This analysis of *The Devils* is entirely convincing in its account of the struggle between G-v's sacred and demonic narrative personae, even if it is rather more difficult to accept Weiner's belief that G-v "is a reflection of Dostoevsky's residual sympathy for the radicals that his narrative nonetheless demonizes."[77] The analysis of *The Devils* offered later in this volume affords no evidence of such "residual sympathy," and its examination of the demonic in that novel follows a rather different line than Weiner's. Nevertheless, the novel as intrinsically demonic is a notion we shall borrow to examine and explain the inserted narratives in works such as *The Idiot, The Devils,* and, especially, *The Brothers Karamazov,* where Dostoevsky attempts to combat Ivan's demonic narrative invention in his poem about the Grand Inquisitor by adopting an entirely different genre, that of the *zhitie,* or saint's life, for the subsequent account of Zossima's life and teachings. He does this, we shall argue, to circumvent the demonic contamination of his message by the novel's narrative contrivances. The fact that he fails in this will provide additional evidence, if such were needed, of the uneasy tension between novelistic and Orthodox imperatives on which his art is founded.

Chapter One

The Electricity of Human Thought:
Defining the Demonic

OUTSIDE HIS MAJOR NOVELS, where generous spatial and temporal dimensions allied to structural and thematic complexity permit it to play a significant and persistent role in the philosophical and symbolic structure of each text, Dostoevsky's engagement with the demonic is uneven. In some works it plays no part at all. In others its appearance is sporadic, its significance narrowly confined to the episode in which it is employed. An example of the latter may be found in a published variant of *Poor Folk*, where Varvara's childhood recollections include memories of forest visits in which she felt she was being enticed toward ravines in the deepest reaches of the wood by some unnamed but hostile spirit (presumably the *leshii*). The lack of overall significance in this early reference to the demonic is eloquently suggested by the fact that it was excised from the final text of the novel (I, 443). The focus of this chapter is on a selection of works, drawn from several points in Dostoevsky's literary career, in which the inscription of demonic motifs is persistent enough to suggest an overarching purpose, but where the demonic markers in any individual text do not coalesce into the sort of coherent semiotic system we find in the major novels. However, taken as a whole these works show how, in the course of Dostoevsky's career, demonic signs come to be attached to a particular cluster of ideas, images, and conditions with a persistence that allows us to develop an understanding of what constituted for him the locus of demonic evil. It is not, however, the purpose of this chapter to discuss at length the nature of evil in any metaphysical system ascribable to Dostoevsky—that would be a separate and major undertaking, and it has in any case been widely treated elsewhere.[1] Instead the focus here is on *how* such ideas, images, and conditions come to attract demonic motifs in preparation for the more systematic process of demonization they undergo in the major, large-scale novels that are the primary object of this study. In early works like *The Double* and *The Landlady*, both written before Dostoevsky's arrest and Siberian imprisonment for association with the Petrashevsky Circle, a politically subversive group, the use of demonic markers was neither precisely targeted nor systematically applied across works. Moreover, it was—if such a term can be applied to literary analysis—"parochial," in the sense of being designed to serve primarily each work's own struggle for thematic clarity and structural integrity. By contrast, Dostoevsky's use of the demonic in works written after his return from Siberian exile acquires a much more consistent and polemical focus and serves not only to structure the poetics of individual texts, but also to clarify the extent to which the author's worldview took firm shape as a result of his Siberian experiences and the years of travel and journalistic engagement that followed his return. His discovery of the buried spiritual treasures at the heart of the simple Russian people, of the extent to which the landed and intellectual classes in Russia had become alienated from that spirituality, and of the primary contribution made to that alienation by those classes' assimilation of the destructively secular and un-Russian principles of Western European civilization, all became entities in an ideological gravitational field that swept up the fragments of Dostoevsky's demonology into a coherent and consistent system.[2]

"ONE TERRIFYING BOOK": *NOTES FROM THE HOUSE OF THE DEAD*

Notes from the House of the Dead, a "fiction" (Dostoevsky included it among his "novels) consisting of the prison memoir of a certain Aleksandr Petrovich Gorianchikov, is indeed an autobiographical work, as most of Dostoevsky's critics have recognized (albeit some more reluctantly than others, given the pains Dostoevsky takes to distance himself from Gorianchikov not only in terms of personal characteristics, but also through the interposition of a narrative frame and fictional narrator between Gorianchikov's memoirs and himself). But what it offers is not so much a fictionally disguised account of Dostoevsky's experiences during his period of imprisonment and hard labor in the 1850s as an insight into the process whereby he came to terms with those experiences and drew from them the lessons that formed the basis of the way he subsequently looked at the world. Robert Louis Jackson, who has provided us with an exhaustive account of the narrative, generic, and ideological complexities of *The House of the Dead,* has probably gone further than anyone else in defining that work's position relative to Dostoevsky's life and art, arguing that it (rather than the more commonly cited *Notes from Underground*) is the watershed in Dostoevsky's career, the centerpiece of his fictional universe, and the key to understanding all his subsequent works.[3] Jackson's approach to this and other works discussed in this chapter, although not specifically focused on analysis of the demonic, provides fertile ground on which to sow such an analysis, and I refer to him often and gratefully in the pages ahead.

This centrality of *The House of the Dead* in Dostoevsky's art extends to the way that work deals with the problem of evil. Aleksandr Herzen's description of the work as "one terrifying book" and "a fearful narrative" alerts us to the stark and emphatic way in which it presents the evil done by humans and to humans.[4] At the heart of this presentation is the "house of the dead" itself, a prison camp that transcends its significance as a human social institution to become a metaphorical depiction of Hell, one that is commonly compared to Dante's in *The Divine Comedy*.[5] In this metaphorical Hell we encounter truly demonic personalities, such as the fearsome Tartar Gazin, whose capacity for acts of unimaginable evil is matched—indeed, refined—by his sharp and cunning intelligence. In this figure, with his Herculean build, his resemblance to an outsized spider, his terrible strength, the "fictions" with which the other convicts surround him, and his delight in the torture and murder of young children, the depiction of human evil almost transcends verisimilitude, skirting the supernatural (IV, 40–41). The same is true of the depiction of the nobleman-convict A-v who, while also being "very clever" (IV, 221), is nonetheless capable of suppressing all moral feeling within himself and committing the most appalling acts. Gorianchikov describes him as "a monster, a moral Quasimodo," "a lump of meat, with teeth and a stomach, and with an insatiable thirst for the coarsest, most bestial physical pleasures," "an example of the lengths man's physical side will go to on its own, when unrestrained by any kind of internal norm or set of laws" (IV, 63).

Examples like Gazin and A-v compel Gorianchikov to rexamine his conception of evil and its causes and to entertain hitherto unsuspected notions about man's capacity for a truly demonic fall from grace:

I have already said that over the course of several years I did not see amongst these people either the slightest sign of repentance or the smallest hint that their crimes might be weighing upon their minds, and that the majority of them inwardly considered themselves to be completely in the right. This is a fact. Of course, vanity, bad examples, high spirits, and false shame are the cause of most of this. On the other hand who can say that he has fathomed the depths of these lost hearts and read in them what is hidden from the whole world? It must surely have been possible over so many years to notice at least something, to catch or pick up at least some feature in these hearts that would attest to some inner anguish or suffering. But there was nothing of the sort, positively nothing. Yes, it would seem that crime cannot be comprehended on the basis of given, ready-made points of view, and that its philosophy is somewhat more difficult than is supposed. [. . .] Only in prison have I heard tales of the most terrible, the most unnatural acts, of the most monstrous murders, told with the most irrepressible, the most childishly merry laughter. [. . .] It's a phenomenon; what we have here is some sort of constitutional defect, some sort of physical and moral disfigurement, as yet unknown to science, not simply a question of crime. (IV, 15–16)

Passages such as this justify Konstantin Mochulsky's assertion that "the fiction of the narrator-prisoner Aleksandr Petrovich Goryanchikov cannot deceive; everywhere is heard the voice of Dostoevsky."[6] Through Gorian-chikov's words we experience Dostoevsky's own loss of faith in the natural virtue of man and in the ideals of humanism and brotherhood which that faith had encouraged in a generation of Russian utopian socialists. Human evil was not explicable simply as the product of an irrational and ill-con-structed environment, one that would disappear with that environment's re-construction on rational bases. Instead, *The House of the Dead* affirms the existence of absolute evil and man's innate capacity for it. Jackson cites the episode "Akulka's Husband" as illustrative of Dostoevsky's approach to the problem of evil in human existence, for in its account of power relations, sex-ual aggression, and mindless cruelty among individuals—what Jackson de-scribes as "the locus of evil" for Dostoevsky—it shows how environmental influences play an entirely secondary role in the exercise of an evil that is in-nate in human nature.[7] Gorianchikov draws explicit attention to the lack of correlation between a person's moral nature, on the one hand, and his high or low social standing, the role he plays in the social power structure, and the level of his education or enlightenment, on the other. A-v, that "lump of meat with teeth and stomach," is a nobleman and not a deprived or excluded social inferior; the prisoner-guards and "gentlemen-executioners" who de-rive sensual gratification from the infliction of corporal punishment can eas-ily match the cruelty and inhumanity of those beneath them (IV, 154–55); and, as Gorianchikov puts it, "not even education is an accurate indicator [of the soul]": "I would be the first to testify that among these sufferers I have met signs of the most refined spiritual development even in the most uned-ucated and oppressed milieu. [. . .] You also come across the opposite: ed-ucation sometimes cohabits with such barbarity, with such cynicism, that you are disgusted, and no matter how good natured or well-disposed you are, you can find in your heart neither excuse nor justification" (IV, 197–98). The conviction chronicled through such examples in *The House of the Dead*—that the problem of evil is a spiritual one, and that salvation must consist in the moral transfiguration of the corrupt individual, rather than the social or political transformation of ill-ordered societies—marks Dostoevsky's final transition from the role of revolutionary conspirator, which he played in the 1840s, to that of religiously driven novelist, played in all his subsequent fiction.

The stark, documentary reality of the events recounted in *The House of the Dead* should not blind us to that work's emphatically metaphorical nature. Jackson writes of the "vital, allegorical dimension of *House of the Dead:* the drama of birth, death, fall, and redemption that constitutes the symbolic structure of the work."[8] On one level this allegorical dimension embraces, as Herzen recognized, the "hell" of Russia under the benighted tyrant Nicholas I (in whose name Dostoevsky found himself in the Dead House of penal servitude) and the nation's transcendence of that hell in the post-Nicholaevan period of reform, relaxation, and renewal.[9] On another, this first literary account of life in Siberian labor camps marks, as Jackson puts it, "the restoration of the image of a 'lost people,' the justification of a pariah people, the symbolic redemption of the Russian people," this justification and redemption flowing from Dostoevsky's account of the humanity, as well as the inhumanity, of the convicts.[10] The process of restoration and redemption described by Jackson does not refer solely to the way *The House of the Dead* awakened the awareness of a Russian readership by revealing a hitherto unknown world and a "lost people." The process goes on inside the work as well as outside it: the figure of Gorianchikov was the means through which Dostoevsky himself was able to transcend the horrors of his own prison experience and the distaste he felt there for the convict population and to learn to see the value and creative potential of the Russian *narod.* Throughout his memoir Gorianchikov reflects on the gulf separating himself and the other educated gentry prisoners from the mass of ordinary convicts, and toward the end he comes to understand the true magnitude of that gulf, if not its nature:

> Now, for the first time, a certain thought that had long been stirring indistinctly within me, nagging away at me, finally took clear shape and I finally understood what I had previously only poorly surmised. I understood that I should never be accepted as a comrade by them, not even if I were to remain a convict until the end of time. (IV, 207)

For Gorianchikov, this is a matter of some regret; for Dostoevsky, such alienation was a matter of profound philosophical and spiritual significance. The historical estrangement of the Westernized Russian nobleman, educated on the basis of European secular culture, from the Russian folk, in whom the wellsprings of Russian nationality and spirituality still flowed, was a concept that came to dominate his conception of evil and the demonic in a specifically Russian context. Indeed, his discovery of the Russian people in Siberia, and his rethinking of the meaning of that people through the fictional memoirs of Gorianchikov, was the process by which Dostoevsky began to exorcise the demons that had possessed him in his youth and had consigned him to Siberia in the first place.

Gorianchikov-Dostoevsky's discovery of the Russian *narod* behind the unappealing facade of the convict population is reflected in the narrative of *The House of the Dead,* which comes to be saturated with folk belief and popular discourse. During his period in the penal settlement, Dostoevsky kept a notebook in which he entered popular sayings that struck him, and many of these are transferred directly to Gorianchikov's memoir.[11] This process of absorption of popular discourse also included, inevitably, popular discourse relating to the demonic, and examination of *The House of the Dead* reveals the presence of many embedded demonic signs derived primarily from the Russian folk tradition, although, as we saw in the introduction to this volume, there was a tendency for such signs subsequently to be appropriated by Orthodox demonology.

The demonic subtext begins to assert itself in the opening description of the prison camp. Both its status as "another world," in a very real sense for Gorianchikov and the other inmates, along with its liminal location "at the edge" (*na kraiu*) of the fortress, under the very ramparts, are replete with significance in the context of popular belief about the "unclean force": Gorianchikov specifically refers to "God's world" as something separate that is glimpsed only with difficulty through apertures in the perimeter fence, while "to those on this side of the enclosure that world seemed like some sort of unrealizable fairy tale. Here we had a world all of its own, no longer resembling anything, with its own particular laws, its own costume, manners and customs, a living House of the Dead, a life like nowhere else and with its own special people" (IV, 9). This society of the fallen and depraved forced into an unnatural brotherhood is obliquely likened to a devil's coven when one of the prisoners speculates on the efforts the devil must have made to get all these people together in the same place (IV, 13). Gorianchikov is puzzled by the extent of, and the importance attached to, cursing among the prison population: "there was no end to their cursing. And what masters of the curse they all were! Their cursing was refined and artistic. They raised it to the level of a science" (IV, 13). Shortly afterward he comments on how a particularly gifted curser, the "dialectician of the curse," would be held in the highest esteem (IV, 25). The demonic nature of the inmates of this hell is suggested further late in the work, when escaped prisoners are searched for and found in woods and ravines, locations firmly associated with the unclean force in folk belief.

However, even the most demonic among the prisoners are drawn into some sense of human communality on religious feast days, days that are "sharply imprinted in the memory of the common people, right from childhood":

These are days of rest from their heavy labors, days when families gathered together. In the prison camp they must have been recalled with torment and anguish. Among the prisoners respect for the solemn feast day was transcended and even became a sort of ritualized formality. There weren't many who made merry; all were serious and as though preoccupied with something, although many had practically nothing to do at all. But even the idlers and the merrymakers tried to preserve a serious demeanor. . . . It was as though laughter had been forbidden.

This passage carries a strong semiotic charge: the feast described is that of Christmas, and we might in the light of folk belief read the renunciation of laughter as an attempt by these outcasts to renounce, at least for that one holy day, the devil's hold over their lives; while the high seriousness of their demeanor in the presence of holiness reflects Dostoevsky's conviction that the Christian spirit is alive even in the most desperate and depraved representatives of the Russian people:

The mood of the prisoners was remarkable, even moving. In addition to his inborn sense of reverence for the great day, the prisoner unconsciously felt that by observing this feast he was in some way coming into contact with the whole world and that consequently he was not a complete outcast, or lost soul or severed limb, and that what was happening in the prison was the same as outside, in the world of men. (IV, 104–5)

At the heart of the demonic semiotics of *The House of the Dead* stands the scene describing the prisoners' visit to the bathhouse. Gorianchikov-Dostoevsky's account fully exploits the demonic potential of the bathhouse in Russian folklore to construct an unforgettable image—one that Herzen described as comparable to a fresco "in the spirit of Buonarroti"—of human souls in purgatory.[12] The hellish associations are made fully explicit, as the following extracts show:

When we opened the door into the bathhouse itself I thought we were walking into hell. Imagine a room about twelve paces long and of similar width, into which were packed perhaps up to a hundred men in one go—at the very least eighty, since the prisoners were divided into two shifts and there were up to two hundred of us arriving at the bathhouse. Steam blinding your eyes, soot, filth, and such a crush that there was nowhere to stand. I took fright and wanted to turn back. [. . .] Even the places under the benches were all occupied; there too people swarmed. Across the whole floor there was not a space the size of a man's palm where huddled prisoners were not sitting, splashing themselves from their tubs. [. . .] On the shelf about fifty birch switches rose and fell in unison; everyone was beating himself into a state of intoxication. The steam increased by the minute. This was no longer heat; it was an inferno. Everywhere there was bawling and cackling at the sound of a

33

hundred chains being dragged across the floor. . . . Some men, wanting to get through, got caught up in the chains of others and themselves caught the heads of those sitting below. They fell, cursed, and dragged along those whom they had ensnared. Filth poured from all sides. (IV, 98)

Sitting over this appalling inferno is the Jew Isai Fomich—the seller of Christ through his religious and racial origins—cackling at the top of his voice and screeching out an aria in a state of mad intoxication.[13] Gorianchi-kov concludes his account with the explicit observation: "It came to me that if at some point we were to find ourselves all together in hell, then it would be very similar to this place" (IV, 99). An equally explicit demonic subtext is to be found in the episode describing the convicts' staging of *Kedril the Glutton,* a popular dramatic fragment in the manner of Don Juan, to which part 1, chapter 11 of *The House of the Dead* is largely devoted. The text of this play has not survived, but a detailed account is given of its demonic con-tent in Gorianchikov-Dostoevsky's narrative. This makes reference to a Russian gentleman and his servant, Kedril, passing a night in an inn room haunted, according to the landlord, by devils. In the course of the night dev-ils indeed invade the room and carry off both master and servant to the nether world. The narrator emphasizes that the events depicted make no sense, and perhaps we should simply accept this assertion of lack of mean-ing and leave it at that, the whole episode merely the incoherent exercise of a demonic rhetoric. On the other hand, we might note that the Russian no-bleman is carried off to hell as the result of a conscious choice he has made, a Faustian pact in which his soul is the price paid for the devil's help. Kedril, the representative of the Russian *narod,* on the other hand, unconsciously falls into the hands of devils, as the result of the folk-demonic snares of drink and gluttony (IV, 125–27).

The notion that human weaknesses, addictions, and criminal actions may be the outward signs of demonic possession is an idea explored on sev-eral occasions in *The House of the Dead.* In a discussion of a particular sort of murderer often encountered in the prison camp, Gorianchikov explains how the murderer appears to be quite normal and benign until suddenly "something in him snaps." He goes berserk, as though possessed, and starts murdering not only his enemies, but anyone who crosses his path:

It is as though the man has become drunk or is in a feverish delirium. It is as though, having once crossed some cherished limit within himself, he is al-ready beginning to exult in the fact that there is no longer anything sacred left for him; as though he can hardly keep from leaping across all limits of law-fulness and authority in one go and delighting in the most unbridled and un-limited freedom. (IV, 88)

He delights in this freedom in spite of his knowledge of the punishment that inevitably awaits him, and Gorianchikov compares this feeling to that of a man standing on a high tower, ready to cast himself at any minute into the depths below. The significance of this episode lies partly in the way this type anticipates the psychology of later Dostoevskian transgressors, like the hero of *Notes from Underground* and Raskolnikov; but it is the specific image of the man ready to cast himself from a high point that has particular resonance for our theme of demonic possession. The image recurs persistently in Dostoevsky's works from this moment on, as Jackson has observed, and we shall trace its progress throughout this chapter; but it acquires an overtly demonic charge when used in the context of the second temptation in Ivan Karamazov's poem "The Grand Inquisitor," where Christ is invited by the devil to tempt God and cast himself from a belfry.[14]

The idea that "the devil has got into" someone is also explored in *The House of the Dead* in the contexts of money and freedom. The two are inextricably linked for the convict, perhaps to an extent greater even than in the outside world. Gorianchikov emphasizes that money has a "terrible significance and power" in the prison, for its possession and the spending of it allow the convict the opportunity, no matter how limited, to exercise his own will and free choice rather than to function merely as part of the fixed routines and relationships of the Dead House. Money allows him to "declare himself and his humiliated personality," and to enact "an anguished, convulsive manifestation of [his] personality," something that can easily go beyond spending and become bingeing, violence, or insanity (IV, 66–67). This desire to enact "a convulsive manifestation of personality," no matter what the cost, also underlies the convicts' passion for gambling, an activity that dominates time free from labor in the Dead House. We have already seen in the introduction to the present study that in popular lore gambling was an activity replete with demonic significance, and Jackson argues that in *The House of the Dead*, as well as elsewhere in Dostoevsky's work, it is a phenomenon rich in symbolic meaning, "a remarkable point of conjunction for so many areas of human thought and experience."[15] Not only does gambling—a concept broadened in Jackson's use of it to include other forms of risk-taking, such as escape attempts—permit a form of existential freedom through the affirmation of selfhood in the face of overwhelming constraints, but it also serves as a metaphor that clarifies the demonic nature of the Dead House and of the convicts' relationship to it. In Jackson's resonant words: "The dead house for [Dostoevsky] later became the metaphor for an enclosed, godless universe, a place where hope or salvation was absolutely denied. Man confined in such a universe could only conceive of the world as being directed by blind fate; that is, he could only relate to it as a gambler."[16] Jackson goes on to demonstrate in an entirely convincing way how the convict's need for gambling and risk—his "desire to determine and affirm his ontological status in a seemingly blind universe"—aligns him psychologically with many of Dostoevsky's later and more individualized characters, such as the Underground Man and Aleksei Ivanovich, the hero of *The Gambler.*[17] The difference is that the convict's desire is unconscious and his ontological status is truly debased by a blind and powerful prison system that bestializes him and tries to strip away all his humanity. Risk and gambling therefore carry a positive and creative charge in the case of the convict, representing his refusal to submit entirely to the meaningless fortunes of a demonic and inhuman universe that for him is coterminous with the Dead House. The Underground Man and the hero of *The Gambler,* however, use risk in order to take up arms not against the Dead House, a demonic universe created by man, but against nature and a universe created by God. Their gambling is thus demonic.

"A PARTICULAR KIND OF HELL": *THE GAMBLER* AND *WINTER NOTES ON SUMMER IMPRESSIONS*

The House of the Dead addresses only indirectly and fleetingly the theme of gambling and the phenomenon of the Westernized nobleman-intellectual who has lost the plot of the Christian narrative of Russian cultural history (along with his place in that plot). The specific demonization of those phenomena begins later, in works written from the 1860s onward. Among those works *The Gambler,* uniquely, exploits the linkages between the two motifs by showing us the lives of Russians living abroad, lives that are centered around the gaming tables of Europe, and it is in this work that the devil really begins to get his act together as a player in the symbolic substructure of Dostoevsky's art.

Like *The House of the Dead, The Gambler* has been widely regarded as an autobiographical and highly personal work, this time drawing on Dostoevsky's own experiences of being a Russian abroad, on his slavish fascination with the casinos of Europe, and on his tortured relationship with Polina Suslova, the highstrung bohemian under whose sway he fell during his European tour of 1862 to 1863. There is much in the text to support this view: Suslova's first name, many of her personal characteristics, and the painful power she exercised over Dostoevsky are all reflected in Polina and her relationship with Aleksei; the writer's own xenophobia and his particular distaste for the French and Poles are displayed in the novel; and his view of the Russian parted from his native soil as a spiritual vagabond is central to the depiction of Aleksei and the general's family. But the work transcends the simply autobiographical through its richly textured characterization and the challenging philosophical questions it raises. Those questions were identified by Dostoevsky right from the start of his work on the novel, as the following well-known passage from a letter of September 1863 to his friend and colleague N. N. Strakhov makes clear:

> The subject matter of the story is this: a certain type of Russian abroad. Note that during the summer there was a big thing about Russians abroad in the newspapers. All this will be reflected in my story, as will be in a general sense the entire present moment in our inner life (insofar, of course, as this is possible). I take a straightforward nature, a man, however, who is highly developed in many ways, but who is in all respects immature; one who has lost his faith *yet is afraid of not believing*, who rebels against the powers that be yet fears them. He consoles himself with the thought that there is *nothing for him to do* in Russia. [. . .] The main thing is that all his vital juices, forces, tempestuousness, and boldness have gone *into roulette*. He is a gambler, and not just a straightforward gambler, in the same way that Pushkin's miserly knight is no straightforward miser. [. . .] He is a poet in his way, but the point is that he is himself ashamed of this poetry, for he deeply feels its baseness, although the need *for risk* also ennobles him in his own eyes.(XXVIII/2, 50–51)

Dostoevsky's mention of newspaper debates refers to items in the periodicals *The Day* (*Den'*) and *The Contemporary* (*Sovremennik*), in the spring and early summer of 1863, in which Russians living abroad were referred to as "guliashchie liudi." This literally means "wandering people," but the verb *guliat'* also has the secondary senses of idling, carousing, or engaging in licentiousness. Dostoevsky was also alarmed at the sheer number of Russians leaving their native land for the enticements of Western Europe: the periodical *Russian Herald* (*Russkii vestnik*) had in October 1862 provided data suggesting that, in 1860 alone, 275,582 Russians went abroad.[18] Such physical abandonment, in Dostoevsky's view, was only the tip of the iceberg: it was the outwardly visible symptom of the renunciation of Russian nationality by those classes that were spiritually corrupted by Russia's love affair with European secular culture in the wake of the Westernization processes that had accelerated in the reigns of Peter the Great and Catherine the Great. The result was the phenomenon of the *obshchechelovek*, a term Dostoevsky uses quite often from this point on. It means literally "general man" or "universal man"—and such suggestions of universality might be read as carrying a positive connotation—but Dostoevsky's use of the term is always unambiguously negative, referring to what he saw as the tragedy of the Europeanized Russian whose loss of all nationality and cultural identity translates into a total lack of purpose, conviction, and meaning—a demonic spiritual atrophy. We shall find the most complete fictional treatment of this figure in the character of Stavrogin in *The Devils,* where its demonic meaning is fully exploited, but Dostoevsky had already attempted a sustained meditation on the effects of Western Europe on the Russian upper classes in his account of his own European wanderings, *Winter Notes on Summer Impressions* (1863), a work close to *The Gambler* in both time and spirit.

Dostoevsky's point of departure for this meditation was one that he shared with the Slavophile tendency in mid-nineteenth-century Russian thought: the conviction that the problematic relationship of the Russian educated nobleman to his nationality was traceable to the Petrine period and to the most visible symbol of the Westernization which that period had foisted on educated Russians: Petersburg, "the most fantastical city, with the most fantastical history of all the cities on earth" (V, 57). However, Peter's attempts to wrest Russia from her true national identity onto an alien path of development touched only the enlightened minority of the Russian population, leaving the masses intact as uncontaminated vessels of the true Russian national identity, a rounded and holistic identity rooted in Orthodox faith rather than the fragmented sense of both selfhood and nationhood produced by the scalpel of rational analysis. Dostoevsky is keen to make the distinction:

> Are we indeed really Russians? Why does Europe produce on us, whoever we are, such a powerful, magical, inviting impression? That is to say, I am not speaking now of those Russians who have remained there, those simple Russians who number some fifty million, and whom we, a mere hundred thousand in number, seriously regard as nobodies and whom our profound satirical journals still ridicule for not shaving off their beards. No, I'm speaking of our privileged and patent few. You see, everything, practically everything we have by way of development—science, art, civilization, humanity, everything—why, it all comes from there, from that land of holy wonders! (V, 51)

The result is the complete estrangement of the educated classes from the mass of Russian people:

> Nowadays the people regard us as foreigners. They do not understand a single word we say, not a single one of our books or a single one of our thoughts—and that, if you like, is progress. [...] While we, on the other hand, are now so self-assured in our civilizing vocation, we resolve questions so condescendingly, and what questions they are: there is no such thing as native soil; there is no such thing as a nation—nationality is merely a means of taxation; the soul is a *tabula rasa,* a piece of wax from which we can now

mould a true man, the universal *obshchechelovek,* a homunculus—all you have to do is apply the fruits of European civilization and read two or three little books. (V, 59)

In *Winter Notes on Summer Impressions* Dostoevsky remains optimistic that the damage of the Petrine period can be undone and that the alienated Russian nobleman-intellectual can be reclaimed for Orthodoxy and true nationality through his discovery of the Russian people. He draws comfort from the fact that, despite unconstrained enthusiasm for that "land of holy wonders," the Europeanized Russian has not yet turned finally into a European. What is it that inhibits this? "Is it really the case that there is some sort of chemical fusion of the human soul and its native land, so that it is completely impossible to tear yourself away from it, and even if you do try to tear yourself away you are nevertheless drawn back?" (V, 52). Such optimism is tempered in later embodiments of the *obshchechelovek,* embodiments such as Stavrogin, in whom the remnants of national memory are insufficient to reclaim him from the identity vacuum he inhabits. But even in *Winter Notes on Summer Impressions* Dostoevsky is in no mood to understate the danger. Despite the occasionally skittish tone of the author of the notes, the characterization of European civilization they afford is one darkened by demonic and apocalyptic symbolism.

That characterization is drawn essentially from Dostoevsky's impressions of two European capitals: Paris and London. His initial description of Paris as "the most moral and virtuous city in the whole world. What order!" (V, 68) is deeply ironic, for the order described is a superficial bourgeois order centered on propriety, formalism, and empty eloquence, and rooted in acquisitiveness and materialism: "To amass a fortune and possess as many things as possible—this has become the most important code of morality, the catechism of the Parisian" (V, 76). Material wealth thus informs the individual's attitude not only to others but also to himself, so that all human values and relationships are reduced, overtly or covertly, to financial transactions. Dostoevsky discerns the same bourgeois materialism in London, but here his account transcends irony to become a truly apocalyptic vision of European civilization ruled by the demonic spirit of industrial capitalism and its consequences. The chapter in question is the very heart of *Winter Notes on Summer Impressions* and it offers a Dickensian description of London by night, in which all Dostoevsky's antipathy to European civilization is condensed into some of his most inspired, poetic, and heartrending pages, where mere social indictment is transcended and raised to a level of profound religious despair, and where the Russian writer abroad is transformed from bemused chronicler of foreign habits into a stern prophet, foretelling nothing less than the end of Western civilization. His descriptions are not those of a traveling paysagist, but are terrible revelations, straining against the very limits of naturalism; the language, too, is revelatory, laden with a sense of doom and saturated with dread of the future foretold by all that he sees:

> This city, bustling day and night, and boundless like the sea; the screeching and howling of machines, the railways built above the houses (and before long beneath the houses too), the boldness of enterprise, the apparent disorder which is in fact the very height of bourgeois order, the poisoned Thames, the air impregnated with coal dust, the magnificent squares and parks, those terrible corners of the town like Whitechapel with its half-naked, wild and hungry inhabitants. The City with its millions and world trade, the Crystal Palace, the World Exhibition . . . (V, 69)

The chapter is entitled, simply and starkly, "Baal," the name of the ancient Phoenician god of material abundance and human sacrifice. The Baal reigning over nineteenth-century industrial Britain was, for Dostoevsky, capitalism; and the human sacrifice demanded was that of man's soul, to be swallowed up in the inexorable, impersonal progress of a society devoted exclusively to material, technological, and financial advancement. Amid the vivid impressions and sharp contrasts that marked out London life from the bourgeois order he had experienced in Paris, Dostoevsky sensed a fundamental paradox, one this society was powerless to resolve: "But all the same here too there is that persistent, smoldering, and already chronic struggle: the fight to the death between the principle of individuality common to Western man and the necessity somehow or other to live together in harmony, to form a community and settle down in the one anthill. Yes, even to become an anthill, just so long as things can be organized without people eating each other—otherwise people will turn into cannibals!" (V, 69). We are here at the very epicenter of Dostoevsky's aversion to Western Europe, the tremors and aftershocks of which may be felt in all his major artistic and journalistic works from this point onward, but most especially in *Notes from Underground* (1864). For him, at a time in his life when his own beliefs were moving toward Slavophilism and faith in Russia's distinctive nature and destiny, European civilization offered only the stark choice of two unacceptably demonic options: either the unfettered pursuit of personal freedom at the expense of social order, as in the revolutions that had shaken the fabric of Europe since 1789, or the sacrifice of the individual to scientific, political, social, material, or economic necessity. There was no third way for a civilization that had lost its spirituality and organic unity—its "binding idea," as Lebedev describes it in *The Idiot*—in its worship of Baal and the pursuit of material advantage.

The demonic nature of Europe's secularized civilization, and by implication of Russian high society's infatuation with that civilization, is suggested in *Winter Notes on Summer Impressions* not only in the hellish descriptions of industrial and working-class London, where the "white negroes" of industrial servitude seek escape in systematic inebriation, but also in the rhetoric used to describe such scenes. Startling images of the "proud and somber spirit" of Baal ruling over this technological hell are matched by consistent reference to the Apocalypse, with its promise of a day of judgment for those who have strayed from the divine path. For Dostoevsky, the World Exhibition held in the Crystal Palace stood as a prophecy of Europe's terrible future. The exhibition, or World Fair, had returned to London in May 1862 and was intended as a celebration of technical and scientific achievement. The Crystal Palace, originally built by Sir Joseph Paxton in 1851, was an enormous iron and glass structure, the architecture of which was entirely in keeping with the new spirit of scientific optimism and heroic materialism. An icon of industrial capitalism, it was also, paradoxically, seen by revolutionary thinkers like Chernyshevsky as a symbol of the secular paradise on earth that man would achieve through socialism. Dostoevsky's description is alert to all these implications:

> Yes, the Exhibition is staggering. You can sense the terrible force which has brought all these innumerable people from all over the world together into one fold; you are conscious of a huge idea; you feel that here something has already been achieved, a victory, a triumph. You even begin to feel a little afraid. No matter how independent you are, for some reason you become fearful. You begin to think "Is this not indeed the attainment of the ideal? Is this not indeed the end of the line? Is this not in fact the 'one fold'? Should you not indeed accept it all as the whole truth and hold your peace?" It is all so solemn, triumphal, and proud that it begins to get you down. You look at these hundreds of thousands, these millions of people obediently flocking here from the four corners of the earth, all coming with the one idea, calmly, deliberately and silently crowding into that colossal palace, and you feel that here something final has come to pass—and come to an end. It is a sort of biblical image, something like Babylon, a prophecy from the Apocalypse taking place before your eyes. You feel it will take a great deal of constant spiritual resistance and denial not to give in, not to succumb to the illusion, not to bow to the fact and worship Baal; not, in other words, to accept what exists as the ideal. (V, 69–70)

It is as though Dostoevsky, in a moment of prophetic insight occasioned by his visit to the Crystal Palace, has realized that what is offered by this glimpse of a rational, technological future is not St. John's prophecy of unity in Christ—"and there shall be one fold, and one shepherd" (John

10:16)—where the freedom of the individual and the interests of the "fold" are held in balance and all are united in mutual love and love of Christ. Rather it is a secular "utopia" concealing the hell of a "brave new world" where the individual is sacrificed to the dumb and implacable machinery of technological and social "progress," yet another house of the dead.

This implied comparison neatly returns us to the discussion of *The Gambler*. In the letter to Strakhov already cited, Dostoevsky goes on to compare *The Gambler* too with *The House of the Dead,* writing that the former presents its own "particular kind of hell, its own particular kind of prison 'bathhouse'" (XXVIII/2, 51). This explicit linkage must be taken seriously, as more than a mere attempt to yoke a forthcoming work to the recent success of an earlier one. Where the "hell" of *The House of the Dead* had taken the form of a Dantean picture of lost human souls confined in the world of the prison house, *The Gambler* shows us the tragedy of the alienated, Western-ized, contemporary Russian, stripped of all true faith and national identity, and caught up in the tyranny of the godless world he has created, one apparently governed by the blind laws of nature, force, and chance. Again, R. L. Jackson's analysis is sharply to the point. Both the convict and the gambler:

> are prisoners in what appears to be an enclosed fate-bound universe. But whereas the convict lives in a prison world not of his own choice, a world from which, moreover, there is really no way out, the gambler lives in a dead house, or underground, of his own making. In the gambler's world everybody is possessed by the illusion of freedom, but nobody is really free.[19]

For Aleksei roulette is not simply a social ritual, nor even primarily a way of making money, needy though he is. It is a form of existential struggle, the futile attempt of an individual trapped in the wastes of unbelief to assert his existence in a meaningless universe. Indeed, as Jackson says, "the very act of gambling becomes a conscious or unconscious affirmation of the meaninglessness of the universe, the emptiness of all human choice."[20] Aleksei's passion for roulette eloquently conveys the exclusion of God from the universe he has chosen to inhabit; his acknowledgment that the universe is ruled by nothing more meaningful than contingency and chance; and his own demonic compulsion to take on that universe and, by mastering it, to fill with his own will the vacuum at its heart. This makes clear the significance of Dostoevsky's comment to Strakhov to the effect that his gambler is no straightforward gambler, in the same way that Pushkin's character is no straightforward miser. The Baron in Pushkin's dramatic sketch *The Miserly Knight* (1830) amasses a huge fortune in gold, not for its purchasing power, but as a means of defining and asserting his own being. In a very real sense Pushkin's miser *is* what he owns, for there are no other bases to his existence.

With Aleksei cast in the role of demonic outcast and pretender to

power, and gambling presented as a displacement of faith in divine authority, it is hardly surprising that the rhetoric of *The Gambler* is contaminated
by demonic signs, some explicit, others less so. Roulettenburg—geographi-
cally indistinct, a place where nobody belongs, its population consisting of
gambling itinerants—is a town constructed in the name of blind, meaningless contingency. It is dominated by two physical features: the casino, set in
a railway station with its implications of impermanence and rootlessness; and
Schlangenberg—"Snake Mountain"—a name replete with demonic meaning.[21] In this modern hell, love, friendship, and the principle of the family
are stripped of value. The "love" between Aleksei and Polina is perverted
into the tragic exercise of morbid self-esteem and destructive egoism; des
Grieux's pursuit of Polina is driven not by idealism, but by greed (his name
surely is intended to suggest an ironic inversion of the moral idealism of the
hero of Prévost's novel *Manon Lescaut*); the general's feelings for his mother
and children turn on the questions of inheritance and financial advantage,
and the respectable Frenchwoman he adores turns out to be an upmarket
courtesan with an eye on his fortune-to-be. And all this takes place not in
Russia, but in that very Western Europe that Dostoevsky held responsible
for a contemporary cultural and spiritual collapse brought about by extreme
individualism, materialism, and religious despair.

The use of roulette as a demonic metaphor in *The Gambler* is richly
suggestive. Jackson has shown how it displaces Polina as the true object of
Aleksei's interest, marking his highly significant transition from lover to gambler, albeit driven by the same aim of engagement with a cruel and implacable mistress—fate.[22] It is specifically used by the Englishman Astley as a
metaphor for the condition of the Russian ruling classes when he asserts to
Aleksei that "Roulette is pre-eminently a Russian game," adding parenthet-
ically, "I am not speaking of your common people" (V, 317). The way it has
displaced religious faith in Aleksei is implied when Polina refers to it as his
"only way out and salvation" (V, 219); and it acts on the otherwise sensible
Grandmother as a form of demonic possession that completely overcomes
her between her arrival in Roulettenburg and her eventual return to Russia,
eliciting from her servant Potapych the shrewd observation: "Akh, that's
enough for me of your abroad—I said it'd come to no good. The quicker we
get back to our Moscow! And what is it they've got that we haven't got back
home in Moscow? We've got a garden, flowers of the sort you can't find
here, fresh air, apples ripening, open spaces—but no, they had to go
abroad!" (V, 281). Gambling also displaces all morality for Aleksei: "What I
have noticed is that latterly it has become somehow terribly repulsive to me
to attribute my actions and thoughts to any moral standard. It was something
else that was guiding me" (V, 218). That "something else" is his sense of the
utter moral relativism of a universe ruled only by chance: "The fact is that
one turn of the wheel and everything could change, and those very same

moralists (I am convinced of this) would be the first to come up with their friendly jokes to congratulate me" (V, 311). The meaninglessness of such a universe, which might reduce many to existential despair, exhilarates Aleksei through the opportunities it offers for risk: "I had dared to risk, and now again I was in the ranks of men!" (V, 312). Its demonic underpinnings are suggested in the repeated use throughout *The Gambler* of the image of leaping from a tower, or in this case Schlangenberg or Snake Mountain, as a sign of the hero's willingness to assume that risk.

In such a universe "everything is permitted," yet nothing is really possible.[23] Aleksei's freedom consists of blind submission to the whims of fate, as he acknowledges in his description of his gambling technique: "At times, however, calculation entered into my thinking. I would go with certain numbers and chances, but I would soon abandon this and bet again, almost unconsciously" (V, 293). His room for maneuver in life is severely curtailed by the path he has chosen. He dreams of a final resurrection and new life, but, as Jackson says, "He will never escape the tyranny of his self-created dead universe."[24] It is the story *Bobok* (1873), rather than *The Gambler,* that provides the most startling image linking gambling, spiritual death, and demonism. The story describes corpses in a graveyard passing the time between physical death and the final extinction of consciousness by playing cards and contemplating a final grand debauch on the basis that, because they apparently have no afterlife, they must be released from all moral constraints, with everything being permitted. The demonic connotations of gambling and debauchery in a cemetery at the liminal moment between life and permanent extinction are entirely self-evident (XXI, 41–53).

The Gambler might have nothing quite to match this, but it does provide striking signs of its own to demonize the world of the Russian gambler abroad. For example, Dostoevsky's well-documented xenophobia always took its most extreme form in his attitude to the French and the Poles. In *The Gambler* this xenophobia is much in evidence, but the Frenchman des Grieux, although presented as a vacuous, self-seeking and unpleasant piece of work, does not attract specifically demonic motifs. Instead, his role in the novel's symbolic substructure is to represent the ease with which Russians are infatuated by the superficial style and forms of the West, to the detriment of their own identity. This role is made explicit by Aleksei late in the novel, when he tries to explain to Mr. Astley the nature of Polina's attraction to des Grieux (V, 315–16). Conversely, the Poles who gather around Grandmother during her "demonic possession," when she completely loses her senses and squanders a fortune at the roulette wheel, are like nothing so much as the squalid petty demons of the Russian folk tradition. These "little polacks" (Dostoevsky uses the offensively diminutive form *poliachki*) flock around and lead astray (*zakruzhit'*) the hapless Grandmother and proceed to confuse her utterly (*sbili babushku s tolku*) in an image that consciously or unconsciously has much in common with the description of how lost travelers are confused and led astray by demons in Pushkin's lyric "Devils" ("Besy" [1830]), where similar vocabulary is used: "We've lost our way (*sbilis' my*). What can we do!/It seems a devil is leading us into a field,/And is whirling around (*kruzhit*) us on all sides." As we shall see, Dostoevsky was to exploit his close familiarity with the demonology of Pushkin's poem in *The Devils,* where it serves as an epigraph to the novel. Grandmother's "little polacks" then squawk "like roosters caught in the hand" when ejected from the casino, but they return with another Pole who is "dressed like a gentleman, but nevertheless looked like a lackey," details again associated with Russian folk conceptions of the devil. Finally, more and more "little polacks," "hitherto unseen and unheard," begin to emerge around the roulette table and even follow Grandmother back to her hotel (V, 282–84).

The Gambler also exploits the demonic motif of imposture. As Jackson writes, "Nothing is what it seems in Roulettenburg. All is deception," and deception is the most fundamental of the devil's dark arts. There is little need to dwell on all the novel's instances of imposture here, since Jackson's analysis is detailed and embraces even the trustworthiness of Aleksei's narrative.[25] We might, though, remind ourselves of Aleksei's assumed role of lover concealing his real identity as gambler, and perhaps of the chameleon-like Blanche, whose apparent respectability conceals a self-seeking courtesan. Aleksei actually describes her as a "devil" and he draws attention to the "demonic" beauty of her face (V, 272); but Blanche slips out of this role too, turning out in the end to possess a decent enough heart in her final dealings with the General and with Aleksei himself.

But it seems to me that the most significant instance of imposture and uncertain identity in *The Gambler* is that of the Englishman Mr. Astley. This figure has been seen as a positive force in the novel by the majority of critics: Jackson, for example, describes him as "the eminently decent Astley"[26]; Mochulsky writes that "Of all the foreigners only the Englishman is portrayed with sympathy. Mr. Astley is an eccentric, timid, taciturn, and virtuous"[27]; while the editors of the Academy edition of Dostoevsky's works compare him to "the kind and noble heroes of Dickens' novels" (V, 402). Moreover, it is a well-documented fact that Dostoevsky's xenophobia was less intense in the case of the English, for whom he had a sneaking admiration.[28] In light of all this, any attempt to suggest that the depiction of Astley is, at the very least, ambiguous, let alone contaminated by demonic markers, must be tentative and well documented. We may start by recognizing that in Russian folk tradition the devil often appears in the guises of foreigner, friend, or gentleman, three roles that define Astley's persona. Right from the start his strangeness is emphasized, along with an almost uncanny ubiquity:

I first met that strange Englishman in Prussia, in a railway carriage where we sat opposite each other, while I was trying to catch up with our group; then I bumped into him entering France, and finally in Switzerland; twice in the course of these two weeks, and now here I suddenly meet him already in Roulettenburg. [. . .] I got him into conversation during our first meeting in Prussia. He told me that this summer he had been to the North Cape and that he would really like to visit the fair at Nizhegorod. (V, 210)

This ubiquity, along with the information that Aleksei and Astley sat opposite each other in the railway carriage, appears to anticipate features of Myshkin's relationship with his demon Rogozhin in *The Idiot,* particularly in light of the fact that Astley's ability to be everywhere at once continues during events in Roulettenburg:

and wherever we happened to be: in the park, in the woods, or on Schlangenberg—you only had to look up suddenly and look around, and without fail there would be a part of Mr. Astley evident somewhere, either on a nearby path or from behind a bush. (V, 222)

We might ascribe this behavior to Astley's reported infatuation with Polina, were it not for the fact that his ubiquity appears to embrace the lives of others, too: Both Blanche and des Grieux seem to know him from elsewhere, for example (V, 221), while Aleksei learns that he has been in Frankfurt "on business" at the same time as des Grieux is there (V, 285, 291). On this latter point Astley is so evasive that Aleksei "little by little came to realize that even if I had spoken with him for two hours, I would have found out absolutely nothing" (V, 285). Sometimes the intimations of Astley's ubiquity are disturbing: During Polina's compromising visit to Aleksei's room, when she is possessed by uncontrollable and hysterical laughter, she suddenly starts talking about Astley, insisting that he is standing under the window of the room at that very moment. Her further comments on him carry surprisingly negative connotations:

"Mr Astley? . . . Well, that one won't be leaping off Schlangenberg, what do you think? (She burst out laughing.) Now, listen: do you know where he's going next summer? He wants to go to the North Pole on some scientific expedition, and he's invited me to go with him, ha-ha-ha! He says that without Europe we Russians don't know anything and are not capable of anything." (V, 297)

This passage contains several potentially demonic markers: Polina's nervous laughter as she speaks of Astley; her recognition that, unlike Aleksei, he is not vulnerable to demonic temptation by leaping off Schlangenberg; the intimation that, like Svidrigailov, Astley is the victim of a demonic, Pechorinesque Romantic ennui that makes him seek relief in travel; and finally the revelation that he shares the demonic illusion that Russia is nothing without Europe. The oblique analogy drawn here between Astley and Pechorin is reinforced later when, in his final encounter with Aleksei, Astley displays a hitherto unsuspected cynicism: "In reality, a man loves to see his best friend humiliated before his eyes; for the most part friendship is based on humiliation, and this is an old truth well known to all intelligent people" (V, 313). So well known, in fact, that Pechorin had made almost the identical observation in his remark to the effect that of two friends, one is invariably the slave of the other.[29] Furthermore, it should be noted in passing that association with Pechorin is not the only oblique literary reference serving to demonize Astley. Earlier we have learned that he "would stand for a whole morning at the gaming tables, without ever playing a stake himself" (V, 224). These words serve to link Astley with the similarly complex and ambiguous figure of Hermann in Pushkin's *The Queen of Spades*, who also watches others gamble for whole nights on end, but "has never taken a card in his hand" himself, and who is also demonized by Pushkin (albeit ironically) through his association with Mephistopheles and his Romantic revolt against convention.

The "particular kind of hell" that is Roulettenburg needs a particular kind of devil to orchestrate its evil, and Astley appears to be cast in that role. Forever enigmatic, always in the corner of one's field of vision, he seems not only to know everything that is going on, but to be the one overseeing it all. He confidently predicts Aleksei's move to Paris (V, 300); the money acquired by the general toward the end of the novel appears to come from Astley (V, 308); Aleksei suspects that his release from prison is Astley's doing (V, 311); and the latter always seems to be one step ahead of Aleksei in understanding the course of events. If he appears as benign benefactor, then we must remember that he does so courtesy of Aleksei's narrative, something we are explicitly warned not to take at face value. For Aleksei the events in which he is caught up are a "chaotic dream" (*bezobraznyi son*), but one whose seductive effects he is reluctant to dissipate and his understanding of which is less than complete (V, 281–82).

"NO LONGER LITERATURE, BUT CORRECTIONAL PUNISHMENT": *NOTES FROM UNDERGROUND*

Like the author of *Winter Notes on Summer Impressions*, the hero of *Notes from Underground* shows himself to be fully alert to the cultural implications of Russia's Westernization in the post-Petrine period when he describes St.

Petersburg, the symbol of that Westernization, as "the most abstract and premeditated city in the whole world" (V, 101). Like a mechanical womb, this city—built in the face of nature and contrary to the spirit of Russia's national character—nurtures not natural beings, not Russians, but homunculi, test-tube men, individuals "who have torn themselves away from their soil and national principles" (V, 107). For the Underground Man such creatures "emerging in the end not from the lap of nature, but from a retort" (V, 104), are the victims of an over-refined consciousness and are spawn of the devil who, like Adam, place "the consciousness of life" higher than "living life." Faced with the immutable and inescapable scientific laws that such consciousness has uncovered and with which it has bound and determined the world of God and nature, these "retort" men, these "mice of aggravated consciousness" (V, 104), have the non-choice of two equally unpalatable options: either to submit to those same deterministic rational laws of nature, losing all dignity and freedom in the process and becoming little more than a "piano key" or "organ stop," or to fly in the face of those rational laws in an orgy of willful existential revolt. The Underground Man adopts the latter course, arguing that the pain that inevitably follows such willful challenges to rationality offers a more "advantageous advantage" than mere self-interest:

> One's own willful, free volition, one's own caprice, however wild, one's own fantasy, inflamed at times to the point of madness—that's what everything comes down to and what constitutes that very same, but overlooked, most advantageous advantage which does not fit into any system of classification and in the face of which all systems and theories go to the devil. (V, 113)

We shall pass over for now the introduction of a demonic motif at the end of this profession of faith, for that faith is self-evidently demonic. The Underground Man embodies the spirit of negation, and his perverse logic compels him to renounce in the name of freedom everything positive. He jealously guards that freedom from the encroachment of anything that might limit it. A finely tuned consciousness is his key tactical weapon in that ongoing struggle, as it allows him constantly to analyze his own behavior, remaining ever alert to the dangers posed by consequentiality, contingency, and necessity, which in the minefield of everyday "living life" prevent man from acting freely, consciously, and capriciously. He argues that man, in order to live authentically as a self-creating being, must resist all self-definition and refuse to submit to anything that would impair his freedom, even if this means acting against his own self-interest, flying in the face of reason, and rebelling against the very laws of nature. Here we see him for what he really is: the embodiment of what Ivan Kireevsky called "the self-propelling scalpel of reason," individual consciousness disengaged from contact with living life to the point of absurdity.[30] He tries, for instance, to get himself thrown from a billiard-room window, for he knows that such an act, although not in his own immediate interest, serves the more "advantageous advantage" of asserting his own independence from such considerations. He acknowledges the logic of mathematics but reserves for himself the right to make two and two add up to five if he wishes, since "twice two is four is no longer life, gentlemen, but the beginning of death" (V, 118–19). He submits to no scientific or natural law, for although he might accept its validity he will not be imprisoned by that acceptance: "What are all these laws of nature and arithmetic to me if I don't happen to like them?" (V, 105). Suffering and pain are the usual consequences of such extreme revolt, but even here the Underground Man derives an advantage, for suffering further sharpens consciousness and refines his sense of freedom.

But what kind of freedom is gained by this sort of revolt? It is certainly not the freedom to act, at least not in any meaningful way, for the heightened consciousness of the Underground Man dissolves every impulse to action in a sea of analysis, doubt, and contradiction. As he says himself, "The direct, lawful and immediate fruit of consciousness is inertia—that is, consciously sitting with your arms folded" (V, 108). Here is the paradox in the Underground Man's condition: "All consciousness is an illness," he says (V, 102), and he envies the "natural" man's capacity for action, but at the same time he despises him for his limitations and stupidity. Yet his own "freedom" is even more constraining, for he cannot move without compromising it. His self-denial at the end of part 1, when he insists that he has been lying "like a cobbler" (V, 121), shows just how demanding his freedom is: He must renounce all he has said in order to avoid defining himself as a man who avoids self-definition! Such freedom is the ultimate denial of freedom; it closes rather than opens up possibilities, and it saps the will it is supposed to liberate. As A. D. Nuttall has observed, the Underground Man is on the run, forever obliged to confirm his frail and sterile freedom in ever more outrageous and meaningless outbursts of irrationality.[31] In the words of Michael Holquist, "He is constantly making experiments in ontology, a mad scientist in the cluttered laboratory of his own identity."[32]

The essential pillars of the Underground Man's identity—a morbid self-consciousness, proud individuality, a rationalistic cast of mind that values the understanding of life more than a feeling for life, an infinite defiance and capacity for revolt, complete withdrawal and isolation, and a sterile freedom consisting of inertia—are essentially those of a demon. As such they attract demonic symbolism in the course of *Notes from Underground,* and this raises the question of the extent to which the hero is aware of the contamination of his first-person confessional discourse by such markers. Is this conscious irony on his part, presenting his "underground" of morbid individualism as a travesty of demonic revolt, or is it a semiotic game played behind the character's back by the implied author and the reader, using a shared language of cultural signs in order to frame with extraneous values the monologue of the Underground Man? The answer is probably a bit of both. As a reasonably educated and intelligent man, the hero is presumably aware of the echoes of Genesis and the fall of man in his bemoaning the way in which consciousness, and the placing of the understanding of life higher than the instinctive sense of life, has excluded him from the easy paradise of natural immediacy. He must also be aware of the potentially demonic identity he invites by the constant application to himself of the adjective *zloi* (a word implying the characteristics of both trivial human nastiness and grandiose metaphysical evil). But is he aware of the demonic subtext discernible in his account of how a man like himself is wont to react to any paradise brought about by the efforts of those socialists intent on restructuring the social order on the basis of rational principles?

> Why I, for example, would not be in the least surprised if suddenly and for no apparent reason there appeared in the midst of all this future good sense some sort of gentleman [*dzhentl'men*], with an ignoble or, to put it better, a retrograde and derisive countenance, who puts his hands on his hips and says to all of us: why, ladies and gentlemen, should we not do away with all this good sense once and for all, kick it away, reduce it to dust, with the sole aim of sending all these logarithms to the devil so that we might once more live on the basis of our own stupid whim! (V, 113)

The use of the stylized word *dzhentl'men*, a guise assumed by the devil in Russian folklore, the direct reference to the devil (*k chertu*), as well as the thematics of irrational revolt against a paradisiacal order in the name of human will—all carry a strongly demonic charge of which the hero may or may not be aware at the time of writing. Similarly, it is questionable whether the Underground Man is inviting us to consider the folk-demonic significance of the word "spoiling" (*porcha*), when he uses it in a discussion of the extent to which his own life might have been invaded by malign forces (V, 102). He would certainly appear to be unaware of the irony in his use of the word, given that his own relationship with the world of nature, normality, and good sense is a travesty of the "spoiling" relationship of the "unclean force" to the world of man in folk tradition. Other demonic markers of which the hero is unlikely to be conscious include possible linkage between his "underground" (*podpol'e*) and the spatially specific demon of Russian folk belief, the *bes podpol'nyi*, and the information that his room—the locus of his figurative underground—is situated "on the edge of town" (*na kraiu goroda*), a strikingly liminal space (V, 101). He also draws attention to the fact that man is the only animal capable of cursing, a quality that both reflects his alienation from the rest of creation and assures his freedom (V, 117). Moreover, that freedom is reinforced by the Underground Man's insistence on seeing all life, including his relationship with the prostitute Liza, as a form of gambling in which he pits himself against the odds. In this way he embodies two further characteristics, cursing and risk-taking, the demonic significance of which has already emerged in our discussion of *The House of the Dead* and *The Gambler.*

Such markers, whether used consciously or not by the Underground Man, serve to delineate an appropriately demonic backdrop to his life's tale. But it is important to recognize that his demonism ultimately resides not just in the content of that tale, but more insidiously in the way that he tells it. It is the Underground Man's willingness to exploit and manipulate both his role as narrator and the potential offered by the confessional device that reveals a truly Luciferian figure, concealing himself behind evasions and generating lies, ambiguity, and confusion in order to justify his tawdry egoism and to mould and recreate the world in accordance with his own whim. The first-person confessional form of *Notes from Underground* has been a consistent focus of attention for critical analysis of that work, and much of this analysis has centered on the paradox of an apparently monological work that exploits every opportunity for dialogical engagement with imaginary interlocutors. The earliest example of such critical analysis is to be found in the text of the work itself, and the Underground Man turns out to be the first to address the formal properties and narrative status of the work he writes. With an eye on Heine's assertion that a truly confessional autobiography is impossible in that a person will always lie about himself, the Underground Man defends the veracity of his own confession by arguing that, unlike Rousseau, he is not confessing to a public and his notes are not designed for publication—they are merely an exercise in self-confrontation and self-indictment, what he later describes as "no longer literature, but correctional punishment" (V, 178). At the same time, however, he recognizes that his words do have an addressee: "And that's another problem for me: why, indeed, do I call you 'ladies and gentlemen' and why do I address you like proper readers?" (V, 122). He attempts to reconcile this apparent paradox by reducing it purely to considerations of form: "I am writing for myself alone, and let me make it clear once and for all that, if I write as though I were addressing readers, then this is only for the sake of appearances, because it is easier for me to write like that. It is a matter of form, pure form; I shall never have a readership." Indeed, he goes on to ask why he writes things down at all, rather than merely recalling them mentally, and he concludes that "on paper it comes out more solemnly" (V, 123). As an excuse, this is both feeble and revealing, for it shows the importance he attaches to the effect of his words.

Similar questions about the confessional and narrative status of the

Underground Man's notes are posed by his attachment of an epigraph to part 2, fourteen lines drawn from Nekrasov's poem of 1846, "When from the Darkness of Error" (*Kogda iz mraka zabluzhden'ia*). We can be confident in attributing this epigraph to the Underground Man rather than the implied author, partly in the absence of any evidence that would point to the contrary and partly because of the mockingly ironic "etc., etc., etc." with which the extract is concluded. These lines, suggesting the moral salvation of a fallen woman through the inspired words of the poem's narrator, clearly imply the Underground Man's intention to frame his recollections of his youth ironically within the idealistic and sentimental conventions that colored the work of writers of the so-called Natural School in the 1840s, a group that included Nekrasov. This, in turn, invites us to recognize that in part 2 it is the Underground Man's intention not so much to recall his life at the age of twenty-four as to *recreate* it within conventions of behavior that he has subsequently drawn not from "living life" (from which he is irrevocably estranged), but from his reading. Indeed, Malcolm Jones has offered a reconstruction on the basis of the text of the likely sources of the sensibilities displayed by the Underground Man, sources drawn largely from the traditions of Romanticism and philosophical idealism as well as from the Natural School.[33] In so doing the Underground Man breaks the terms of the confessional contract he has just, at the end of part 1, negotiated with both himself and his imaginary reader and interlocutor. His notes are now clearly no longer confined to truthful self-confrontation, to literature as "correctional punishment": He is now openly guilty of what Adam Weiner terms "the demonism of authorial pride" and of "openly challenging [the] Creator's exclusive rights to creation."[34] The epithet "correctional" is still applicable to what he writes, but only in the sense of attempting to rewrite an uncooperative reality in accordance with the behavioral conventions and self-image he has adopted.

The Underground Man thus uses narrative to posture, deceive, and reinvent himself through aesthetic reformulation and the deft use of rhetorical flourishes. The contrivance of an interlocutor of his own making is a more disturbing achievement than the mere adoption of a convenient "purely formal" device, as he implicitly recognizes in the following response to one of his interlocutor's imagined interjections: "Of course, all these words of yours I've made up myself just now. They too are from the underground. I've spent forty years on end there listening to those words of yours through a crack. I thought them up myself" (V, 122). The point about the Underground Man's relationship with his interlocutor is that, unlike in real-life relationships, he calls all the shots—even to the extent of determining the identity of his audience and the nature of its interventions. As Malcolm Jones suggests, as readers we come to feel uncomfortable with the identity the Underground Man thrusts on us.[35] We sense we are being coerced into an unequal "dialogue" in which we can speak only words preinvented for us as part of a script designed to serve the interests of the hero. Our originality and autonomy are written out even as we "speak," and our very predictability becomes a bulwark shoring up the Underground Man's self-image and superiority. Even when he describes his own shortcomings and humiliations it is on his own terms as author, as in the following example where he turns an initially negative statement about himself to his own advantage:

> I was a coward and a slave. I say this without any embarrassment. Every decent man in our time is and must be a coward and a slave. It is his normal condition. I am profoundly convinced of that. [. . .] Only asses and mongrels are bold, and then only until they reach a wall. It is not worth paying attention to them, since they signify nothing at all. (V, 125)

Our identity and autonomy as coparticipants in a "dialogue" do not extend as far as the freedom to object to this sleight-of-hand.

Indeed, perhaps we need to rethink our use of the word "dialogue" here. Bakhtin's well-known analysis of the dialectical underpinnings of the Underground Man's monologue is founded on the assumption that he incorporates the anticipated responses of others into his own discourse:

> What the Underground Man thinks about most of all is what others think or might think about him; he tries to keep one step ahead of every other consciousness, every other thought about him, every other point of view on him. At all the critical moments of his confession he tries to anticipate the possible definition or evaluation others might make of him, to guess the sense and tone of that evaluation, and tries painstakingly to formulate these possible words about himself by others, interrupting his own speech with the imagined rejoinders of others.[36]

The emphasis on anticipation here suggests the Underground Man's implicit acknowledgment of others and of the potential force and viability of other points of view, whereas the emphasis should perhaps fall on his denial of the autonomy and viability of others. He does not anticipate the response of others: He creates it from his own experience, and in so doing he inevitably excludes the possibility of unanticipated questions he might not be able to deal with. This is not dialogue, but the denial of dialogue; not "living life" with its unpredictable relationships, but demonically created life in which monologue is disguised as dialogue, authority is disguised as reciprocity, and power over others is disguised as tolerance.

Having created the hero of his notes, a suitably enhanced self, as well as a compliant and predictable readership, the next step is to script a plot and a cast of other characters. The result is the tale entitled "Apropos of Wet Snow," in which the Underground Man tells of his attempts to insinuate himself into a group of former school acquaintances and of his relationship with, and eventual abuse of, the prostitute Liza. In this tale he uses narrative in the service of self, rather than of truth, employing it both to reconstruct himself and his past in accordance with behavioral patterns derived from his reading, and to gain power over others. For example, when, having been slighted by his school acquaintances, he follows them to a bordello and dreams of challenging one of them, Zverkov, to a duel, the Underground Man is acutely aware that he is basing his planned behavior on that of Silvio in Pushkin's well-known tale "The Shot," as well as on the plot of Lermontov's drama *Masquerade* (V, 150). Similarly he attempts to bend Liza to his will by consciously seducing her with narratives constructed from sentimental literature. Although she is sharp enough to sense on at least one occasion the false note in his bookishness (V, 158–59), his tactic works:

> I had sensed for some time now that I had turned her whole soul upside down and broken her heart, and the more I became assured of this, the more I wanted to achieve my aim as quickly and forcefully as possible. The game, it was the game that drew me on; or rather, not just the game. . . .
>
> I knew that I was speaking in a forced and constructed manner, even bookishly, but in a word I knew no way other than "just as in a book." But this did not worry me: you see, I knew, I sensed that I would be understood and that this very bookishness might help matters even more. (V, 162)

He is fully aware of how his own self-serving literariness contrasts with the flowery, but deeply felt style of the love letter Liza once received from a medical student, and which she has kept and now shows to her "savior" (V, 163). But this does not disturb him since for him language is not a means of achieving intimacy with Liza (or anyone else, for that matter), but rather a way of enslaving her and recreating her according to his whims:

> "And how little," I thought to myself in passing, "how few words, how little of an idyll (an idyll, moreover, so affected, so bookish, so contrived), were necessary in order there and then to turn an entire human soul into what one wanted." (V, 166)

Even the dramatic change of identity he thrusts on her at the end— when, having appealed to her innocence by sketching out Romantic narratives of moral rebirth, he then confirms her status as prostitute by giving her money—turns out to be prescripted and part of his need consciously to create life rather than live it:

For a moment I was on the point of lying here, by writing that I did this unintentionally, without knowing what I was doing, flustered, not thinking. But I don't want to lie and therefore I'll say straight out that I forced her hand open and put the money in it . . . out of malice. It came to me to do it when I was running back and forth across the room and she was sitting behind the screen. So I can say the following with certainty: even though I committed this cruelty on purpose, it did not come from my heart but from my malign head. This cruelty was so affected, so cerebral, so deliberately composed, so *bookish,* that I could not restrain myself even for a moment. (V, 176–77)

He then runs after Liza "in shame and despair"—but only in order, we feel, to impose yet a further change of identity on her in order to reflect his latest change of heart.

His relationship to Liza is essentially that of author to his own fictional character. He constructs her in order that she might inhabit the narrative he contrives in the place of "living life." Indeed, he dreams of her as "my creation" (V, 167), and he is both incensed and confused on those occasions when she asserts her autonomy, does something unscripted, and manages to escape momentarily from the prison of his narrative. Such an occasion arises when, contrary to his expectations, she sees the extent of his unhappiness behind the mask of hero and savior he has donned and kneels to comfort him:

I am so used to thinking and imagining everything according to books, and presenting everything to myself in the way I myself have previously composed it in my dreams, that I did not immediately comprehend then that strange circumstance. What had happened was that Liza, although humiliated and crushed by me, had understood much more than I imagined. [. . .] It also came into my agitated head that our roles had shifted completely: that she was now the heroine, while I was precisely that humiliated and crushed creature that she had been before me that night. (V, 174–75)

In his underground retreat, swamped by his own evasive rhetoric and by the narratives that take the place of reality, the Underground Man succumbs to a demonic solitude that is a denial of life, and in which human relations are perverted into the exercise of tyranny and supremacy over others. He compares himself—significantly—to a cripple, excluded from life and indeed no longer capable of recognizing it: "Why, we don't even know where the living lives these days, what it is or what it's called. Leave us alone without our books and we are immediately confused and lost." At the very end of his notes he even renounces his right to be called a man, offering instead the by-now highly suggestive term *obshchechelovek* as an apt description of those who, like himself, are stillborn fetuses, poisoned by consciousness:

We are stillborn, and indeed for a long time now we have been born not of living fathers, and we are getting to like this more and more. We are developing a taste for it. We'll soon come up with a way of somehow giving birth to ourselves from an idea. (V, 178–79)

These demonically charged notions of human solitude, of stillborn homunculi unable to distinguish living life in a landscape of desolate abstraction, of human relationships reduced to power struggles, of trying to impose one's own narratives on life, as well as the ultimately blasphemous act of trying to create another human being—all are to be explored further in the equally demonic context of suicide in *A Gentle Creature,* a tale that appeared in, and was framed by, Dostoevsky's *Diary of a Writer* for 1876.

"LONG LIVE THE ELECTRICITY OF HUMAN THOUGHT!": *A GENTLE CREATURE* AND *THE DREAM OF A RIDICULOUS MAN*

> The destruction of one's own self is a serious matter, no matter how *chic* it may appear, but the epidemic of self-destruction that is growing among our intellectual classes is an excessively serious matter and one deserving tireless observation and study. (XXIV, 54)

Dostoevsky's words, from his *Diary of a Writer* for December 1876, only a month after the publication of *A Gentle Creature,* reflect his real concern at what he truly took to be a phenomenon significant in both its extent and its implications. The theme of suicide dominates the *Diary* in the final months of 1876, with articles devoted to discussion of those who have felt the need to take their own lives "in the absence of a higher idea of existence in their souls" (XXIV, 50), articles that perfectly frame the November issue in which *A Gentle Creature* appeared. But it was two particular instances of suicide, and the stark differences between them, that really focused Dostoevsky's thinking. In June 1876 he was told by his influential friend Konstantin Pobedonostsev, a man of extreme conservatism who was close to the Russian royal family, of the suicide of the seventeen-year-old daughter of the émigré socialist, Alexandr Herzen; then at the beginning of October he read in the newspaper *New Times* (*Novoe vremia*) an account of the suicide of a Moscow seamstress, Maria Borisova. The latter had thrown herself from a sixth-floor window while clutching an icon of the Madonna, details Dostoevsky appropriated for the death of the heroine in *A Gentle Creature.* This suggests how struck he was by Borisova's actions and particularly by the icon: "a strange and hitherto unheard-of feature in a suicide!" (XXIII, 146). The case of Borisova clearly ran counter to the conventional view of suicide as a demonically incited act that was the ultimate blasphemy, the presence of the icon instead suggesting that this was "a somehow gentle and humble suicide. Here, apparently, there was not even any grumbling or reproach, it just became impossible to carry on living, 'God did not wish it,' and so she died whilst praying" (XXIII, 146).

In the *Diary of a Writer* for October 1876, in an entry entitled "Two Suicides," Dostoevsky contrasts the meek and submissive suicide of Borisova with the entirely different tone discernible in the suicide note left by Herzen's daughter, Liza, a creature "Russian by blood, but practically not at all Russian by upbringing." The note, written in French, reads:

> I am about to undertake a long voyage. If my suicide is not successful then let everyone gather to celebrate my resurrection with a bottle of Cliquot. *If it does succeed,* then I pray only that I should be buried only when it is sure I am dead, for it would be extremely unpleasant to wake up in a coffin under the ground. *That would not be at all chic!* (XXIII, 145)

Dostoevsky is offended by that "chic," discerning in the glib tone of the note "a challenge, perhaps indignation, and malice," and in the suicide itself a willful refutation of yet another "house of the dead": a life constructed on the meaningless struggle against "the tyranny of principles of inertia, with which it is impossible to become reconciled" (XXIII, 145). Put more simply, Liza—raised in the family of a prominent émigré who had turned his back on Russia in favor of the West, and who most completely embodied for Dostoevsky the tragedy of the *obshchechelovek*—died from a lack of the oxygen of native Russian spirituality and faith: "She simply died from 'cold darkness and tedium,' with a suffering that was, so to speak, like that of an animal and beyond her control; it simply became suffocating to live, as if there were not enough air" (XXIII, 146). In the entry that immediately follows "Two Suicides" and which is entitled "The Verdict," Dostoevsky develops at greater length his conception of the sort of person who commits suicide out of tedium in the face of an outrageously meaningless existence. The entry purports to be the confession of a rational, atheistic suicide who lacks faith in eternal life and who is aware that his own consciousness brings him into disharmony with creation. Confronted with the absurdity of life in the face of inevitable and apparently senseless annihilation, he is driven to rebel against his situation in an act of demonic self-destruction. This figure clearly has much in common with the indignant suicide Ippolit in *The Idiot*, as well as with the main character in *The Dream of a Ridiculous Man,* whose solitude and solipsistic conviction that "nothing matters" (*vse ravno*) is finally penetrated by an encounter with a suffering young girl, an encounter that heads off his intention to kill himself. Accused by some readers of inciting and attempting to justify suicide, Dostoevsky later explained that "The Verdict" was designed to show how suicide is an inevitable consequence of lack of faith, and that "without Christianity it is impossible to live" (XXIII, 408; XXIV, 44–50)

If the heroine of *A Gentle Creature* was suggested by the suicide of Borisova, then the narrator-protagonist of the tale, her pawnbroker husband, emerges from the ranks that include the Underground Man, Ippolit, and the author of "The Verdict." Like them, his existence is not validated by faith in anything beyond himself, in any "higher idea, without which neither a man nor a nation can exist," and what for Dostoevsky was synonymous with God and the immortality of the human soul (XXIV, 48). Instead, if the pawnbroker emerges from self-absorption at all, it is only to contemplate a universe governed by inertia (*kosnost'*) and contingency, a universe itself stripped of all meaning and one that also renders human life purposeless by reducing it to blind accidentality, and from which true choice, self-determination, and responsibility are excluded. This is a universe from which God has fled, and, as Liza Knapp argues, the insensible, repellent, metronomic tapping of the pendulum reported by the pawnbroker at the very end of his tale suggests that blind celestial mechanics have been left in charge.[37] As is the case with the other figures with whom we are comparing the pawnbroker, this state of spiritual desolation has been achieved through the consumption of living life by a voracious and completely self-contained individual consciousness. This is the essence of his demonism: As he lies still, feeling his wife's revolver against his forehead and contemplating the possibility of immediate death, his primary thought is admiration for the speed at which ideas storm through his mind. "Long live the electricity of human thought!" he writes, but it is that very electricity that has already burned out the life in him (XXIV, 21). As Jackson puts it: "At the core of his mentality is the persistent striving of pure thought to rupture or deny the crucial 'connections' that distinguish the moral universe of man from an amoral world of disconnected and meaningless happenings."[38] It is the absence of these connections in the pawnbroker's accidental and abandoned universe that gives rise to his moral nihilism and, yet again, the conviction that "everything is permitted." Life is not "living life"—unpredictable, boisterous, and irresistible—but inert material for his own mental creativeness, plasticine to be molded by his touch: Like the alienated dreamer heroes of Dostoevsky's tales of the 1840s, the pawnbroker is "the artist of his own life" (II, 116). The result is an implicit denial of the "otherness" of other people and other things, which in turn leads to a bleak and impenetrable solipsism. As was the case in *Notes from Underground,* what

Jackson calls "the tragedy of solitude, silence, alienation," inevitably determines the narrative shape of *A Gentle Creature:* "The very form of the narrative, the interior monologue, expresses its central theme—solitude. Monologue is the medium of a man locked within himself, talking only to himself. Alone in himself, the pawnbroker speaks words that echo endlessly in the chambers of consciousness and conscience. The words are not spoken, but thought in silence. Silence is the man."[39] Denied the test-bed of contact with reality, the pawnbroker's words are not validated by any external measures of their truthfulness; like those of the Underground Man, they constitute a demonic narrative in which he is constantly trying to "get his thoughts into order" and impose on events a shape and a meaning acceptable to him. In his notebook, Dostoevsky draws specific attention to this aspect of the pawnbroker's narrative: "Words fly out that are too impatient, they are naïve and unexpected, they are inconsistent and contradictory; but they are sincere, even if at the same time terribly mendacious, for man sometimes lies very sincerely, especially when he himself wishes to believe in the truth of his lie" (XXIV, 319).

The pawnbroker's solipsism, his denial of the "otherness" of others, means that his relationship with those others is inevitably perverted into possessiveness and the struggle for power, and this is the essence of his "love" for his "gentle" wife. She, of course, turns out to be far from meek, and their relationship is, as Jackson and others have shown, structured around the motif of the duel. The pawnbroker comments several times on the strong sensual pleasure afforded by mastery of others, and at the end of his monologue he even momentarily contemplates keeping possession of his dead wife's body, rather than releasing it for burial (XXIV, 35). It is in such possession that he finds the only confirmation of his own identity, and, like the baron in Pushkin's *The Miserly Knight,* mere consciousness of the power possession brings is enough for him (XXIV, 23). Unfortunately for his wife, that consciousness needs to be constantly fed by reconfirmation and reassertion of that power, a power that extends eventually to embrace the blasphemy of seeking to create a human being in his own image. At first this takes the form merely of "writing the script" of the girl's behavior, as when he insists that she herself recognize, without any prompting from him, the extent of his "worth":

> I was always silent, and especially with her, right up until yesterday. Why was I silent? Because I was proud. I wanted her to find out for herself, without my help, and not by relying on the stories of scoundrels, but *so that she herself should guess* the nature of this man and comprehend him! In taking her into my home, I wanted complete respect. I wanted her to stand before me in supplication for my sufferings—and I deserved that. (XXIV, 14)

It also includes the smug satisfaction he derives from accurately predicting her behavior, as when he listens to her rejection of the advances of Efimovich: "Let me repeat once more: to my credit, I listened to this scene without any surprise. It was as though I had encountered only what was already known to me" (XXIV, 20). Later, though, a more chillingly possessive note creeps into the pawnbroker's words: "She was the only person I was preparing for myself, there was no need for another" (XXIV, 24).

Unlike God's, the pawnbroker's creation of a human being is creation driven by egoism, arrogance, and pride. It is informed neither by love and respect for the integrity of others, nor by willingness to take responsibility for that creation. It casts him in a truly demonic role that attracts in the course of his narrative an appropriately demonic subtext, of which, like the Underground Man, he appears to be only partially aware. When he makes direct reference to Goethe's *Faust*, introducing himself to the girl in the same words Mephistopheles uses to introduce himself to Faust, we see the pawnbroker's complicity in the process of his own demonization. But his words carry little real authority, even for himself: They are merely a rhetorical flourish, designed to show off his literary knowledge before his young visitor. Nevertheless, as other critics have pointed out, the use of *Faust* as a source text for *A Gentle Creature* does contribute to the tale's demonic subtext.[40]

Like Mephistopheles, the pawnbroker is in the business of snaring human souls and possessing them: indeed, the down-at-heel and subordinate quality of Goethe's demon casts him in the role of a sort of metaphysical pawnbroker, and Faust's soul is safe as long as he remembers to "redeem" it. The relationship of the girl to the pawnbroker is a loose reworking of the Faust story, as she sells or pawns her soul to her tormentor, but affords him in the end only a Pyrrhic victory. She also pawns her icon but, in a highly symbolic gesture, reclaims it at the moment of her death. Given the attention already paid to this by other critics, there is little need to dwell further here on the role played by *Faust* in the subtext of Dostoevsky's tale. Let us remind ourselves instead that it is not the only literary text with a demonic charge invoked in the pawnbroker's narrative. The girl's question as to whether he is avenging himself on society (XXIV, 9) brings to mind the demonic Romantic heroes of Lermontov's works,[41] while the pawnbroker himself quotes from Pushkin's lyric "The Demon" (XXIV, 14). He also dramatizes himself as a fallen hero, an outcast, and a victim, in terms that recall the Demon of Lermontov's narrative poem and that figure's relationship to, and desired possession of, Tamara as a sort of reward for past suffering:

Yes, *I had the right* to want to look after myself then and open that pawnshop: "You rejected me, you, people that is, you drove me away with silent contempt. You responded to my passionate impulse toward you by wounding me with a hurt that will last my whole life long. I am therefore within my rights to wall myself off from you, to amass that thirty thousand rubles, and to end my life somewhere in the Crimea, on some southern shore with mountains and vineyards, on my own estate, bought with that thirty thousand, and, most important, far away from all of you, but with no malice toward you and with an ideal in my soul, and with the woman of my heart, and a family if God so wishes." (XXIV, 16)

But there are other points in the pawnbroker's confession where demonic motifs are invoked, apparently without his conscious knowledge or complicity. For example, he complains of the difficulty of getting his account into order (by which he means a narrative that suits his own purposes) because of "all the little details": "The fact is, I now want to recall all of this, every little thing, every tiny detail. All the time I am trying to get my thoughts into order, and I can't—because of those little details, those little details [*chertochki*]" (XXIV, 8). Jackson has suggested that the Russian *chertochki* is the diminutive plural form of both "detail" (*cherta*) and "devil" (*chert*), implying that the pawnbroker's task is confounded not only by his failure to grasp detail, but, more importantly, by the devils that inhabit his self-justifying and therefore demonic narrative account.[42] We may assume that he is similarly unaware of the connotations attending his proposal of marriage, which takes place in the liminal space of the entrance gateway of the girl's dwelling, a fact that is much repeated, but unremarked on, in the pawnbroker's narrative (XXIV, 11). Likewise, he assumes the identity of the risk taker or gambler in the scene where he calculates the odds of his wife shooting him, and in the same scene he compares himself to a man about to precipitate himself from a great height (XXIV, 21). As we have seen, both these motifs acquired demonic connotations in Dostoevsky's use of them in the works discussed in this chapter, but the pawnbroker does not appear to be party to those connotations.

But it is the final paragraph of the pawnbroker's narrative that most clearly exposes his demonism and the desolate landscape of his soul:

Stagnation! O, nature! People are alone in the world—that's the trouble! "Is there anyone left alive in the field?" cries out the Russian folk hero. I—no folk hero—cry out too, but no one answers. They say that the sun gives life to the universe. The sun rises, but—look at it—is it not a corpse too? Everything is dead, and everywhere there are corpses. There are only people, alone, and around them silence—that's the earth for you! "People, love one another"—who said that? Whose bidding was that? The pendulum clicks insensibly, repellently. It's two o'clock in the morning. Her little shoes are standing by her little bed, as though awaiting her. . . . No, seriously, when they take her away in the morning, what will become of me? (XXIV, 35)

This vision of the pawnbroker's bleak universe is a vision of hell, where inertia, stagnation, death, silence, and solitude reign. Only the mechanical pendulum moves, ticking out an eternity of nothingness. The very symbol of life, the sun, is extinguished in an image replete with apocalyptic connotations: "And I beheld when he had opened the sixth seal, and, lo, there was a great earthquake; and the sun became black as sackcloth of hair, and the moon became as blood" (Revelation 6:12). As the editors of the Academy edition of Dostoevsky's works point out, the same pawnbroker who can quote verbatim from a secular text like *Faust* cannot remember that it was Christ who enjoined men to love each other in St. John's Gospel.

The pawnbroker's final words in *A Gentle Creature* leave him in that hell of solitude, nonbeing, and solipsism from which the hero of *The Dream of a Ridiculous Man* begins his escape from the demonic. This tale also appeared as an embedded fiction in *The Diary of a Writer* for April 1877, squeezed between discussion of the Russo-Turkish war, which had been declared on April 12, and further debate of the outcome of the trial of the peasant-woman Kornilova, who had thrown her stepdaughter from a fourth-floor window. Like *A Gentle Creature*, it is subtitled "A Fantastic Story" and its point of departure is the act of suicide: however, the fantastic quality of this tale resides in its supernatural content, rather than in the stream-of-consciousness narrative form, as was the case with *A Gentle Creature*. Moreover, the thematic focus is now on how the intention to commit suicide is overcome in "a modern progressive and vile Petersburger," who, like the Underground Man and the pawnbroker, is a victim of that complete existential solitude that is the consequence of an existence powered only by "the electricity of human thought." At the start of the tale we find him reduced to nonbeing, a demonic specter haunting the barren urban landscape of St. Petersburg. So complete is his introspection, so total his estrangement, that he now doubts even the reality of the world about him. His ego, so long deprived of human contact, floats in a silent vacuum where the only certainty is that of its own inviolability and isolation: "I suddenly felt that it would be *all the same* to me whether the world existed or there was nothing anywhere. I began to hear and feel with all my being that *there was nothing out there around me*" (XXV, 105). Crushed by the burden of such spiritual solitude, the Ridiculous Man, as he terms himself, turns to the act of suicide as a logical way out of the tedium and tyranny of a meaningless universe. He is deflected from his purpose by his response to an encounter with a lost girl and his realization that he is not completely indifferent to everything. This in turn prompts a dream in which, having taken his life, he is raised from the dead and transported to a world that is an idyllic double of Earth, a paradise peopled by innocents who have not experienced sin, but whom the Ridiculous Man unwittingly infects with the scourge of rationalism. In their newly discovered prioritization of the understanding of life over the sense of life, these beings sacrifice their paradise and repeat all the mistakes of humankind, leaving the Ridiculous Man, on awaking, transfigured by his vision of paradise on Earth and determined to preach it to others.

Much has been made of the prophetic and utopian qualities of *The Dream of a Ridiculous Man,* and of the glimpse it offers of a world capable of redeeming our own on the basis of man's love for man. But this should not obscure the demonic markers that accompany the Ridiculous Man's vision, nor blind us to the fact that the basis for that vision is the act of suicide (albeit imaginary), driven by lack of faith and tedium in the face of a Godless universe. It is a demonic act, and it demonizes what follows. Although the hero's dream may lead, on his awakening from it, to his spiritual rebirth, it is in itself a demonic vision not of an unsullied paradise of humanity at one with creation, but of the *corruption* of that paradise. The hero's continuing consciousness after his "death" reflects the fact that, as a suicide, he now joins the ranks of the *zalozhnye pokoiniki.* Moreover, his afterlife is at first no different from his everyday life in that it consists initially, as he lies in his coffin, of inert and mute submission to the blind and meaningless laws of nature. The senselessness of his continuing existence is forcefully brought home by the drops of water falling, it would seem for eternity, on the hero's eye, but the response this eventually provokes, like that of the Underground Man, is confined to rational outrage and impotent revolt: "Whoever you are, if you exist and if there is something more rational than what is happening at this moment, then let it make itself known here. If, though, you are taking revenge on me for my ill-judged suicide by means of a continued existence that is absurd and senseless, then know that no torment you may inflict upon me will ever compare with that contempt which I shall feel in silence, even if my martyrdom lasts millions of years!" (XXV, 110). It is this challenge that provokes the appearance of a creature who transports the Ridiculous Man to the alternative world of his utopian vision, but what kind of creature, angel or devil, has his outrage summoned? The editors of the Academy edition point to the contemporary popularity of Swedenborg, and to Dostoevsky's apparent familiarity with his works, in order to argue that the creature is something like Swedenborg's "angels" (XXV, 401), but this is to overlook the deeply ambiguous nature of Dostoevsky's creature and of the circumstances in which he operates. He is described as "a dark and unknown creature" with a human face. Like the hero himself, the creature is silent and he provokes a feeling of "profound revulsion." The world to which he transports the Ridiculous Man is a *double* of Earth, suggesting all the demonic associations attached in folk belief to mirrors, doublings, and "other worlds." Moreover, the purpose of the creature's journey is to insinuate a serpent—the Ridiculous Man himself—into this Garden of Eden, thereby precipitating its fall, followed by what Chris Pike has called "a light-speed review of human history" from Genesis to the baleful individualism and demonic questioning of the divine order characteristic of contemporary man.[43]

Edward Wasiolek has been almost alone in arguing that the Ridiculous Man's dream should be read as blasphemy rather than sacrament in its presentation of a golden age of Earthly paradise:

> The Golden Age, like every important concept in Dostoevsky's world, is a dialectical concept: it can be sacrament or blasphemy, the vision of regeneration in Christ or the vision of degeneration in the imitation of Christ. *The Dream of a Ridiculous Man* is *blasphemy*, and yet it has been taken universally by Dostoevsky's interpreters as *sacrament*. [. . .] The dream of the Ridiculous Man is *his dream*, and it is as good as his motives, and his motives are self-interested.[44]

Wasiolek's argument thus turns on his recognition of what Gary Saul Morson has called "the irony of origins," the impossibility in a fictional narrative of separating an idea from the psychology of the bearer of that idea.[45] Everything the Ridiculous Man describes in his narrative—his alienation, his "suicide," his dream vision, and his subsequent life of preaching his "truth" to others—everything is driven by the same sense of his own isolated superiority, and it serves the interests not of others, but of himself. In his demand that he be crucified he thus becomes a demonic travesty of Christ himself.

But although the Ridiculous Man's dream may be demonically sourced, contaminated by demonic signs and blasphemous in its vision of a paradise rooted in egoism rather than Christian love, Wasiolek's argument misses perhaps a greater "irony of origins" in its failure to locate *The Dream of a Ridiculous Man* in its context of the *Diary of a Writer.* As Morson writes, critical disagreement over whether *The Dream* is sacrament or blasphemy is ultimately reducible to the vexed question of that work's genre. Wasiolek is right to insist on a psychological reading of ideas and visions within a work of psychological fiction, but there are other genres, such as religious narratives of conversion, medieval dream visions, and hagiographical lives of saints, in which such a reading would be inappropriate.[46] In fact, we can go further and argue that the success of such genres is dependent on the exclusion of such a reading. *The Dream of a Ridiculous Man* is generically ambiguous: It looks like a psychological short story, it is called a "fantastic tale," and it is framed within an apparently journalistic work that turns out to be an "adventure of the soul among Utopian inquiries," a work that, taken as a whole, reveals Dostoevsky's "complex attitude toward his own utopianism"[47]:

> *The Diary*, in short, is itself an ambiguous context, and the story appears to be not only a boundary work—that is, one that has been interpreted according to contradictory generic conventions—but also a threshold work, that is, one *designed* to resonate between opposing genres and interpretations.[48]

Morson's fine analysis of the generic complexity of the *Diary of a Writer*, and of *The Dream of a Ridiculous Man* within it, relieves us of the need to take the matter further here. But issues raised in ambiguous form by *The Dream* take on great significance in other works that we have yet to address. The question of whether the assumption of certain generic forms might legitimize the suspension of a psychological reading of the "truths" proclaimed in them, a reading in which the "irony of origins" must be respected, is central to any discussion of the account of Father Zosima's life in book 6 of *The Brothers Karamazov*. While the question of whether demonic solitude can be breached, and "the electricity of human thought" short-circuited, by means of an aesthetic experience, determines our whole approach to Raskolnikov's crime and subsequent salvation in *Crime and Punishment*.

Chapter Two

The Fear of Aesthetics:
Crime and Punishment

SHORTLY AFTER Raskolnikov has revealed to Sonia that he is responsible for the murders of the old pawnbroker Alena Ivanovna and her sister Lizaveta Ivanovna, the following conversation takes place between the murderer and the prostitute:

> "Oh, be quiet, be quiet!" cried Sonia, clasping her hands. "You've deserted God, and God has struck you down and given you over to the devil [*d'iavolu*]!"
>
> "So, Sonia, when I was lying in the dark and the whole idea was coming to me, that was the devil confusing me, eh?"
>
> "Be quiet! Don't laugh, blasphemer, you understand nothing, nothing at all! O Lord, he won't understand anything, anything!"
>
> "Be still, Sonia, I'm not really laughing at all, for I myself know that a devil [*chert*] was dragging me on. [. . .] A devil dragged me on then and only afterwards made clear to me that I had no right to go since I was exactly the same sort of louse as everyone else. He made a fool of me, and that's why I've come to you now! Welcome your guest![. . .] Did I kill the old woman? I killed myself, not the old woman! [. . .] It was the devil [*chert*] that killed that old woman, not I." (VI, 321–22)

This scene, which occurs late in *Crime and Punishment,* is the first point in the novel when Raskolnikov's crime is explicitly linked to the agency of the devil, or devils, although a whole network of demonic markers throughout the text thus far has implicitly identified the demonic nature of the act and prepared the reader for this moment. The "confession" scene, as it is often referred to, is thus a defining point when the murderer confronts his diabolical actions. It is, though, less effective as a confession since, although Raskolnikov *reveals* his responsibility for the murders, he does not fully *assume* that responsibility, using the devil as a convenient fall guy, playing word games with the gullible Sonia, and manipulating the act of confession so that it deceives and skirts around the motivation for his behavior. As Philip Rahv has neatly concluded: "In the end, for all the keenness with which Raskolnikov explicates his act to Sonya, we are still left with a crime of indeterminate origin and meaning."[1] Such indeterminacy extends even to the nature of the devil as evoked in this exchange: Sonia's Christian convictions and her use of the word *d'iavol* suggest that she sees Raskolnikov as a victim of *the* devil as envisaged in Orthodox tradition; Raskolnikov's deliberate refusal to continue her use of *d'iavol* in favor of the more generic term *chert* signals perhaps his unwillingness to allow such conventional religious symbols of good and evil into the discussion of his crime, as well as his growing awareness of the unheroic and shabby scale of his deed. We shall return to this richly suggestive scene later, but for the moment our attempts to understand what, apart from the devil, might have "dragged" Raskolnikov to his crime, along with what that crime might mean for him, are better served by his bête noire, the amoral sensualist Svidrigailov, who later undertakes to summarize the processes behind the crime for the benefit of Raskolnikov's sister, Dunia:

"It's a long story, Avdotia Romanovna. What we have here—how can I put it to you?—is a theory in its own way: the same sort of thing as if, for example, I were to find that a single act of evil is permissible if the main aim is good. A single act of evil and a hundred good deeds! It is also, of course, offensive for a young man of merit and with immeasurable vanity to know that if he had, for example, just three thousand or so then his whole career, the whole future of his purpose in life, would turn out differently—and yet he hasn't got that three thousand. Add to that the irritability arising from hunger, from his cramped room, from his rags, from a keen awareness of the beauty of his social position, along with the situation of his sister and mother. Most of all vanity, pride and vanity—though, God knows, perhaps even with good inclinations. . . . I am not blaming him, please don't think that, for it's none of my business. There was also a certain little theory of his own here—a reasonable enough theory—according to which people are divided, you see, into raw material and special people, in the sense of people to whom, because of their elevated position, the law does not apply, but who themselves on the contrary devise laws for the rest, for the raw material, for the rubbish. Not bad, a decent enough little theory, *une théorie comme une autre.* He got terrible carried away by Napoleon—that is to say, strictly speaking, he was carried away by the fact that a great many men of genius took no notice of the single act of evil, and stepped across it with no hesitation. He seems to have imagined that he too was a man of genius—that is, he was sure of it for a time. He has suffered greatly, and is still suffering, from the idea that he knew how to devise a theory, but was not capable of stepping across without thinking about it, which means that he is not a man of genius. Now for a young man of vanity that is degrading, especially in our age." (VI, 378)

There is deception and "indeterminacy" here too, of course, for all Svidrigailov's words and deeds are compromised by the designs he harbors on Dunia; but the shape of Raskolnikov's crime, its origins, motivation, and diabolical implications, emerge clearly enough from Svidrigailov's performance. For a start, the crime embraces and serves ostensibly altruistic as well as egoistic purposes, appearing to benefit both the "greater good" of humanity and Raskolnikov's own vanity. Interestingly, in both respects it is invested with diabolical meaning by the implicit value system deployed throughout the novel. In the former "altruistic" guise the crime is, as Svidrigailov tells Dunia, underpinned by "a theory in its own way" that seeks to justify the single act of evil if the consequences and purpose of that act are generally beneficial. It is in this way that the motivation for the crime is first suggested in the novel, when Raskolnikov overhears a student and a young officer talking "theoretically" of how the murder of Alena Ivanovna would be fully justified in terms of the socially advantageous consequences such an act would bring:

> "on the one hand a stupid, meaningless, insignificant, wicked, sick old hag, of no use to anyone but quite the reverse, harmful to everyone, who herself does not know why she lives, and who tomorrow will die anyway of her own accord. [. . .] On the other hand, the fresh forces of youth that are being wasted for lack of support. [. . .] Kill her and take her money in order to use it to devote oneself subsequently to serving the whole of humanity and the social good. What do you think? Would not a single tiny little crime be erased by thousands of good deeds? In exchange for one life, thousands of lives saved from putrefaction and disintegration. One death and a hundred lives in exchange—now there's arithmetic for you!" (VI, 54)

In a letter of September 1865 to his publisher M. N. Katkov, a letter that may be regarded as the earliest identifiable draft of what was to become *Crime and Punishment*, Dostoevsky describes a crime committed on an identical basis by a criminal who, "having given in to some of these strange 'half baked' ideas that are floating about in the air," has become convinced of the uselessness of his victim and the absurdity of regarding her murder as a "crime" (XXVIII/2, 136–37). The reference here to "'half-baked' ideas that are floating about in the air," along with the information that the action of the proposed novel is to take place "in the present year," make it clear that the utilitarianism displayed by the murderer, as well as by the student and officer, is not sporadic but forms part of a theoretical fashion espoused at the time. Raskolnikov's "decent enough little theory, *une théorie comme une autre*" lies at the core of Dostoevsky's polemical engagement with the young radical "nihilists" of the 1860s, whose rationalism and rejection of all spiritual values he found so distasteful. The materialist basis from which the ideas of "the men of the sixties" sprang was most effectively dramatized in the figure of Bazarov in Ivan Turgenev's novel *Fathers and Sons* (1861) and most systematically described in the journalistic writings of Nikolai Chernyshevsky (1828–89), whose editorship of the literary section of the periodical *The Contemporary* in the late 1850s turned that publication into the major rallying point for radical opinion in Russia. Chernyshevsky's work, as well as that of Nikolai Dobroliubov, his successor as literary editor of *The Contemporary*, was derivative and of little real philosophical significance in itself, but it proved inspirational to a younger generation of Russian intellectuals who had tired of the vapid theorizing of their intellectual "fathers" in the 1840s and who took advantage of the climate of liberalization and reform that followed the death of Tsar Nicholas I in 1855 to demand a much more hardheaded approach to Russia and her problems. The philosophical roots of Chernyshevsky's thought lay in the respect for the natural sciences that had developed from the European Enlightenment, when such sciences and the knowledge they yielded had seemed to offer mankind the key to understanding and resolving the problems that beset it. In works such as *The Anthropological Principle in Philosophy* (1860), Chernyshevsky had sought to bring to the understanding of moral questions the same confidence and certainty that the natural sciences were bringing to the understanding of the natural world and empirical questions. In seeking to demonstrate that the human "sciences" were just as amenable to the rational method and rationally deducible laws as the natural sciences, Chernyshevsky and his followers fell into a crude utilitarianism that appeared to yield the following sequence of deductions: Man is a unitary being consisting solely of matter, with no empirical evidence for the existence of a spiritual dimension separate from his physical being; man's values must therefore derive from his physical, rather than his (nonexistent) *meta*physical being; the primary, scientifically demonstrable law of an individual's existence is self-interest; the individual defines as good what serves his self-interest and he may be helped by reason in the identification of where that self-interest ultimately lies; society consequently defines as good what serves the greater interest of the greater number.

This is a crude summary of an already crude deductive process, but Chernyshevsky's ideas, as well as Dostoevsky's scandalized reaction to a "philosophical" system that he felt degraded man by reducing his moral existence to a sort of shadow thrown by his physical needs, have been well documented already.[2] Of more immediate interest to us are the demonic implications of the ideas popularized by Chernyshevsky and the way Dostoevsky builds those implications into the value system supported by *Crime and Punishment*. The most immediately apparent of these implications is the fact that the utilitarian ethic advanced by the nihilists sacrifices the notion of an absolute morality derived from some higher, metaphysical source in favor of a relativistic morality derived from human reason and its "mathematical" deductions. This foregrounding of human reason over divine wisdom has the "demonic" effects, already described in chapter 1, of allowing man to prioritize his own conceptions over those of God and of reducing evil to the outcome of human political and social preferences. This in turn possesses profound biblical resonances in that it takes us back to Genesis, to original sin, and to the pivotal role of the devil in the process of man's fall from grace and subsequent exclusion from paradise. The decision to eat the fruit from the tree of knowledge of good and evil and to ignore God's command—"But of the tree of knowledge of good and evil, thou shalt not eat of it: for in the day that thou eatest thereof thou shalt surely die" (Gen. 2:17)—marked an implicit challenge to God's authority and a desire to prioritize human reason over submission to divine wisdom. As the serpent says to Eve: "In the day ye eat thereof, then your eyes shall be opened, and ye shall be as gods" (Gen. 3:5). The utilitarian ethic espoused by Raskolnikov represents a similar ambition—albeit one masked by pretensions to social altruism—to be as a god and to decide matters of good and evil for himself, with his eyes opened by reason. His "decent enough little theory" thus assumes the stature of an ideological restatement of the process by which man first succumbed to the subtle persuasiveness of the forces of evil: It is the voice of the devil whispering in his ear, and the crime it provokes may in turn be construed as a personal reenactment of the fall and exclusion from paradise, an analogy strengthened by Raskolnikov's profound sense of alienation and estrangement in the days following the murders.

Such biblical resonances provoked by his theory and crime are strengthened in the scene where Raskolnikov first visits Sonia with a view to enlisting her as a fellow transgressor against the established moral order. Using as a basis Luzhin's recent attempt to compromise her by accusing her of the theft of a large sum of money, Raskolnikov seeks to provoke in Sonia a similar assumption of the right to decide the nature of good and evil and, on that basis, the fate of others:

> "I would be particularly interested to know how you would now resolve a certain 'question,' as Lebeziatnikov would say. [. . .] Imagine, Sonia, that you knew all Luzhin's intentions in advance, that you knew (for certain, that is) that as a result of them Katerina Ivanovna would be completely destroyed, the children too, and with you also thrown in for good measure (I say 'thrown in' since you attach no significance to yourself). Polechka, too . . . because she'll go the same way. Well, so, here's the question: if all this were suddenly given to you to decide: is it for him or for them to go on living, that is should Luzhin live and commit abominations, or should Katerina Ivanovna die?

Then how would you decide which one of them was to die? That's what I am asking you."

Sonia looked at him anxiously: she detected something peculiar in this hesitant speech, which was approaching something in a roundabout way.

"I had already felt that you would ask something like that," she said, looking at him inquisitively.

"Fine. Be that as it may, but all the same how would you decide?"

"Why do you ask about what cannot be?" Sonia said with revulsion.

"So, it's better for Luzhin to live and commit abominations! You won't dare to decide even in this?"

"But how can I know divine Providence. . . . And why do you ask what it is impossible to ask? What's the point of such empty questions? How could it come about that such a matter would depend on my decision? Who set me up to judge who is to live and who is not to live?" (VI, 313)

Although Sonia is not yet fully aware of Raskolnikov's responsibility for the murders of Alena and Lizaveta, the reader quickly senses how this discussion bears on his crime and his willingness to assume the role of judge that Sonia refuses. But there is much more going on here than we first recognize: Raskolnikov is not confessing to Sonia—at least not yet; he is *tempting* her with fruit from the tree of knowledge of good and evil by inviting her to judge, as he has done, the value of the lives of others. He is thus implicitly cast in the role not only of victim of diabolical temptation, but also of serpent-tempter himself, inviting others to collude in the usurpation of God's identity and prerogatives. Having succumbed to his own demonic "little theory," he in turn becomes the voice of the devil whispering in Sonia's ear. Her revulsion, anxiety, suspicion that something "roundabout" is going on here, and final triumphant affirmation of her willingness to subordinate her own feelings to the workings of Providence, all testify to her acceptance of divine wisdom (a concept embodied in her name, derived as it is from *Sophia*) in recognizing that her role is to articulate God's will, not appropriate it.

The demonic identity thus ascribed to Raskolnikov is clarified throughout this scene through a network of semiotic markers that link him to the conventional typology of the Romantic demon. Indeed, the very relationship between Raskolnikov and Sonia—wherein the fallen rebel against the divine order is torn between his proud isolation and his desire to find solace in company, seeking a meaning to his existence through the love of an innocent woman—is emblematic in its closeness to the basic plot structure of Lermontov's *The Demon*, where the Demon's sense of alienated superiority is both the primary purpose of his existence and the major barrier to his happiness. The descriptive clichés traditionally attending the depiction of the Romantic hero (in both his demonic and human guises) are discernible in the description of Raskolnikov's demeanor throughout this scene with Sonia. His face is "deathly pale" and provokes terror in Sonia's heart when she contemplates him; he speaks "gloomily" (*ugriumo*) or "with a melancholy smile." "His eyes burned with feverish fire. He was almost beginning to ramble; a restless smile played around his lips. A terrible impotence was discernible behind his agitated spirit" (VI, 320). He confesses to possessing "an evil heart" but is also shown to be receptive to finer feelings: "A feeling long unknown to him washed over his soul like a wave and immediately softened it. He did not resist it: two tears sprang from his eyes and hung on his eyelashes" (VI, 316). He describes his own character in terms redolent of Romantic malice and ennui: "I'm vain, jealous, spiteful, loathsome, vengeful, and, if you like, inclined to madness. [. . .] I turned spiteful and didn't want to [work]. That's it exactly: *I turned spiteful* (that's a good way of putting it!). And then like a spider I hid in my corner" (VI, 320). He then finally describes his crime as nothing more than an act of Romantically defiant aggression and self-affirmation:

> "It was not to help my mother that I killed—that's nonsense! I did not kill so that, having obtained the means and the power, I might become a benefactor of mankind. Nonsense! I simply killed; I killed for myself, for myself alone; and at that moment it ought to have made no difference to me whether I would later become anyone's benefactor or would spend the rest of my life catching everyone in my web like a spider and sucking their vital juices out of them! And the main thing: it was not money I needed when I killed, Sonia; it was not so much money as something else[, . . .] at that moment I needed to find out, and find out quickly, whether I was a louse like everyone else or a man. Did I have the right to overstep or not? Did I dare bend down and seize [power] or not? Was I a trembling creature, or did I have *the right* . . . ?" (VI, 322)

Finally, at the end of Raskolnikov's exposition of his "gloomy catechism" of Romantic revolt, he and Sonia sit side by side, "sad and crushed, as if they had been cast ashore alone on an empty shore after a storm" (VI, 324), imagery almost identical to that used by Lermontov's hero Pechorin to describe his own Romantic desolation in *A Hero of Our Time*.[3]

Such markers, identifying Raskolnikov with the conventional typology of the Romantic demon, emphasize of course the egotistic, rather than altruistic, side of both his nature and his crime. The absence of any real financial advantage to the murder, his unwillingness to contemplate robbery without killing, and the way he buries and then forgets the few trinkets he has taken, all confirm Raskolnikov's confession that he did not kill for money and that he was not driven by the desire to benefit society through the judicious redistribution of "irrationally" distributed wealth. Instead, we contemplate a crime driven by arrogance, unlimited vanity, and Promethean revolt against the established order, be it social, moral, or divine. Raskolnikov's very name, suggesting as it does one who has broken away (*raskol'nik*: "schismatic"), and the word for crime used in the title and throughout the novel (*prestuplenie*: "transgression," "stepping across"), help to confirm the hero's association with demonic revolt.

The use of semiotic markers to signal the presence of the demonic is by no means confined to the scene with Sonia that we have just examined, nor are such markers confined to signaling Romantic demonic conventions. Several key scenes in the novel are richly inscribed with demonic markers that serve to suggest the value system against which we are encouraged to measure Raskolnikov's crime. Pace those Bakhtinian analysts who would argue that authorial values are largely dissipated in the relativized world of the Dostoevskian polyphonic novel, there can be little doubt of the presence of such a value system in *Crime and Punishment,* or of the fact that such a system derives from the moral position of its author, Dostoevsky. From outside the text we have the evidence of Dostoevsky's letter to Katkov, which envisages the murderer's moral need for punishment as "unsuspected and unanticipated feelings torment his heart" and reveal to him the inescapability of absolute divine morality. Within the text there is the authoritatively "monologic" statement of Raskolnikov's moral conversion in the novel's epilogue. Earlier in the text the use of demonic markers to stigmatize both Raskolnikov's crime and his motivation for it serve to prepare the reader for the moral certainties revealed in that epilogue. Of course, such markers are supplied by the novel's narrator, and their "authority" is dependent on that narrator's trustworthiness and position vis-à-vis the author on the one hand and the hero on the other. Whereas it would be unwise to assume a straightforward relationship between Dostoevsky and the narrator of *Crime and Punishment* (by the naive assumption, for example, that the narrator's voice *is* that of Dostoevsky), it is nevertheless clear that the narrator in this novel is by no means as evasive, deceitful, and generally untrustworthy as those found in later novels, such as *The Idiot* and *The Devils.* Dostoevsky originally intended *Crime and Punishment* to be narrated in the first-person confessional form but settled eventually on "narration from point of view of author, a sort of invisible but omniscient being who does not leave his hero for a moment" (VII, 146). The narration in the final novel is more complex than this notebook comment suggests, in that the narrator does leave his hero—to describe the suicide of Svidrigailov, for example—and he also relies on other secondary narrating consciousnesses, such as that of Razumikhin.[4] But it is probably safe to assume that in carrying out Dostoevsky's notebook injunction to shadow the actions and consciousness of the central character, the narrator does not depart too radically from the "point of view of author" as far as his system of values is concerned.

Early in the novel Raskolnikov—sick, exhausted, tormented by uncertainty over the crime he plans, and disorientated by having drunk a glass of vodka—dreams of himself as a child wandering with his father beyond the limits of their little town and witnessing the cruel beating of a defenseless mare unable to draw the weight of her cart. The dream is prompted by Raskolnikov's own anticipated violence and it is clearly designed to foreshadow his subsequent revulsion from an act of cruelty. The scene is graphic and is inscribed with a variety of markers, drawn largely from popular conceptions of the demonic. Before analyzing these, however, we should pause to consider their origins. On the one hand, the events of Raskolnikov's dream are narrated by the sort of omniscient narrator anticipated in Dostoevsky's notebook comment cited above; but, on the other hand, it is the product of Raskolnikov's consciousness that is being narrated. It is therefore legitimate to ask whether these demonic signs, lodged in the narrated content of the dream rather than in its narrative frame, derive from the narrator's value system or whether they suggest that even at this early stage Raskolnikov's own innate sense of morality implicitly demonizes such acts of violent cruelty. The latter interpretation is suggested by the fact that the motive for the killing of the mare is a grotesque travesty of the motive inspiring Raskolnikov to the murder of the pawnbroker: Both victims are judged by the authors of the violence against them to be *useless*. The flogging of the mare takes place outside the entrance to a tavern and it is witnessed by a crowd of drunkards urging on Mikolka, the cart driver. We are told that this tavern "always made an extremely unpleasant impression [on Raskolnikov], almost one of fear, whenever he passed it while out walking with his father. There was always such a crowd there, shouting, guffawing and swearing so much, singing in such an ugly and hoarse way and so often fighting; there were always such drunk and scary mugs loitering around the tavern" (VI, 46). The scene is one of drunken bedlam, and drunkenness, we recall, is associated with demonic possession in Russian folk belief. Moreover, the scene takes place at a liminal time, toward evening, and in a liminal space, the tavern is located at the very edge of town, "a few steps beyond the very last kitchen garden." The road skirting the tavern is covered in black dust and winds on a further three hundred paces to the town cemetery, another space possessing profound liminal significance, where Raskolnikov often visits the grave of his younger brother who, having died in infancy, would fall into the category of *zalozhnye pokoiniki*. The emerging pattern of demonic signs is enriched by the uncontrollable laughter that seems to have taken possession of the crowd as they witness the slaughter of the mare: "Suddenly a volley of loud laughter rings out and covers everything. The mare was unable to withstand the blows that had become quicker, and in its impotence began to kick out. Even the old man was unable to restrain himself and started to grin" (VI, 48). This old man, the last to succumb to this wave of malignant laughter, has already accused Mikolka of having no fear of God (literally, not possessing a crucifix: "na tebe kresta, chto li, net!"), referring to him as a "wood demon" (*leshii*). The crowd subsequently takes up the theme that Mikolka "has no crucifix on him" after he has finally dispatched the unfortunate animal (VI, 49). Raskolnikov's first response on awaking is to invoke God—"Thank God, it was only a dream!"—and to dismiss his dream as "ugly" (*bezobraznyi*), a highly suggestive term in light of the inseparability of ethical and aesthetic categories in Dostoevsky's moral system. The initial invocation of God is repeated several times as Raskolnikov draws conclusions from his dream:

"God!" he exclaimed, "will I really, will I really actually take an axe, start to beat her about the head, smash her skull, slip about in the sticky, warm blood, break the lock, steal and tremble; to hide myself, all covered in blood . . . with the axe. . . . Lord, will I really?" [. . .]

"No, I shall not be able to bear it, I shall not bear it! Even if there were no doubt about all these calculations, even if everything that has been decided in this last month were as clear as day and arithmetically just—Lord, I should still not be able to decide on this!" [. . .]

"Lord!" he prayed, "show me my path, and I shall tear myself away from this accursed . . . dream of mine!" (VI, 50)

Demonic signs similar to those deployed in the mare-beating scene also surround the description of Raskolnikov's preparations for the eventual commission of the crime, although in this case they appear in due course to derive primarily from the value system of the narrator-author himself. First he reports Raskolnikov's increasing tendency toward superstition and his sense of the presence in his life of "some sort of peculiar influences and coincidences" (VI, 52). An example of this is the coincidence of Raskolnikov overhearing the army officer and student discussing the "morality" of murdering Alena Ivanovna. As the narrator puts it, no doubt reporting Raskolnikov's own analogy: "It was as if someone had taken him by the hand and pulled him along behind him, irresistibly, blindly, with unnatural force, without objections. It was as if he had caught a piece of his clothing in the cog of a machine and he had begun to be dragged into it" (VI, 58). Apart perhaps from the passing mention of "unnatural force," neither Raskolnikov nor the narrator has so far suggested that these influences and coincidences might be attributable to the workings of the "unclean force," but this is soon to change. Having carefully planned to take an axe from the kitchen in order to commit his crime, Raskolnikov is nonplussed to find that at the critical moment the servant girl Nastasia is in the kitchen. However, standing aimless and humiliated in the gateway, he notices another axe glinting in the open closet of the caretaker, who happens to be absent at that moment. Seizing his chance, he grabs the weapon and moves on unnoticed: "'If not reason, then the devil!' he thought, grinning strangely. This incident encouraged him remarkably" (VI, 60). This notion that the force encouraging him and "dragging him on" might be diabolical is also suggested by an event that occurs as he tries to gain unseen access to the building in which his victim lives: "Fortunately for him, everything again turned out well at the gateway. Moreover, as if by design, an enormous load of hay entered the gates at that very moment, just in front of him, concealing him completely all the while he was passing through the archway" (VI, 60). The semiotics of popular demonology are present here not only in the liminality of the gateway, marking the moment when Raskolnikov crosses the threshold from innocent citizen to criminal anxious to conceal himself, but also in the crucial assistance offered by a load of hay, which, we recall, was held in popular belief to be an inanimate form often assumed by the "unclean force."

Once Raskolnikov is inside the building, the description of events leading finally to the murders of Alena and Lizaveta is also heavily semioticized with markers drawn from popular conceptions of the demonic. For a start, the initial encounter between murderer-to-be and victim-to-be occurs on the threshold of Alena's apartment, before Raskolnikov finally forces his way in. The narrator then begins to refer to him as the "uninvited guest" (*nezvanyi gost'*), a taboo name for the devil in Russian folklore. All the windows and doors in the pawnbroker's flat are tightly locked shut, "despite the suffocating heat" (VI, 62)—a reference perhaps to popular belief that the devil makes his appearance through apertures. Similarly, the murder of Lizaveta is given diabolical resonance by Raskolnikov's realization that she gained access to the apartment because the front door had been left open after his entrance (VI, 66). When Alena's business associate Koch tries to get into the flat where Raskolnikov is secreted with the corpses of his victims, he too is referred to by the devil's taboo names "uninvited guest" and "that one" (*tot*), while the verbal exchanges that punctuate this stand off at the doorway to Alena's flat are embellished by conventional demonic invocations, such as, "The devil knows, I almost broke the lock"; "Hm . . . the devil . . . ask him"; "The devil, there's nothing to be done, let's go!"; "Ah, the devil . . . !"; and, when one of the housepainters bursts from the apartment below, "Eh, wood-demon, devil! Stop him!" (VI, 67–69).

The richest concentration of demonic signs, however, is to be found in those scenes describing the activities of Svidrigailov, Raskolnikov's malignant alter ego and the counterbalance to Sonia in the struggle for the hero's soul. Some might object to this wholly negative view of Svidrigailov, pointing out—quite rightly—that he is also the source of some good in the novel, as he secures the future of the Marmeladov orphans and makes it financially possible for Sonia to accompany Raskolnikov to Siberia. There is no doubt that much of the demonic pollution of Svidrigailov, to be described in the paragraphs that follow, derives from Raskolnikov's own demonized consciousness and perceptions, but equally many of the demonic signs that stigmatize him, particularly those accompanying his final hours, are conjured in Raskolnikov's absence and must be attributed to the implied author. The resultant ambiguity of Svidrigailov is yet another demonic sign and a further instance of the novel's indeterminacy.

As Faith Wigzell has noted, Svidrigailov is associated throughout the novel with one particular liminal space, the threshold, an association that exploits his demonic potential through the magical significance specifically attributed to the threshold in Russian folk belief.[5] He first appears outlined in the threshold of Raskolnikov's open door, looking at the hero intently, in what the latter takes to be a continuation of a dream he has just experienced in which he has failed to kill the pawnbroker, who laughs diabolically in his face, and in which he has been forced to concede the gulf that separates him from the truly Napoleonic figure. This dream—itself, of course, the product of a liminal condition exploiting the borderline between consciousness and unconsciousness—has in turn followed a strange episode in which Raskolnikov has been confronted by a mysterious artisan who has accused him of murder. He wonders who this man is "who has emerged from under the ground," a detail reminding us that the gallery of spatially specific demons identified in folk belief included the "devil from under the floor" (*chert podpolnyi*).[6] Raskolnikov finally parts from the artisan at the crossroads, another particularly liminal space, when the latter goes off to the *left*, the devil's side. This cluster of demonic markers anticipating and surrounding Svidrigailov's arrival in the novel culminates in his first narrated action: "Suddenly he stepped cautiously across the threshold, [and] carefully closed the door behind him" (VI, 214). The Russian verb used to describe the act of crossing the threshold (*perestupit'*) also means "to overstep" or "to transgress": It is related closely to the word "crime" in the novel's title (*prestuplenie*), and this serves to establish an immediate connection between Svidrigailov 's apparently innocent first move and Raskolnikov's demonic act.

The chronotope of the threshold possesses a broader metaphorical as well as narrowly literal identity in Dostoevsky's novels, and this is perhaps especially so of *Crime and Punishment*. As Bakhtin says, it is impossible to enumerate "all the 'acts' that take place on the threshold, near the threshold, or that are permeated with the living sensation of threshold in this novel":

> The threshold, the foyer, the corridor, the landing, the stairway, its steps, doors opening onto the stairway, gates to front and back yards, and beyond these, the city: squares, streets, facades, taverns, dens, bridges, gutters. This

is the space of the novel. And in fact absolutely nothing here ever loses touch with the threshold, there is no interior of drawing rooms, dining rooms, halls, studios, bedrooms where biographical life unfolds and where events take place in the novels of writers such as Turgenev, Tolstoy, and Goncharov.[7]

The "living sensation of threshold" embraces also, as Sidney Monas has observed, such physical and psychological states as "the boundary between life and death, the familiar and the strange, health and illness, reality and illusion, sanity and madness, waking and sleep, clear-sightedness and hallucination,"[8] in which guises it is particularly prominent in the scenes involving Svidrigailov and his relationship with Raskolnikov. In their first encounter, as we have seen, Raskolnikov is unsure of whether his visitor is real or a continuation of his dream, to the extent that after Svidrigailov's departure he is anxious to confirm with Razumikhin that the latter has actually seen him (VI, 225). It soon emerges, if obliquely through references to a forthcoming "voyage," that Svidrigailov is indeed a man existing on the threshold between life and death, in that he is already seriously contemplating taking his own life (VI, 222–23). Raskolnikov is unsure whether his visitor is sane or not (VI, 221), and he finds him a morally ambiguous character to the extent that his feelings toward him exist constantly on the boundary between revulsion from Svidrigailov's actions and identification with his readiness to "overstep" conventional law and morality. The "living sensation" of Svidrigailov's liminality is continued in his description of the "other world" of the afterlife as a dirty peasant bathhouse inhabited by spiders (VI, 221), a description replete with demonic meaning in Russian folk belief. Moreover, he is regularly visited by ghosts from that "other world" who cross the threshold of life and death in order to return and trouble the conscience of the man they hold responsible for their deaths (just as the "ghost" of Alena Ivanovna has returned to trouble Raskolnikov in his recent dream). What is more, Svidrigailov attributes these liminal phenomena to the effects of a different one, the transition from health to sickness:

> "Ghosts are, so to speak, bits and pieces of other worlds, the point where they begin. Naturally, there is no reason why a healthy man should see them, because the healthy man is the most earthly of men and ought therefore to live according to this life alone, for the sake of completeness and good order. But as soon as he falls sick, as soon as the normal earthly order breaks down in his organism, then the possibility of another world begins to make itself known; and the sicker he is, the closer his contact with that other world, so that when he dies altogether he goes straight to that other world." (VI, 221)

The ghosts Svidrigailov "sees" include his wife, Marfa Petrovna, whom it is rumored he killed, a young girl he abused and who subsequently committed suicide, and a manservant, Filipp, who hanged himself after being subjected to ridicule by Svidrigailov. All three cases would be assigned in popular belief to the category of *zalozhnye pokoiniki* and would thus form part of the "unclean force."

Apart from threshold motifs, other demonic markers are attached to Svidrigailov from his initial appearance onward. He is persistently implicated in the demonic act of suicide, either his own or that of others[9]; the narrator refers to him as Raskolnikov's "guest" (*gost'*); he travesties Raskolnikov's own thinking, projecting his most revered ideas back at him, but in a form that now arouses the hero's revulsion; he is prone to fits of hostile, mocking laughter; and he prides himself on his own evasiveness and duplicity. Moreover, in his account of the *tedium vitae*, aimlessness, cynicism, and craving for intensity that have come to possess him, he emerges as an embodiment, albeit in unappealing form, of those very qualities that once distinguished the demon figure in Romantic literature. (We shall return to this last aspect of Svidrigailov's characterization in due course.) Later in the novel, Svidrigailov's arrival at the Marmeladovas', shortly before the death of Katerina Ivanovna Marmeladova, is immediately preceded by a description of the landlord Kapernaumov who, despite the biblical resonances of his name,[10] possesses marks characteristic of popular and Orthodox depictions of the devil, in that he is lame and his hair stands on end. Moreover, in the same scene the Kapernaumov children stand with their mouths open, a condition the demonic implications of which we have already encountered (VI, 332). Later again, Raskolnikov, having lost his sense of direction, "coincidentally" encounters Svidrigailov sitting in the window of a tavern. "This struck him terribly, to the point of horror," the narrator tells us; and we can understand why, for Raskolnikov has inadvertently turned *left* (the devil's direction) rather than right from the Haymarket (VI, 355–56). The same sort of play on the demonic implications of directional signs is to be found at the very end of this scene, a scene throughout which Svidrigailov has sought to emphasize the closeness of his behavior to that of Raskolnikov, even implicitly comparing his own desire to find "salvation" and "resurrection" through his pursuit of Dunia to Raskolnikov's relationship with Sonia (VI, 365). As they part company he reaffirms this moral identification by saying first, "You go to the right, and I to the left" (VI, 368), but then changes this to:

> "You go right and I'll go left, or, if you like, the other way around; only adieu, mon plaisir, until the pleasure of meeting you again!"
> And he turned right toward the Haymarket. (VI, 372)

In this way the novel signals that even at this late moment the "Svidrigailov solution"—that is, willfulness and suicide rather than contrition and salvation—is still very much open to Raskolnikov too. The physical description of Svidrigailov that accompanies this encounter suggests his role as Raskolnikov's demon in its ambiguity and in the way it emphasizes the mask-like quality of his face; and we should note that despite the third-person form the narrative here quickly moves to reporting Raskolnikov's impressions:

> Raskolnikov rested his right elbow on the table, propped up his chin on the fingers of his right hand and gazed intently at Svidrigailov. He examined his face for about a minute, for he had always previously been struck by it. It was a strange sort of face, rather like a mask: white, but with red cheeks and crimson lips, with a light blond beard and blond hair that was still fairly thick. The eyes were somehow too blue and their expression too heavy and still. There was something terribly unpleasant in that handsome and extraordinarily young-looking face. (VI, 357)

In addition to the superficially unpleasant aspects of this description—the implicitly signaled sensuality and unsettling combinations of disparate elements—there is the overtly demonic marker of the mask with its connotations of deception and its liminal status at the threshold between identities.

In the scene describing Svidrigailov's final night and his suicide, the demonic markers are particularly insistent. He spends the early part of the evening in various taverns and cesspools, although without drinking anything stronger than tea. There is something unsettling, although not explicitly demonic, about the characteristics of those whose company he seeks: two wretched, squabbling scriveners with crooked noses, one crooked to the right, the other to the left—something that particularly strikes Svidrigailov. The weather is appalling: lowering clouds, driving rain, thunder and lightning—precisely the sort of weather associated in folk belief with the appearance of the devil. When Svidrigailov later arrives at Sonia's, wet to the skin, the Kapernaumov children recoil from him "in indescribable terror" (VI, 384). He speaks to Sonia of his intention to "go to America," a euphemism for his imminent suicide, and the reader will pause to wonder at this conjunction of what was for Dostoevsky an act driven by the greatest spiritual desolation and the country that most embodied the spiritual desert spawned by Western materialism. Having left Sonia's, he crosses a bridge over the Neva "precisely at midnight," a conjunction of profound temporal and spatial liminality, before settling in a cheap hotel room where, shivering, he recalls the bridge and the river and remembers that he has always been afraid of water, the devil's element in folk belief (V, 388–89). He then falls into feverish sleep and experiences dreams punctuated by conventional invocations of the devil (for example, "the devil take it!") and demonically charged images such as mice,[11] flies, rising water levels, and the body of a young girl who has committed suicide by drowning. This last image, and its setting during Trinity week, strongly suggest, as Ivanits has argued, an affinity with the folk figure of the water-nymph (*rusalka*), a representative of the "unclean force" whose malignant powers were especially effective during Trinity week.[12] Finally, a five-year-old girl is transformed before his eyes into a demon-child bursting into mocking laughter and outraging him with her insolent and depraved sensuality (VI, 393). As Ivanits tells us, "Virtually every Russian village knew stories of 'accursed' children (*prokliatye*) [the very term used by Svidrigailov to exorcise his apparition] snatched away by devils (or *leshie* [wood-goblins] or *rusalki*) after being damned by a parent."[13] The account of Svidrigailov's eventual suicide recalls his initial entry into the novel in its emphasis on "spatial imagery suggesting transition."[14] The threshold chronotope is revived in the form of the locked gates of a large house with a watchtower, guarded by a Jew in a soldier's greatcoat, in front of which Svidrigailov shoots himself. Even the figure of the Jewish sentry contains demonic implications, for, as Wigzell reminds us, "In the anti-Semitic lore of the time, Jews were excluded from heaven for their crucifixion of Christ."[15]

The motif of the mask applied to the physical description of Svidrigailov also serves to focus attention on a further theme with demonic resonances in the novel: that of Raskolnikov as a *pretender*. Dostoevsky's treatment of dualism and role usurpation in *The Double* served as an early introduction to this theme and its demonic implications, and we shall encounter it in a yet more suggestive form in our discussion of *The Devils* in chapter 4. In *Crime and Punishment* the theme is centered on Raskolnikov's desire to rise above the ordinariness of his own identity and assume the power of the "superman" to shape destiny for himself. The model for the role he aspires to play and the identity he attempts to assume is the figure of Napoleon, and the theme of pretendership is given dynamic form in the novel through the hero's ambiguous and vacillating attitudes to that figure: On the one hand Raskolnikov admires Napoleon's "beautiful and monumental deeds" (VI, 319), but on the other he fears and recoils from the violence, loneliness, and responsibility that go with the role of superman. This ambiguity emerges most effectively in the dream in which Raskolnikov tries unsuccessfully to kill his victim again and where he senses his own falseness in the role of Napoleonic transgressor. As Bakhtin has pointed out, this scene is replete with hostile, mocking laughter directed at Raskolnikov:

[H]e quietly freed the axe from its loop and struck the old woman on the crown of the head, time and again. But strangely she did not even stir from the blows, as though she were made of wood. He became frightened, bent down closer and began to look at her, but she bent her head even lower. He then bent down right to the floor and glanced up into her face, glanced and was mortified: the old hag was sitting there and laughing—simply dissolving into soft, inaudible laughter which she was trying her hardest to conceal from his hearing. Suddenly, it seemed to him that the bedroom door had opened a little and that there too there seemed to be people laughing and whispering. He was overcome by rage: he began to strike the old woman on the head with all his strength, but with each blow of the axe the laughter and whispering from the bedroom became louder and more audible, and the hag heaved all over with laughter. He made to run away, but the whole of the entrance hall was now filled with people, all the doors to the staircase were wide open, and on the landing, on the stairway, and further down, there were people packed head to head, all looking—but all hushed and waiting, silent. . . . His heart shrank, his legs would not move, as though rooted to the spot. . . . He tried to cry out—and woke up. (VI, 213)

Predictably, yet nonetheless convincingly, Bakhtin identifies the carnival resonances of this scene, arguing that before us "is the image of communal ridicule on the public square decrowning a carnival king-pretender."[16] He further identifies literary sources for the scene in the works of Pushkin, first in the story *The Queen of Spades*—where another Napoleonic pretender, Hermann, is subjected to mocking laughter by the "ghost" of the old woman he has killed—and second in the prophetic dream of the tsar-pretender, Grishka Otrepev, in the historical drama of role usurpation *Boris Godunov*. The similarities offered by the latter are particularly striking:

I dreamed I climbed a *crooked stair* that led
Up to a tower, and there upon that *height*
I stood, where Moscow like an ant hill lay
Under my feet, and in the *marketplace*
The *people* stared and pointed at me *laughing;*
I felt ashamed, a trembling overcame me,
I fell headfirst, and in that fall I woke.[17]

The historical figure of Grishka Otrepev, the idea of the "False Dmitry," and indeed all reference to the historical period of the Time of Troubles (*smutnoe vremia*), when leadership of the Russian state was seized by various "pretenders," all carry a strong semiotic charge in Dostoevsky's fiction, signifying the demonic aspects of role-play and pretendership.[18] The most explicit condemnation of a character through association with Grishka Otrepev is to be found in *The Devils*, where Stavrogin is caught up in an inescapable web of cultural-historical markers associated with the Time of Troubles, and we shall explore this in chapter 4. Raskolnikov's links with the historical pretender are implicit rather than explicit, and they derive largely from his own constant consciousness of the falseness of his Napoleonic aspirations and the role he is playing. This is to be found right from the start, when he questions his own ability to proceed with the murder: "Am I really capable of *this?*" he asks, before crying out to God for guidance (VI, 6, 50). He later confesses to Sonia that he "wanted to become a Napoleon, and that is why I killed," before admitting that he knew he was not a Napoleon even before murdering his victims, and that no real Napoleon would have thought twice about carrying out such an act (VI, 318–19). Finally, the identification of Raskolnikov with the False Dmitry is obliquely hinted at by Porfiry Petrovich, the examining magistrate, who, having revealed that he knows that Raskolnikov is the murderer, urges him to give himself up with the words: "Be a sun and all will see you. Above all a sun must be a sun" (VI, 352). This is a strange formulation, but the image of the sun is later to be applied to another pretender—Stavrogin—in which context it is significant that, as Boris Uspensky points out, the term "sun of righteousness" (*pravednoe solntse*), applied to Christ in liturgical texts, was also used to describe the False Dmitry. [19]

The period of the *smutnoe vremia* (1598–1613) and the historical phenomenon of royal imposture predate by about a century the foundation of the city of St. Petersburg in the reign of Peter the Great. But in Dostoevsky's works the northern capital of Petrine Russia is often associated with the ideas of imposture, falseness, deception, and identity usurpation which that historical phenomenon embodied, and partly through such association St. Petersburg acquires a very considerable demonic charge of its own. *The Double* was subtitled "A Petersburg Poem," as though to imply that the incidents of madness and imposture it narrates were somehow attributable to, and explicable in terms of, its Peterburg setting. The city is similarly implicated in the events of *Crime and Punishment* and the mind-set of its characters. Svidrigailov in particular is alert to the fact that Petersburg is much more than a merely neutral setting for its people and their actions: It somehow seems to be the progenitor of those people and actions. He describes to Raskolnikov how he arrived in Petersburg from the countryside:

"On the very day of my arrival I went around visiting all these various cesspools—well, after seven years, I really threw myself at them. [. . .] You know, on Marfa Petrovna's estate in the country I was tormented to death by the memory of all these mysterious places and little corners where, if you know what you're looking for, you can find quite a lot. The devil take it! The people are drinking, the educated youth are burning themselves up in unrealizable dreams and fancies out of idleness, crippling themselves with theories; Jews come flocking from somewhere or other, hiding their money away, and all the rest sinks into depravity. In this way the city breathed its familiar breath on me from the first hours." (VI, 370)

Svidrigailov also offers a memorable image of Raskolnikov himself as a mechanical, mad demon spawned by Petersburg, a phenomenon unthinkable in any other setting. He is trying to account for the fact, discussed above, that Raskolnikov has somehow managed to turn left rather than right from the Haymarket:

> "The address got stamped on your memory automatically. So you turned here automatically, strictly following the directions I gave without realizing. [. . .] And another thing: I am convinced that in Petersburg there are many people who walk around talking to themselves. This is a city of half-crazy people. If we had any science, then doctors, lawyers and philosophers would be able to do the most valuable research on Petersburg, each in their own field. It's rare to find a place where so many murky, sharp and strange influences have their effect on man's soul as in Petersburg. The climatic influences alone are worth a fortune! And at the same time this is the administrative center of the whole of Russia, and its character must be reflected in everything. But that's not what I'm getting at. The point is, I've already observed you several times from the side. You come out of the house with your head still held high, but after twenty paces you allow it to drop and you put your hands behind your back. You look but apparently no longer see anything either in front of you or to the side. Finally, you start to move your lips and talk to yourself, sometimes freeing one hand and declaiming, and at last coming to a halt in the middle of the road for a long period. It's really not good, sir." (VI, 357)

Shortly before this passage, the housepainter Mikolka, who has falsely confessed to the murders, has also been described as a product of Petersburg by Porfiry, and the crime referred to as a "fantastic, dark, and contemporary" Petersburg crime, the result of withdrawal from reality and life (VI, 347–48). Such an association of the city with the malignant products of an alienated consciousness goes right back to Dostoevsky's works of the 1840s and his linkage of the figure of the Petersburg dreamer with solipsism and spiritual death.

Moreover, as Bakhtin points out, in Dostoevsky's fiction, and especially in *Crime and Punishment*, Petersburg is above all else a *liminal* city: it "is on the borderline between existence and nonexistence, reality and phantasmagoria, always on the verge of dissipating like the fog and vanishing. Petersburg too is devoid, as it were, of any internal grounds for justifiable stabilization; it too is on the threshold."[20] Sidney Monas makes the same point with reference to Russian literature in general, arguing that the hero of the Petersburg tale (Monas cites here Evgeny from Pushkin's narrative poem *The Bronze Horseman*) "is always somehow caught on the threshold of the public and the private, the conscious and the unconscious, the real and the illusory."[21] However, Monas takes the argument one important step further by developing the view that the liminality of St. Petersburg is *reflected in*, rather than *created by*, the products of Russian literature, and that the city itself is in its historical, topographical, and cultural essence a "threshold city." He finds evidence of this, as have many before him, in the ambivalence sustained by the contrast between Petersburg's architecture—its magnificent "ensembles of palaces" and "mannerist vistas"—and its natural setting: caught up in a watery swamp, beset by a "tubercular climate," its inhabitants the victims of optical illusions created by its northern light and of attempts by nature to claim back its own.[22] In cultural and historical terms, too, Petersburg has traditionally been seen as a threshold, marking the transition from pre-Petrine Russian civilization, with its emphasis on native or Byzantine cultural values and models, to Westernized imperial Russia with its attempts to renegotiate Russia's historical meaning and destiny on the basis of its assumption of a European identity: "as the capital and major port, it was the city into which everything Russian made its way, and everything European as well. It was the threshold-city, the window to and from the West, the *limen*."[23] This is an idea familiar enough in Russian intellectual and cultural history to require no further elaboration here, other than to emphasize yet again the demonic implications of the threshold and the window, implications that do not form part of Monas's argument.

The association of Petersburg not only with the specific concept of the threshold, but with the generally demonic too, is an idea that also has a considerable pedigree in Russian cultural history. As Pamela Davidson has recently argued, the effect of Peter the Great's reforms as a whole was to initiate a new and more secular phase in Russian culture, which inevitably challenged the previously religious worldview and its aspirations. Given the binary "either/or" tendency modeled in Lotman and Uspensky's view of Russian culture, allied to Peter's assault on the institution of the Patriarchate of the Russian Church, this inevitably encouraged a view of the post-Petrine cultural order and its products as intrinsically demonic and it eventually fostered the identification of the Tsar-Reformer with the Antichrist.[24] As the most visible symbol of that cultural order and its displacement of the past, St. Petersburg was fully implicated in the demonic dimension ascribed to it, to the extent that the depiction of the city in post-Petrine Russian literature formed, and continues to form, a coherent tradition in which the supernatural, ungodly, destructive, and deceptive aspects of the city are emphasized. The most significant contributions to this tradition—at least as far as their impact on Dostoevsky was concerned—are to be found in the works of Gogol and Pushkin. The former supplied the topography and "demonography" of Dostoevsky's Petersburg in his tales of soulless victims of the devil's deceits drifting wraithlike through an urban landscape of narrow streets, frozen canals, and empty squares—a world in which "everything is a lie, everything is a deceit" and "the demon himself lights the lamps in order to show things as they really are not."[25] Pushkin, on the other hand, in the introductory section of *The Bronze Horseman,* suggested an explanation of the city's demonic nature in the hubris of the man who ordered its creation. As Davidson neatly puts it, the "parallel drawn in the introduction between God, the creator of the universe, and Peter, referred to simply as 'He,' the creator *ex nihilo* of a new city and a potent symbol of the artist contemplating his impending act of creation, can be read in two ways: as an extreme form of praise for Peter, or as an indictment of his idolatrous pretensions."[26] The latter reading is favored by Pushkin's initial identification of Peter as "he" (*on*), italicized for emphasis in the text and a traditional taboo term of reference for the devil.[27] *Crime and Punishment* exploits the contributions made by both Gogol and Pushkin to the "Petersburg tradition" in its own attempts to demonize the city. The debt to Gogol is perhaps most evident in the novel's presentation of a "fantastic" urban reality where dream and hallucination invade waking reality to the extent that it is not always possible to decide where Raskolnikov's consciousness ends and St. Petersburg begins. The weight of Pushkin's poem is felt in Raskolnikov's dualism and in the linkages the novel implies between, on the one hand, Raskolnikov and Peter the Great—both aspiring to overstep conventional limits and sacrificing the innocent along the way—and, on the other, Raskolnikov and Evgeny, who both end up as victims of their attempts to challenge authority.

Although the use of such "source texts" in *Crime and Punishment* serves to signal the presence of the demonic in Dostoevsky's Petersburg, it does not necessarily serve to clarify its nature. The views expressed in *The Diary of a Writer* and Dostoevsky's other journalistic and polemical writings make it clear that what demonized St. Petersburg for him was not primarily the hubris of Peter the Great in godlike creating it from the Finnish swamps nor the deceptive nature of its topography. Rather, it was its status as a symbol of post-Petrine Russia's withdrawal from everything truly Russian and its rejection of national identity and healthy Orthodox spirituality in favor of the gloomy intellectual phantoms spawned by Western rational culture. *Crime and Punishment*'s account of Raskolnikov's spiritual journey from the demonic wastes of his "decent enough little theory," and from the arrogant intellectualism that gave rise to it, to the haven of grace offered by Sonia's Orthodox Christianity, was a journey that in Dostoevsky's view had to be made by the whole of Russia's alienated, Westernized intellectual classes. This view is thematized to a greater or lesser degree in all of the major novels that followed *Crime and Punishment,* but it forms the polemical core of *The Devils,* in particular—a novel whose very title points to Dostoevsky's willingness to assign the Russian intellectual classes, and especially those with revolutionary aspirations, to the realm of the demonic.

Raskolnikov's spiritual journey from demonic intellectual pride and revolt to the sort of acceptance of God's will anticipated in the novel's epilogue is of course signaled in the very title of *Crime and Punishment,* and this is another indicator of the fact that Dostoevsky approached this work with a clearly defined polemical purpose and subsequently invested it with a clear and unambiguous value system. The concept of punishment was inseparable from that of crime from the moment Dostoevsky first set out his plans in the letter to Katkov, where we are told that the murderer:

> passes almost a month after the crime before the final catastrophe. Nobody suspects him, nor could they. And here the whole psychological process of the crime unfolds. Insoluble questions confront the murderer, unsuspected and unanticipated feelings torment his heart. Divine justice and the earthly law claim their rights, and in the end he is *compelled* to give himself up, compelled so that even if he is to perish in penal servitude he might once again be united with people; the feeling of separation and isolation from mankind, which he has experienced since the crime was committed, torments him. The law of justice and human nature take their course and destroy his convictions with little difficulty. The criminal himself decides to accept suffering in order to expiate his deed. But here I find it hard to elaborate my thought fully. (XXVIII/2, 137)

Dostoevsky's sense of the vagueness of his design and the ill-defined references to "insoluble questions," "unsuspected and unanticipated feelings," "divine justice and the earthly law," and "the law of justice and human nature" do not disguise his clear desire to demonstrate that, although the murderer's demonism may have come from outside him through the absorption of the "half-baked ideas" of the radicals, the need for punishment comes somehow from within, from an area of his being unsuspected and untouched by his radical convictions.

This desire is carried over into the novel itself, but simply to attribute Raskolnikov's salvation to the effects of his "conscience" or his innate "sense of morality" would be to resort to the same vague terminology used in the Katkov letter. More importantly, it would be to overlook a striking feature of that "salvation": the fact that until the very last moment before his confession, and even for the first year of his Siberian punishment, Raskolnikov appears to remain convinced that his crime is *morally* acceptable. In an interview with Dunia shortly before his confession, he vigorously defends the ethics of his act:

> "Crime? What crime?" he cried in a sort of sudden frenzy. "That I killed a vile, harmful louse, an old hag of a moneylender of no use to anybody, for whose murder one should be forgiven forty sins, and who bled poor people

dry. Can that be called a crime? I don't think about it, and I have no desire to wipe it out." (VI, 400)

Something drives him to submit to the shame, degradation, and physical hardships that follow his confession and arrest, but that something is clearly not simple moral contrition. Instead, Raskolnikov's behavior before, during, and after his crime dramatizes Dostoevsky's belief, discussed in the introduction to this volume, in the inseparability of moral and aesthetic categories, and his conviction that a man's aesthetic sense is more likely to alert him to the presence of evil than any "decent enough little theories" generated by an intellect invaded by demonic pride and pretensions. In this regard, too, *Crime and Punishment* sustains its polemical campaign against the "half-baked ideas" of the radical thinkers of the time.

The men of the 1860s, led again by Chernyshevsky through the ideas developed in his dissertation "The Aesthetic Relations of Art to Reality" (1855), had sought to deny the unity of aesthetic and moral categories. But, whereas the "aesthetic confusion" of the Romantics, discussed by Dostoevsky in "Mr. -bov and the Question of Art," had arisen from an inversion of idealist aesthetics through the deliberate association of beauty with evil, the radicals of the 1860s diminished the value of beauty by assigning it a status secondary to that of utility. The moral value of, for example, a work of art was to be measured by that work's usefulness, not its beauty. Writers and artists were urged by the utilitarian critics associated with *The Contemporary* to communicate moral truths and to appeal to their audience's ethical sense without feeling obliged, as Dobroliubov put it, to "cultivate the aesthetic taste of the public."[28] Dostoevsky mounted his own arguments against the utilitarian aesthetic in "Mr. -bov and the Question of Art," where he reaffirmed his faith in the unity of content and form by criticizing the tales of the Ukrainian writer Marko Vovchok, tales that had been welcomed by Dobroliubov (Mr. -bov) despite their lack of artistry.

In *Crime and Punishment* Raskolnikov's crime is conceived with a total disregard for form in the face of moral content that is characteristic of a man of the 1860s. Rationally, and in terms of the "new" utilitarian ethic to which he thinks he subscribes, Raskolnikov can justify his crime as *good* in terms of its likely social consequences, and this explains his lack of any overtly *moral* remorse until his final spiritual epiphany in the epilogue. Konstantin Mochulsky has famously dismissed this epiphany as a "pious lie" on Dostoevsky's part, an instance of authorial moral bullying as, after five hundred or so pages of being a psychologically convincing murderer-demon, Raskolnikov is nudged unconvincingly into God's camp, where he serves his author's polemical purpose but loses all artistic credibility.[29] This view is probably unfair in that throughout much of the novel Raskolnikov's crime, so justified by reason and the utilitarian ethic, is censured by his aesthetic sense, and this prepares both us and the hero for his eventual submission to the authorities and punishment. Put simply, Raskolnikov right from the start finds all thought of the crime, as well as its commission, ugly and disgusting, and he cannot understand why it should so revolt him when he thinks he can justify it ethically. He is brought to the realization that although his generation of radical thinkers may aspire to the creation of a new ethic, it has not discovered a workable new aesthetic. Beauty is shown to be an absolute and permanent ideal: A new age cannot create a new beauty.

Like Ivan Karamazov after him, Raskolnikov is a rationalist whose rationalism is flawed by the "irrational" residue of a highly developed aesthetic sensibility. The conflict between his rational and aesthetic responses accounts for much of his confusion throughout *Crime and Punishment*. This confusion affects him even before the crime is committed, and it is evident in the doubts he voices about what he is intending to do. Careful examination of these doubts reveals that they are couched in a vocabulary more appropriate to an aesthetic, rather than ethical, sensibility, suggesting that when Raskolnikov is troubled by thought of the crime, he is disturbed not by its lack of morality, but by its lack of aesthetic form, by its ugliness. Consider, for example, his reaction to his early "rehearsal" visit to the pawnbroker's flat:

> Raskolnikov went out in a decidedly confused state. This confusion became stronger and stronger. As he went down the staircase he even stopped once or twice as though suddenly struck by something. Finally, when he was already in the street, he exclaimed: "O God! How repulsive [*otvratitel'no*] this all is! And will I, will I really. . . . No, this is nonsense [*vzdor*], this is preposterous [*nelepost'*]!" he added decisively. "And really, how could such a horror [*uzhas*] enter my head? Is my heart really capable of such filth [*griaz'*]? The main thing is it's filthy [*griazno*], foul [*pakostno*], and disgusting [*gadko*], disgusting!" (VI, 10)

In a comparable passage that we have already cited and that follows his dream of the beating of the mare, Raskolnikov again demonstrates that his revulsion when confronted with an act of violent evil is aesthetic, rather than moral, in nature. Having dismissed his dream as *bezobraznyi,* a term literally meaning "ugly" but carrying also implications of formlessness and absence of iconic beauty, Raskolnikov then continues:

> "No, I shall not be able to bear it, I shall not bear it! Even if there were no doubt about all these calculations, even if everything that has been decided in this last month were as clear as day and arithmetically just—Lord, I should still not be able to decide on this!" (VI, 50)

This is an intriguing admission, implying as it does that the whole of Raskolnikov's system of rational and mathematically "infallible" ethics may be brought to nought by a sense of aesthetic revulsion. At this stage in the novel the would-be murderer has reached an impasse. Moral and intellectual justification for what he plans to do is not enough: He must overcome his disgust and somehow invest his proposed crime with aesthetic *form* in order to render it more than just intellectually attractive to himself. This he attempts to do by invoking the Romantic myth of Napoleon—although "attempts" suggests a conscious strategy and is perhaps inappropriate given Raskolnikov's imperfect understanding of the forces at work in him. At the time *Crime and Punishment* was written, the cult of Napoleon as a historical superman was well established and had found significant treatment—usually ironic—in works of Russian literature. Pushkin had used him in *The Queen of Spades* to suggest the Romantic grandeur that Hermann so conspicuously lacked; and Tolstoi's unsympathetic account of Napoleon's attempts to orchestrate the historical processes in *War and Peace* was serialized alongside installments of *Crime and Punishment* in *The Russian Herald.* Romantic mythography had depicted Napoleon as a great historical figure who had embodied in his person and deeds many of the qualities and ideals affirmed in the course of the Romantic movement, most notably individualism and revolt. Through sheer force of will he had changed the very course of history and the face of Europe. He had torn a gaping hole in the fabric of accepted historical thought and had, through his example, elevated man to unprecedented heights of freedom. It is in this form that the image of Napoleon invades Raskolnikov's consciousness, becoming the very embodiment of the superior man described in his essay on crime. But Raskolnikov is attracted to Napoleon not only intellectually, as the model for his own transgression against the established order, but also aesthetically. Indeed, he seizes on the Romantic image of Napoleonic grandeur as the aesthetic formula that will allow him to come to terms with his own planned crime, for in his eyes—as in the eyes of Romantic historiography—Napoleon had brought form, elegance, style, and greatness to the act of violence. As Kirpotin has remarked in a stimulating discussion of the Napoleonic myth in *Crime and Punishment*: "Raskolnikov is attracted not by the historical Napoleon, but by the myth of Napoleon. [. . .] Myth has aestheticized Napoleon and surrounded his name with an iridescent halo."[30] In this way Napoleon becomes Raskolnikov's demon, tempting him with the idea that willful cruelty, violence, and evil can be noble and beautiful, and this leads us to suspect that when Raskolnikov eventually concedes to Sonia that "a devil dragged me on. [. . .] It was the devil that killed the old woman, not I," it is the *chert* Napoleon, rather than Sonia's "orthodox" *d'iavol*, that he has in mind.

The aesthetic appeal of Napoleon's example—his "beautiful and monumental deeds" (*krasivye i monumental'nye veshchi*)—is enough to allow Raskolnikov to proceed, but the illusory nature of this example is fully revealed to him afterward. The point is that the real Napoleon has taken refuge from his violent actions in a prettified myth, but Raskolnikov cannot do so. In the aftermath of his crime, alone in his coffin-like room, he is forced to confront the full horror of what he has done, and again it is aesthetics rather than ethics that torment him. He is shocked at the way he has been deceived by a myth, and he despairs at the aesthetic gulf separating the grandeur of Napoleon from his own squalid crime:

> "No, those people are not made in the same way; a real *ruler of men*, to whom all is permitted, takes Toulon by storm, causes wholesale carnage in Paris, *forgets* an army in Egypt, *throws away* half a million lives in his Moscow campaign, and gets away with a pun at Vilna. And after his death monuments are erected to him—for him it would appear *all* is permissible. No, such men are not made of flesh and blood, but of bronze!"
>
> A sudden, not quite relevant thought almost made him laugh:
>
> "Napoleon, the pyramids, Waterloo—and a scraggy, vile old hag, a moneylender with a red box under her bed: what could Porfiry make of it? Could he make anything of it? No, his aesthetic sense would not let him. A Napoleon crawl under an old woman's bed? Nonsense!" (VI, 211)

The recognition that Napoleon is made of bronze, rather than flesh and blood, represents Raskolnikov's tacit acknowledgment that he has been guilty of demonic idolatry. Even the reference to Napoleon's pun at Vilna is significant, for that pun was not without relevance to the situation in which Raskolnikov now finds himself: "From the sublime to the ridiculous there is only one step, and posterity must judge."

Raskolnikov further demonstrates the essentially aesthetic nature of his despair in the discussion he has with Dunia, shortly before giving himself up to the police. Here, as we have already seen, he vigorously defends the ethics of his crime, but condemns its form: "Ah. It did not have the form; it lacked the aesthetically right form! Well I just cannot understand why lobbing bombs at people or killing them by regular siege is a more respectable form" (VI, 400). The answer, of course, is that it is not. Only myth can invest a diabolical act with beautiful form—and in this respect posterity has judged Napoleon very kindly indeed. Raskolnikov's crime leads not only, as Kirpotin points out, to the debunking of the Napoleonic myth: In its ugliness it also serves to reaffirm Dostoevsky's belief that the morally repulsive cannot truly be realized in beautiful form.

If the myth of Napoleon serves to promote for Raskolnikov the illusion of aestheticized evil, then the more immediately present figure of Svidrigailov—surrounded by a constellation of demonic markers—is there to dispel that same illusion. He emerges from a penumbra of rumor and suspicion to become a counterbalance to Napoleon in the process of Raskolnikov's growing self-knowledge. He also comes to stand as a travesty of the Byronic demonic hero, embodying the same qualities of languid world-weariness, unorthodoxy, moral freedom, and apparent indifference to the sufferings he causes others, but now presenting those features in a form that is repellent, rather than "shining with an unearthly beauty." As we have seen, Raskolnikov's reaction to this figure is one of profound ambiguity. On the one hand, he is fascinated by him, a fascination that derives from the unwilling recognition that there is much in common between Svidrigailov and himself. The rumors that precede Svidrigailov persuade Raskolnikov that here is someone who, like himself, has transgressed common laws and morality through the willful act of violence. Svidrigailov also recognizes this affinity and compares himself and Raskolnikov to "berries of the same field" (VI, 221). Each is drawn to the other, seemingly anticipating some sort of lead or example. However, Raskolnikov is loath to acknowledge this affinity, unable to reconcile it with the overwhelming aesthetic disgust Svidrigailov arouses in him. On almost every occasion in which he addresses Svidrigailov the words "with revulsion" (*s otvrashcheniem*) occur, for he finds the latter's actions an aesthetic far cry from the "beautiful and monumental deeds" of a Napoleon.

Raskolnikov is affected initially by the ugliness of Svidrigailov's mind—he shudders to see his own ideas about the right of the strong individual to transgress presented in so repulsive a form, just as in *The Devils* Stepan Trofimovich Verkhovensky recoils from his generation's ideals when those ideals are travestied by the younger generation and can be found in the "second-hand market, unrecognizable, covered in filth, clumsily set up at an angle, without proportion, without harmony" (X, 24). In his conduct too Svidrigailov debases Raskolnikov's Napoleonic ideal by stripping it of its pretensions to grandeur. He revels in the dirt and squalor of backstreet Petersburg, and he is most at home in seedy restaurants and bars, where he indulges his predilection for depravity. Whereas Napoleon exercised his moral independence in great historical deeds, Svidrigailov exercises his moral indifference in the brothels and taverns of St. Petersburg. Napoleon takes Toulon by storm, Svidrigailov seduces young children. It is, we recall, only a small step from the sublime to the ridiculous, or indeed to the squalid, but this is a step Raskolnikov cannot accept. He can come to terms with his superman only when the latter is cloaked in the grandeur and nobility bestowed by myth; he cannot accept the gross distortion represented by Svidrigailov. In this respect he is, as Svidrigailov insists, a "Schiller" and an idealist, whose aesthetic sense prevents him from accepting the devilish horrors invented by and carried out in the name of reason.

"The fear of aesthetics is the first sign of weakness!" exclaims Raskolnikov to Dunia (VI, 400), and in these words he reveals his acuity of insight into his own predicament. His fear of ugliness serves to demonize his crime as surely as it demonizes his Napoleonic ideal through the figure of Svidrigailov. His aesthetic sense prevents him from completing the act of transgression that his reason condones. He is caught on yet another threshold, torn between the intellectual-ethical freedom of the superman and the aesthetic inhibitions of a louse. "I am an aesthetic louse!" he acknowledges. "I was in too much of a hurry to step across. . . . I didn't kill a person, I killed a principle! I killed a principle, but I didn't step across, I remained on this side" (VI, 211). The principle he has destroyed is his notion that ethical criteria may be determined by reason alone, without reference to that sense of beauty that in Dostoevsky's view allowed man to identify his true ideals. The moral freedom to which Raskolnikov aspires is possible only in the absence of a sense of aesthetic discrimination, but such an absence would transform a man into a demon, as the figure of Stavrogin is later to show. Ivan Karamazov, too, is to stumble over aesthetics in both his rebellion and his conception of the devil. The "devil" produced by his rational imagination takes the form of his Grand Inquisitor, an ideal figure like Raskolnikov's Napoleon, impressive in its Romantic grandeur. But the devil who later appears in Ivan's nightmare is, like Svidrigailov, an aesthetic reappraisal of that ideal, an irrational product of his unconscious mind, and a shabby little demon who offends Ivan's sense of form:

> "Moderate your demands [says Ivan's devil]. Don't demand from me 'everything great and beautiful' and then you'll see how well we'll get on together. You are really angry with me because I did not appear before you in a red glow, with 'thunder and lightning' and with scorched wings, but introduced myself in so modest a form. You are offended first of all in your aesthetic feelings and secondly in your pride. How could such a vulgar devil appear to such a great man. I'm afraid you have that romantic strain so derided by Belinsky." (XV, 81)

The aesthetic sense for both Ivan and Raskolnikov is thus an impediment to their respective acts of rebellion and the means through which their demonism is exposed. For both, it may indeed be "the first sign of weakness," but it is also the key to their eventual salvation. As a touchstone of healthy normality, a template for moral idealism, and a sort of devil alarm alerting us to the presence of evil, man's innate sense of ideal beauty described by Dostoevsky in his essay "Mr. -bov and the Question of Art" has the potential to "save the world," and it is perhaps fitting that this simple faith should be articulated unequivocally by the writer's own favorite hero, Myshkin, "the positively good man" of *The Idiot*.

Chapter Three

The Abbot Pafnuty's Hand: *The Idiot*

The law of self-destruction and the law of self-preservation are equally strong in man! The devil rules equally over mankind until a point in time still unknown to us. You are laughing? You don't believe in the devil? Disbelief in the devil is a French idea, a frivolous idea. Do you know who the devil is? Do you know what his name is? Yet without even knowing his name you laugh at his form, following Voltaire's example. You laugh at his hoofs, tail and horns, which you yourselves have invented; for the unclean spirit is a great and dread spirit, but he does not have the hoofs and horns that you've invented for him.

Lebedev's words to the company assembled at Prince Myshkin's birthday party in part 3 of *The Idiot* (VIII, 311) are surely a warning to us that, in a novel ostensibly centered on the iconic representation of "the positively good man," as opposed to the depiction of the sort of criminal egoism displayed by the major characters in most of Dostoevsky's other novels, we should expect the devil to make his approaches indirectly and to assume forms other than those traditionally depicted. That is not to say that *The Idiot* does not avail itself of the sort of semiotic markers that signal the devil's presence elsewhere in Dostoevsky's fiction, nor to overlook the fact that it produces in the figure of Myshkin's alter ego, Parfen Rogozhin, perhaps the most conventionally complete embodiment of gothic demonism Dostoevsky ever created. Indeed, at times it is difficult to take Rogozhin seriously as a character in a nineteenth-century realist novel, with his haunting and tempting Myshkin and the tragic heroine Nastasia Filippovna as well as the consumptive youth Ippolit, with his disembodied piercing eyes, his ubiquitous knife, his encroachment into their dreams, and his strange omnipresence. Right from the novel's start he is established as a dark and disturbing counterpoint to Myshkin's iconic Christ-like demeanor and as the inevitable agent of Nastasia's violent demise, always liable to emerge from liminal spaces like staircases, crossroads, railway stations, bridges, and doorways, or from liminal conditions like dreams, and always shadowing the hero from opposite locations such as the facing seat in a railway carriage, a reflection in a shop window, or the pavement on the other side of the street. Add to this his generally dark demeanor, offset only by the sort of hauntingly pale face usually associated with the demon figure of Romantic literature, and Rogozhin is inescapably established as an emissary from the "Other World," a highly conventionalized *diabolus ex machina,* carrying out the dirty work of the Unclean Spirit.

He may be the novel's most insistent demonic marker, but he is not the only one. We also recognize the presence of the devil in Ippolit's strident rebellion against an order he cannot accept, in the hyperbolic lying of General Ivolgin, in the petty-demon-cum-jester Ferdyshchenko, in the satanic pride of Nastasia Filippovna, described by her despoiler Totsky as "a serpent under the flowers" (VIII, 42),[1] and in Gania Ivolgin's blasphemous association of the title "King of the Jews" with Rothschild and his own mercenary ambitions. Demonic markers emerge, as they do elsewhere in Dostoevsky's fiction, indirectly in casual speech, such as General Epanchin's fond description of his daughter Aglaia as "a demonic personality" (*kharakter besovskii* [VIII, 298]), or Aglaia's mother's equally fond opinion that she is "wicked" (*zlaia*) and a "little devil" (*besenok* [VIII, 273]). The conditions of insanity and epilepsy, widely held to be not only pathological but also symptomatic of possession by the evil spirit, are intimately associated with Nastasia Filippovna and Myshkin respectively, while the similarly demonic motifs of lameness and irritability are attached to the "nihilists" Burdovsky and Ippolit. Nastasia Filippovna's "madness" and satanic pride are complemented by her quite literally bewitching "demonic beauty" (VIII, 482) as well as by her willingness to espouse diabolical behavior. It is not for nothing that she warns her seducer Totsky: "If you're afraid of the wolf, don't go into the woods" (VIII, 121): The wolf is a form assumed by the devil in Russian folk belief, while the woods were a favorite place for the snaring of souls. Finally, in this brief survey of the conventionally demonic paraphernalia of *The Idiot,* we should note that, like *Crime and Punishment,* it exploits the demonic potential of its status as a "Petersburg novel," drawing heavily on the demonic semiotics of that city's history in both life and literature as a counterbalance to the trees and parks of the dacha suburb of Pavlovsk.[2]

The import of Lebedev's words, however, are that we should look beyond the conventionally demonic in order to understand the devil's true meaning and purpose. At the same birthday gathering Lebedev displays his skills as an interpreter of the Apocalypse, but earlier in the novel he tells Myshkin of how he has already confronted Nastasia Filippovna with his essential conclusions:

"She agreed with me that we are in the time of the third horse, the black one, and of the rider with the balance in his hand, since everything in our age is weighed in the balance and settled by agreement, and people are only interested in seeking their rights: 'a measure of wheat for a dinarius and three measures of barley for a dinarius,' but with all this they still want to preserve a free spirit, a pure heart, a healthy body, and all the rest of God's gifts. But they won't preserve them by demanding their rights alone, and there will follow the pale horse, and he whose name is Death, and after him comes hell." (VIII, 167–68)

This apocalyptic vision, which along with Holbein's painting of Christ taken from the cross forms the core imagery of *The Idiot,* is also the key to its demonic meaning. As David Bethea has pointed out, this is Dostoevsky's first major work "in which the apocalypse, as metaphor for 'anti-life' (death), 'anti-history' (timelessness), and indeed 'anti-narrative' (end, silence) is ironically the prime mover of plot."[3] Here we shall be less concerned with that apocalypticism's contribution to the novel's structure as with the way it frames its demonism. Apocalyptic notes are sounded everywhere in the text, to the extent that it is quite legitimate to talk—as Robert Hollander does—of an "apocalyptic framework" to *The Idiot.*[4] These notes resonate in the novel's sense of the imminent spiritual disintegration of the society it describes; in its insistent preoccupation with the themes of justice, judgment, and condemnation (introduced right from the start in Myshkin's anecdotes about execution); and in the teleological urgency of the narrative structure, its constant "end-directedness" as, aided by the symbolism of Rogozhin's ubiquitous eyes and knife, it gallops toward a dénouement identified right from the start: the murder of Nastasia Filippovna. This apocalyptic "end-directedness" is picked up also in Ippolit's "Necessary Explanation," first in the epigraph he chooses for it ("Après moi le déluge!"), then in his assertion that afterward "there will be time no more" (a direct quotation from Revelation), and finally in his melodramatic breaking of the large red seal attached to his confession, so reminiscent of the opening of the seals by the Angel of the Apocalypse (Revelation 5:6). We should also note the use made of what Michael C. Finke calls "talking names," especially those that seem designed to keep our attention focused on Lebedev's primary image of the apocalyptic horsemen.[5] Nastasia Filippovna's patronymic is derived from the Greek for "lover of horses," Ippolit Terentev's given name is also horse related, with its particularly apocalyptic connotation of unleashing horses, while the society grande dame Princess Belokonskaia, whose tastes and opinions shape the entire behavioral basis of the corner of society depicted in *The Idiot,* has a name that is a direct translation of "white horse." This clearly suggests the fourth horse of the apocalypse, Death, but it also links in with the doomed Nastasia Filippovna's predilection for driving about in a carriage drawn by white horses (see, for example, VIII, 250, 262).[6]

Other talking names in the novel are derived from birds, and their use seems to me to suggest a parallel between the fallen state of nineteenth-century Europeanized Russia, with its emphasis on pecuniary imperatives, and the fall of Babylon as described in St. John's apocalyptic dream. Revelation 18:2, for example, describes a Babylon that has become "the habitation of devils" and "a cage of every unclean and hateful bird." For Dostoevsky, writing *The Idiot* from the depths of a self-imposed exile in Western Europe in order to escape the demands of creditors, his native Russia must indeed have seemed to teem with all kinds of "devils"—social-ists, nihilists, atheists, moneylenders, and a Westernized and alienated edu-cated class, to name but a few—so it is hardly surprising that his novel is overrun with a multitude of "unclean and hateful birds": There is the moneylender Ptitsyn, whose name derives from the Russian word for "bird" (*ptitsa*); There is the mendacious Lebedev himself (*lebed'*: "swan"), as well as the avaricious Gania Ivolgin (*ivolga*: "oriole"). There is even mention of a General Sokolovich (*sokol*: "falcon"), an old "friend" of General Ivolgin who is probably only the product of the latter's mendacity (VIII, 108). Like the biblical Babylon, Dostoevsky's Russian equivalent is presided over by a "whore," the fallen woman Nastasia Filippovna, seduced as a young woman by the businessman Totsky and now bent on a perverse course of revenge through self-destruction. Details from the biblical account of the fall of Babylon are woven through Dostoevsky's text. Revelation 18, for example, describes how "the kings of the earth, who have committed fornication and lived deliciously with her [the Whore], shall bewail her, and lament for her, when they shall see the smoke of her burning. [. . .] And the merchants of the earth shall weep and mourn over her [. . .] and shall stand afar off for the fear of her torment, weeping and wailing" (verses 9, 11, and 15). In Dostoevsky's apocalypse the kings of the earth are, as Gania Ivolgin recog-nizes, the merchants themselves, the men of money; and three of them—Epanchin, Totsky, and Ptitsyn—at the end of part 1 explicitly lament the self-destructive course pursued by Nastasia Filippovna, and yet at the same time they fear her and "stand afar off." As well as being the "Whore" at the heart of this modern Babylon, Nastasia Filippovna Barashkova is also asso-ciated by her surname with the "Lamb" (*barashek:*"lamb"), the biblical sym-bol of innocence and forgiveness. As we shall see, the Lamb introduced into Dostoevsky's allegorical reworking of God's final apocalyptic struggle with the devil is the novel's Christ-like hero, Prince Myshkin.

Such apocalyptic notes, struck throughout Dostoevsky's text, are or-chestrated into something coherently demonic by Lebedev's "reading" of the contemporary age, first in his interpretation of the apocalyptic horsemen, already cited, and then in his assertions at Myshkin's birthday gathering. This latter performance—on the surface a mixture of arrant nonsense, self-important pontification, mendaciousness, and outlandish anecdotalism—in fact turns out to be a pivotal moment in the novel's polemical design and one that replicates concerns and issues that are expressed more seriously by other characters in other novels, as well as by Dostoevsky himself in writings more easily identifiable with his own views. Lebedev's insistence that "the law of self-destruction and the law of self-preservation are equally strong in man" and that "the devil rules equally over mankind" is a consequence of his belief in the third horseman as the ruling symbol of mankind in the present age. The materialism, utilitarianism, and self-interest represented by that figure, along with the contemporary predominance of "objective" laws of scientific and social development, have stripped existence of all spiritual purpose and divine meaning, reducing it to a bleak and demonic landscape devoid of God and driven by money, that potent symbol of life as transaction rather than transcendence. This in turn is accompanied by an erosion of human brotherhood and an insistence on personal power and personal rights that eventually result in the demonic figure of the isolated individual, confronting the rest of existence solely as an arena for self-aggrandizement and insisting on what Radomsky—another lesser character who, like Lebedev, seems chosen to articulate some of the novel's most central concerns—calls "the right of might" (VIII, 245). For Lebedev, the whole spirit of the modern age, with its lack of "any moral basis save the gratification of personal egoism and material necessity"—a spirit he associates with the spread of railways, a realization of the apocalyptic prophecy of the star of wormwood—is quite literally accursed (VIII, 309–10). The emergence of self-interest as "the normal law of existence" produces an abstract humanitarianism in which the individual act of charity is displaced in favor of "universal peace and universal happiness out of necessity!" The results are symptoms such as atheistic socialism with its rumble of "carts bringing bread to the whole of humanity without a moral basis for that act" (VIII, 312), which leads Lebedev to the conclusion that "the friend of humanity with an unsteady moral basis is the cannibal devouring humanity." It emerges in the course of the novel that Lebedev's views on socialism are shared, and in a sense validated, by the far less buffoonish figure of Myshkin. Indeed Myshkin goes further, arguing that atheistic socialism and the spiritual bankruptcy to which it gives expression are in turn merely contemporary by-products of the true seat of the antichrist, the Roman Catholic Church. Myshkin's views on socialism and on Catholicism as an "unchristian faith" (VIII, 450) are, of course, localized fictional fallout from Dostoevsky's own vehement antisocialism and anti-Catholicism, which explode with emphatic megatonnage elsewhere, in his letters, journalism, and *Diary of a Writer.*

Myshkin's views, voiced on hearing the news that his benefactor Pavlishchev has converted to the Roman church, do though bring to the rout of Catholicism that same penumbra of demonic rhetoric that also attaches to it in Ivan's tale of the Grand Inquisitor in *The Brothers Karamazov:*

> Pavlishchev possessed a lucid mind and was a Christian, a true Christian. [. . .] how then could he submit to a faith that is . . . unchristian? [. . .] Roman Catholicism is even worse than atheism itself, that's my opinion! Yes, that's my opinion! Atheism merely preaches a void, but Catholicism goes further: it preaches a distorted Christ, one that it has traduced and abused itself, the opposite of Christ! It preaches the Antichrist, I swear, I can assure you. That is my own long-held conviction, and I myself have been much tormented by it. . . . Roman Catholicism believes that without universal temporal authority the Church cannot survive on earth, and it cries: "Non possumus!" In my view Roman Catholicism is not even a faith, but a continuation of the Western Roman Empire, and everything in it is subordinated to that idea, starting with the faith. The Pope seized the earth, an earthly throne, and took up the sword; since then everything has gone the same way, only to the sword have been added lies, intrigue, deception, fanaticism, superstition, and villainy. They've played with the most sacred, truthful, innocent, and ardent feelings of the people, and bartered away the lot, everything, for money, for base temporal power. Is that not the teaching of the Antichrist?! (VIII, 450–51)

Like Dostoevsky himself in *Winter Notes on Summer Impressions*, Myshkin makes clear his belief that the spiritual collapse of which socialism, atheism, and Catholicism are symptomatic has its roots in the essential nature of Western European civilization, a civilization that has taken possession only of those educated Russians who have lost their nationality in their rush to embrace the "benefits" offered by Western rationality, materialism, and scientific progress. He advocates a form of Russian religious messianism, essentially indistinguishable from Dostoevsky's own, in which the West is both resisted and itself reborn through "our Christ, whom we have preserved and whom they have not known" (VIII, 451). The attempt thus to lay the blame for the Antichrist, for the demonic, and for the threat of Apocalypse squarely at the feet of the West is therefore no eccentric aberration of a socially inept "idiot prince." It is the be-all and, quite literally, end-all of a novel whose parting shot is the prophetic warning of Mrs. Epanchina: "And all this, and all this abroad, and all this Europe of yours, all this is just an illusion, and all of us Russians abroad are just an illusion. . . . Mark my words, you'll see for yourself!" (VIII, 510).

Lebedev illustrates the attack on the Western-inspired spiritual poverty of the modern age with an absurd but revealing anecdote about a twelfth-century cannibal who, after a lifetime's gourmandizing on fat monks and the occasional tender infant, confesses and goes to the stake. What was it, Lebedev asks, that impelled him to such an act when he knew the fate that would befall him? Lebedev's answer is that there must have been in those days "something more powerful than the stake and the flames and even the habit of twenty years! There must have been an idea stronger than all misfortunes, famines, tortures, plagues, leprosy, and all that hell which mankind could not have endured without that binding idea which guided the heart and made fecund the springs of life" (VIII, 315). Conversely, it is the absence of precisely such a binding idea in the modern age that loosens the individual's attachment to life and allows Lebedev's apparently paradoxical conclusion, prompted by Radomsky, that the opposing laws of self-destruction and self-preservation, of death and life, of the devil and God, are now equally strong in man. In the absence of a binding idea the individual may be reduced to despair and may confront the "dead house" of a meaningless prison-universe in the only way left open to him—through the personal revolt of suicide. Here we see clearly the relationship of Lebedev's apparently nonsensical ramblings to the ideas on the contemporary phenomenon of suicide later expressed by Dostoevsky in his *Diary of a Writer* entries for late 1876, entries already examined in chapter 1 of this study with regard to the tale *A Gentle Creature*.

Lebedev's performance immediately precedes Ippolit's reading of his "Necessary Explanation." This is significant, for it also provides the framework in which we must seek to understand both that "explanation" and Ippolit's subsequent attempt to take his own life. In part Ippolit's attempt is an obvious act of demonic individualism and rebellion against a universe he cannot understand and an existence over which he no longer has any power, except insofar as he is still able to choose the moment to end it. As he admits to the assembled company, "It's not much in the way of power, not much in the way of revolt," but it is the only act he is still able to complete on the basis of his own free will and individual choice (VIII, 344). On the other hand, Ippolit's comment that if he had had the power not to be born, "I would not have accepted existence on such derisive terms," and his admission that he cannot bring himself to continue living "in a life that assumes such strange and offensive forms" (VIII, 341), indicate that he sees not himself, but the universe against which he is rebelling as the embodiment of demonic evil. This places him squarely in the same frame as the Ridiculous Man and "N.N.," the author of "The Verdict" (*Diary of a Writer* for October 1876), both of whom resort to suicide out of despair in the face of a universe of truly terrifying inertia and emptiness. As the author of "The Verdict" concludes: "And so, as I cannot eradicate nature, I shall eradicate only myself, solely out of tedium at having to endure a tyranny for which no one is to blame" (XXIII, 148). Suicide is thus implicitly linked to forms of risk-taking such as gambling and escape, first seen in *The House of the Dead,* where they serve to give expression to a humiliated individual and represent "an anguished, convulsive manifestation of personality" against the tyranny of inertia (IV, 67).

Ippolit's comparable existential despair is mediated through his interaction with certain people, objects, events, and images that for him articulate the essence of an enclosed, godless universe-void, so drained of values is it, and so indifferent to human hopes and desires. The name of the medical student who pronounces the death sentence over him is Kislorodov, from *kislorod* ("oxygen"), an oblique echo of the view expressed by contemporary Russian nihilists to the effect that the universe consisted solely of objective matter like oxygen and hydrogen and was not the meaningful creation of some transcendental intelligence. Ippolit's nightmarish dream of being stalked by a hideous, but unidentifiable, scorpion-like creature offers a striking symbol of the "dark and godforsaken force" that is indifferently to crush him "like a fly" (VIII, 326). Later he confesses to another dream-vision in which he is shown a "huge and repulsive tarantula" and is assured by an unidentified figure that this is the embodiment of that same "deaf, dark and dumb" force, something that prompts him to wonder: "Can that which does not possess form appear as an image?" (VIII, 340). Ippolit then imagines that Rogozhin enters his room, and it is the intriguing association of the demonic Rogozhin with such images of a godforsaken universe that leads Ippolit to his conclusion that: "That vision humiliated me. I cannot bring myself to submit to a dark force taking the form of a tarantula" (VIII, 341).

It is Ippolit, significantly, who gives the novel's fullest description of the copy of Hans Holbein's *Christ in the Tomb* that hangs "in one of the gloomiest rooms" of Rogozhin's house. The presence of this painting above a door effectively transforms that house into a supremely demonic location: a mausoleum for a dead and vanquished Christ. It stands at a crossroads (VIII, 170), it is associated with religious heresy through its links with the sects of castrates and old believers (VIII, 173),[7] it is described by Ippolit as "like a cemetery" (VIII, 338) and by Myshkin as "gloomy" and "completely lacking in architectural form" (VIII, 170), while Nastasia Filippovna is convinced that a corpse rots below the floor (VIII, 380). Myshkin's earlier reaction to this painting, which depicts a dead Christ displaying signs of physical decomposition and which appears to hold out little hope of the resurrection on which the entire Christian faith is erected, is that it is an image that could cause one to lose one's faith (VIII, 182). But for Ippolit the painting is a compelling confirmation of his own demonic cosmology, representing as it does the consequences of a universe in which there is "only nature" (VIII, 339):

Here you unwillingly admit the thought that if death is so terrible and the laws of nature are so strong, then how can you overcome them? How can you overcome them when even He could not overcome them now, He who vanquished nature during his lifetime, He whom nature obeyed, who said *"Talitha cumi!"* and the maid arose, who cried "Lazarus, come forth!" and the dead man came forth. Looking at that picture, one gets the impression of nature as some sort of huge, implacable, dumb beast, or more accurately, much more accurately, strange to say, as some sort of huge machine of the latest construction which has pointlessly seized, dismembered and swallowed up, mutely and insensibly, a great and priceless being, a being who alone was worth the whole of nature and all its laws, worth the entire earth which perhaps was created merely for the coming of that creature! That picture somehow gives expression to that notion of a dark, insolent, and senselessly eternal force to which everything is subordinated. (VIII, 339)

As Jostein Børtnes has commented, Holbein's Christ is the central symbol of *The Idiot,* but in Ippolit's interpretation it has been "emptied of divine content" and has therefore lost its Christian meaning.[8] But a Christ emptied of its divine content is no Christ at all. It is a pretender, an impostor, a deceit, and is thus ultimately blasphemous and demonic. Ippolit's apparent sorrow for a "great and priceless being" swallowed up meaninglessly by a mute universe is in fact sorrow for his own predicament. Moreover, far from being the helpless victim of such a universe, Ippolit is in fact the author of it. His vision of demonic desolation, inertia, and despair is the inevitable consequence of his own lack of faith, which in turn is attributable to his narrowly self-centered and intellectualized approach to existence. It is the sort of universe that emerges when puny human reason displaces a sense of the divine and individuals cease to experience "a higher idea of existence in their souls" (XXIV, 50). Like the Underground Man, the pawnbroker from *A Gentle Creature,* and the Ridiculous Man, Ippolit is destroyed not by a mutely indifferent nature, but by "the electricity of human thought."

The symbol of Ippolit's alienation—his dream of a fly instinctively knowing its place in a divine feast of universal harmony (VIII, 343)—ironically betrays his recognition that such a harmony might indeed exist beyond his own demonic egocentrism and arrogant rationality. This rebellious consciousness smolders with the desire for reconciliation and the need for existence to be not merely a matter of indifference (*vse ravno*). He betrays himself in his need for his confession to create an effect—hence his spite when his audience feigns indifference, his attention to the dramatic paraphernalia with which he surrounds its reading, and, above all, the fact that he has a second copy ready to be given to Aglaia Epanchina. His confession and attempted suicide are thus driven equally by a demonic desire to confront an unacceptable reality in "an anguished, convulsive manifestation of personality" (notice how he uses the by-now demonically charged image of leaping from a bell tower—VIII, 345, 347), and by the need to make contact in the only way he knows with those about him.

The image of the fly at peace with God's creation links Ippolit with Myshkin, who experiences an identical dream but who responds to his own alienation-by-illness with faith, humility (which he insists is a "terrible force" [VIII, 329]), and an acceptance that he now urges on Ippolit with the words: "Pass us by and forgive us our happiness" (VIII, 433). This relationship between demon-rebel and Christ-like advocate of humility is characteristic of Myshkin's role in the novel, which would appear to be one of confronting and attempting to negate its various manifestations of the demonic. His spiritual simplicity stands in stark contrast to the duplicity and emptiness of Russian high society. His initial indigence and ignorance of money matters set him apart from the materialism of all about him. He advocates the novel's core values of humility, spirituality, and compassion in the face of utilitarianism and egoism. He retains faith in a meaningful universe despite the hardships of his own life and the existential despair of those he encounters. And he is consistently set in opposition to the arch-demon Rogozhin: positionally, as in the opening and closing scenes; physically, in the fair complexion and tranquil demeanor that contrast so sharply with Rogozhin's swarthiness and passionate intensity; and symbolically, as rivals for the soul of the fallen Nastasia, who, as both angel and whore, needs Myshkin to confirm her innocence as much as Rogozhin to confirm her guilt.

All this would appear to be in line with Dostoevsky's intention, set out in a well-known letter of January 1868 to his niece, Sofia Ivanova, to depict in *The Idiot* "the positively good man," despite the difficulties in so doing "particularly nowadays." It was not only the nature of the present godless age that militated against the convincing depiction of moral beauty and Christlike goodness, but also, in Dostoevsky's view, the nature of the novel form itself that, in its reliance on sustaining the illusion of reality, was intolerant of the ideal and tended to compromise its depiction:

> All those writers who have set out to depict the *positively* good man have always shirked the job—and not just our writers, but European ones as well. For this is a boundless task. The good is an ideal, and neither we ourselves nor civilized Europe have come anywhere near working out an ideal. There has existed on earth only one positively good man—Christ; so that the appearance of this boundlessly, infinitely good figure is in itself, of course, an endless miracle. (This is the whole thrust of the Gospel according to John: for him the whole miracle is contained in the incarnation alone, in the mere appearance of the good.) [. . .] Of all the good characters in Christian literature

the most complete is Don Quixote. But he is good only because at the same time he is ridiculous. (XXVIII/2, 251)

It is perhaps for this reason that Dostoevsky ascribes to Myshkin, in his confrontation with a Westernized and demonized Russia, a series of recognizable identities, drawn from Russian and European cultural and religious tradition and directly or indirectly appropriate to that purpose. On reflection, "allows to be ascribed" might be more accurate here, in that often those identities emerge from "readings" and "misreadings" of Myshkin by the other characters he meets. Among the more obvious examples of this are Aglaia's identification of Myshkin with the chivalrous knight errant, achieved through her reading of Pushkin's poem about a "poor knight" and her placing of his letter in a copy of *Don Quixote;* the Christ-like identity ascribed to him by the insistence of various members of the Epanchin family that he is a philosopher who has come to teach them; and Rogozhin's comment to the effect that he is a religious fool (*iurodivyi*) and that "God loves the likes of you!" (VIII, 14).

The relationship of Myshkin to the identity models of chivalrous knight, Christ figure, and holy fool has been thoroughly studied in the critical literature.[9] But there is a further, less widely examined cultural identity attributable to him, one that is particularly appropriate to his apparent function in the novel to struggle against demonic temptation: that of the saintly monk, familiar from the tradition of hagiographical literature. That tradition was well known to educated Russians of the mid-nineteenth century, who would have been exposed as children to religious and hagiographical literature, both through the formal processes of education and through the popular editions of saints' lives current at the time. Moreover, hagiographical texts and motifs found their way into the works of many Russian writers during Dostoevsky's lifetime.[10] As a child, Dostoevsky himself was familiar with one of the most popular collections of saints' lives, the *Chet'i Minei,* or *Monthly Readings,* which consisted originally of the translated lives of Greek saints, with the lives of native Russian saints added in later editions. He read the work again while imprisoned in the Peter and Paul Fortress in 1849, and an abridged modern Russian edition was to be found in his library.[11] The collection is mentioned right at the beginning of *The Idiot,* when Rogozhin comments that his mother reads it (VIII, 10).

The hagiographical tradition gradually evolved a series of *topoi*—in the sense of what Margaret Ziolkowski has called "flexible narrative components," rather than precise formulae—that became associated with the depiction of the holy man,[12] and many, although by no means all of these, attach to the figure of Myshkin. Usually the offspring of respectable, Christian parents, the hagiographical hero shows an early disdain for worldly matters and is indifferent or resistant to property ownership. He undertakes demanding ascetic feats, resisting the tests of demons in the process. He may exert a positive, soothing effect on wild animals and may effect miracle cures. He displays great mystical insight and usually dies a peaceful death, joyfully meeting his maker. But the most striking characteristic of the monastic saint and holy man is his kenoticism, "the imitation of Christ's extraordinary humility,"[13] which became a common feature through the *vita* of the abbot Feodosy of the Kievan Caves Monastery, one of the most widely read saints' lives. The *topos* of humility may take the form of dressing so badly that the holy man is mistaken for a beggar, as Myshkin is on his arrival at the Epanchin household, or by dressing in a way that is inadequate to the elements, as Myshkin does on arrival in wintry Russia in a light summer cloak. It may also take the form of a willingness to undertake menial work (compare the copying job offered to Myshkin by General Epanchin), or of happily enduring the ridicule of others (compare, again, Myshkin's arrival at the Epanchin's). Once the kenotic tradition took hold in Russian monastic life and literature, it helped to produce the phenomenon of the "God's fool," or *iurodivyi*, which, as Rogozhin recognizes, is another identity ascribable to Myshkin.

Other ways in which Myshkin embodies the *topoi* of the saintly monk or holy fool include his asexuality—like Russian saints he is chaste—and his lack of familiarity with Russian ways as a result of having spent many years abroad. As Ziolkowski points out, many of the holy fools depicted in hagiographical accounts were of foreign origin.[14] Like the holy fool, whose combination of insight and apparent simplemindedness often allowed him to get away with expressing opinions that would have caused offense if expressed by others, Myshkin's naivety takes the offensive edge off of some of his less well-judged comments. (Although, on the other hand, his directness is equally capable of causing deep offense in those who, like Gania and Ippolit, cannot deal with the truth.) His humility emerges in his oft-expressed acknowledgment of his inferiority to others, in his reluctance to pass judgment, in his willingness always to take blame on himself, even when he is struck by Gania (VIII, 99), and in his advocacy of meekness as a "terrible force." He complies with the Epanchin manservant's request that he not smoke in the house with the unusually apt response: "However, as you wish; there's a saying, you know: 'When in another's monastery . . .'" (VIII, 17). His command of medieval calligraphy also serves to suggest the figure of the saintly monk or holy chronicler, and it is the handwriting of the fourteenth-century Abbot Pafnuty, "the head of a monastery on the Volga, in what is nowadays Kostroma province," that he selects as the first example of his skills (VIII, 46). The choice of the name Pafnuty is highly significant, particularly since it recurs late in the novel attached to Rogozhin's servant

Pafnutevna. The editors of the Academy edition of Dostoevsky's works identify Myshkin's words as referring to Abbot Pafnuty, the founder of the Avraamieva-Chukhlomskaia Monastery on the River Viga (IX, 431). However, in signing himself as one Pafnuty, Myshkin inadvertently aligns himself with another: Pafnuty of Borovsk (died 1477), whose life appears in the *Chet'i Minei*, was the abbot who guided and tonsured Joseph (Iosif) of Volokolamsk, who was to become leader of the so-called Josephian movement against the "heretical" monastic practices and religious views held by the Transvolgan elders and their followers. The essence of the dispute between Josephians and Transvolgans boils down to the twin issues of the appropriateness of monastic property and the extent to which "heretical" departures from religious and monastic norms were to be tolerated. The Transvolgans were renowned for their kenoticism, mysticism, and quietism (Hesychasm); they celebrated internal spiritual achievements over and above the external observance of fasts and other ascetic undertakings, and they objected to the acquisition of property by monasteries to the extent that they were known as "nonpossessors." The Josephians, on the other hand, favored strict monastic codes, external displays of piety, and the rigid observance of ritual and prescribed disciplines. They were also "possessors," in favor of monastic property. The Josephians were zealous in their pursuit of religious heresy, whereas the Transvolgans, although not sympathetic to heresy, were reluctant in their humility to rush to judgment over others.[15] The implications of all this for Myshkin are clear, for at the moment he emulates "the Abbot Pafnuty's hand" he is unwittingly poised to shift from being a "nonpossessor" to a "possessor" as he learns of his inheritance. He is also on the point of shifting from a position of nonjudgmentalism to one in which he rushes to snap judgments about others, including his conviction that Rogozhin will murder Nastasia Filippovna.

In his role as hagiographic hero Myshkin is subjected, as hagiographic tradition demands, to a series of "trials" (*mytarstva*) and demonic temptations. His increasing intimacy with Ippolit and Rogozhin confronts him with the values of two demonic alter egos, who embody in their persons malign qualities from which he has hitherto been insulated during his period of "monastic retreat" in the sterile environs of Schneider's Swiss clinic. It is surely not coincidental that these qualities—Ippolit's arrogance in setting human intellectualism above acceptance of the divine order, along with his sense of exclusion from that order, and Rogozhin's destructive sexual egoism—are qualities that attend the account of the fall of man in Genesis. In his relationship with these two figures Myshkin plays out a contemporary variation on the demonic temptation of Adam.[16] The "positively good man" also finds his values at odds with, and tested by, the pecuniary ethic of Totsky, Ptitsyn, and Gania, particularly after his unexpected inheritance reveals to him the extent to which money maketh the man in the world of nineteenth-century capitalism. His views on humility, compassion, and personal charity are rudely challenged by the strident utilitarianism of Burdovsky's band of nihilist demons; and his personal simplicity is shown to be inadequate in the face of the duplicitous norms of "proper" social behavior. But perhaps the demonic temptation confronting Myshkin that most insistently evokes the typology of the hagiographic saint is that offered by Nastasia Filippovna. His initial familiarity with her is achieved through an anecdote that takes on for him the significance of a parable in which she functions as a Mary Magdalene figure, and through a portrait, to which his kiss attributes iconic importance. But later Myshkin is compelled to recognize the demonic nature of Nastasia Filippovna's suffering and the huge reservoir of pride that lurks beneath her self-humiliation. In a dream he experiences while waiting on a park bench for his meeting with Aglaia, shortly after Ippolit's "Necessary Explanation" and failed suicide attempt, Ippolit's face is displaced by that of Nastasia Filippovna, "but strangely she did not seem to have the same face as he had always known, and he desperately wanted not to acknowledge her as the same woman. In this face there was so much remorse and horror that it seemed to be the face of a great criminal who had just committed a terrible crime. [. . .] His heart froze; nothing, nothing at all would allow him to admit that she was a criminal; but he sensed that at any moment something terrible was about to happen, something he would remember for the rest of his life" (VIII, 352). The transformation of Nastasia Filippovna's face from an iconic symbol of suffering innocence to one of demonic destructiveness suggests the hagiographic motif of the temptation of the innocent and chaste saintly monk by what Christopher Putney has termed "the demonized and harlotized female," the devil assuming the form of a beautiful and seductive woman in order to test the resolve of the ascetic man of God and only subsequently revealing his true identity.[17] The same motif is to be replicated in Grushenka's attempted seduction of the novice Alesha in *The Brothers Karamazov*.

The dynamics of *The Idiot* consist in Myshkin's failure fully to grow into any of the traditional identities that the reader and the other characters tend to ascribe to his appearance. It is by now a commonplace of critical opinion on *The Idiot* to conclude, for example, that Myshkin is not only an *imitatio Christi*, but is also a failed Christ—but it is a conclusion that is no less true for its frequent repetition. Myshkin reduces the divine ideal to a combination of benign humanism, strident Russian chauvinism, and extreme religious intolerance. There is little wrong with what he stands for; it is how he stands for it that turns out to be problematic. His ideal of compassion provokes the murderous passions of Rogozhin; his treacly meekness provokes the outrage of Ippolit; his attempts to mediate between others creates chaos and dissension. The symbol of his failure to embody successfully his own most cherished ideals lies in his breaking of the delicate china vase at the height of his naively utopian attempt to embrace the Epanchin's disdainful and self-interested guests in a celebration of human brotherhood (VIII, 451). During that same scene Myshkin reveals that he is only too aware of his failure to realize what he would wish to stand for when he says: "I am always afraid of compromising the sense and the *main idea* by my ridiculous appearance. My gestures are all wrong. They always come out in the opposite way to what I intend, and this gives rise to laughter and belittles my idea" (VIII, 458). The relationship of Myshkin to Christ is thus one of a failure of embodiment to the very symbol of successful incarnation: the word made flesh. Myshkin emerges in the course of *The Idiot* as a distorted and malfunctioning Christ preaching paradise on Earth. Like Holbein's *Christ in the Tomb,* he represents a Christ "emptied of divine content" and blasphemous, and thus no Christ at all.

He also fails as a knight-errant, driving one of his ladies to the point of Rogozhin's knife and the other, Aglaia, into the clutches of the despised Catholic Church. He fails as a holy fool, compromised by his wealth and increasing desire to live more for himself. And he fails as the hagiographic ideal of the saintly monk, succumbing to "double thoughts" and suspiciousness and manifesting a form of "mystical insight" that turns out to be not only pathological, but also associated with demonic possession. It is highly significant that the epilepsy that is the source of Myshkin's belief in a higher and more harmonious mode of being is also the condition that brings to such an ignoble end his attempts to articulate his beliefs at the Epanchin soiree, and that returns him to darkness at the end of the novel. The narrator's account of the former fit is alert to its demonic condition, as it describes "the wild cry of 'the spirit that threw down and tore' the unfortunate man" (VIII, 459). The reference, set off in quotation marks, is to the demonic possession of a child described in Mark 9:17–27 and Luke 9:42.

The idea of failure seems to have run alongside and contaminated Dostoevsky's very conception of "the positively good man." The letter to his niece setting out the main idea of the novel also contains the striking admission: "I am terribly afraid it will be a positive failure" (XXVIII/2, 251). This initial ambiguity in the depiction of Myshkin feeds through into the finished novel, with characters like Lebedev's odious nephew expressing the view, shared by others, that Myshkin is "either a little too innocent or a little too cunning" (VIII, 235). The ambiguity has been taken up by several critics, with Robert Lord in particular going so far as to argue that Myshkin is a monster at heart, scheming and duplicitous and held in check only by his epilepsy.[18] While we shall argue that Myshkin's goodness is indeed compromised by his actions and by events, the view of him as consciously and deliberately evil seems counterinstinctive and difficult to square with what we read in the novel (as opposed to the notebooks and drafts on which Lord is excessively reliant for his analysis). It is more realistic to speak of the emerging *potential for demonism* in Myshkin as he attempts to translate the abstract ideals and views worked out in the isolation of his Swiss retreat to the characters and situations confronting him in the reality of Russian society. The essence of Myshkin's demonic potential lies in the particular way he chooses to relate to others and in the way he fails to give due regard in his own actions to the advice he offers the Epanchin family at the very start of his period in Russia, when he urges against the easy pigeonholing of people with the words: "It's people's laziness that makes them categorize each other at first sight, so that they can't see anything" (VIII, 24). In pursuing this idea, I should like to draw at some length on the findings of Michael C. Finke's analysis of Myshkin as an "author figure," in the sense that "authoring becomes a metaphor or model for the way Dostoevsky's hero approaches the others around him."[19]

The core of Finke's argument is an attempt to explain Myshkin's failure in terms of the "genre in which he has conceived his activities": On entering Russia with a set of behavioral models, formulaic abstractions, and generic types derived from a Rousseauesque and untested Swiss idyll, he then tries unsuccessfully to impose these on the "Petersburg tale" in which he finds himself immersed. Just as the form of his clothing proves to be unsuitable for the world he is about to enter, so his form of thinking and the way he reads others prove to be equally inappropriate. The behavioral models that bring about the "resurrection" of the fallen woman Marie in Switzerland lead instead to the murder of Nastasia Filippovna. The context of Finke's argument means that he does not pursue the demonic implications of what he describes as Myshkin's tendency to respond to live human beings "with aesthetic rather than ethical activity."[20] But our familiarity with the demonism implicit in the way the Underground Man and the pawnbroker from *A Gentle Creature* relate to those around them in an "authorial" way alerts us to those implications: Both in the parables he narrates and in his relations with those he meets in Petersburg, Myshkin tends to reduce live models to generic types of his own making, turning them from individuals into mere characters in his own authored "fiction" and stripping them of their "otherness" in the process. This tendency is most evident in his dealings with Nastasia Filippovna. Finke points out neatly how several others, including Totsky, Epanchin, Gania, Rogozhin, as well as public opinion as a whole, have been "incubating their own plots" for Nastasia, and how in seeking to release her from their authorship Myshkin ensnares her in his own, slotting her into a plot of redemption and resurrection modeled on that of Marie. In her subsequent relationship with Myshkin, Nastasia wavers between sub-

mission to that plot, with its sentimentally literary denouement of confirmation of her innocence, and asserting her otherness and independence as
what Finke terms a "resistant hero."[21] Incidentally, Finke sees Ippolit, too,
as a "resistant hero," but the authorship he resists is that of God and his suicide is conceived as an attempt "to finalize himself and transform his life into
a self-authored aesthetic event."[22]

Myshkin shows an early interest in the instruments of authorship, ad-
miring General Epanchin's pencils, pens, and high-quality writing paper
(VIII, 25). He signals early his tendency to encroach on the otherness of others by appropriating for his own purposes the Abbot Pafnuty's signature, a
highly personalized form of discourse which Myshkin is prepared to invade
like a parasite. He also demonstrates a remarkable talent for constructing
narratives and deploying them to great effect. In the novel's early chapters
Myshkin's narratives are centered on the theme of the condemned man, and
he regales the Epanchins' manservant with an account of an execution in
which he describes the condemned's face as "white as a sheet of paper"
(VIII, 20). The mention of paper alerts us to what is about to happen: Myshkin sees the condemned man's face as a blank sheet on which he writes his
own impressions. When he takes up the same theme in his story to the
Epanchin family, he once again appropriates for his account the life and
death of another person, inhabiting the most intimate moments and feelings
of that person's life just as he had earlier inhabited Pafnuty's signature.
Aglaia is clearly disturbed by Myshkin's apparently parasitic ability to live in
an authorial sense off the sufferings of a fellow human being, and she comments dryly that he is equally capable of making a laudable deduction
whether he is confronted with an execution or "a finger" (VIII, 53). Driven
as much by his ignorance of life as by the moral and narrative templates he
has constructed in his sterile Swiss clinic, Myshkin sucks up the lives of others as mere material for the enactment of those templates. Again, Aglaia is
quick to recognize this when she asks how he can claim always to have been
happy abroad when he actually witnessed an execution there (VIII, 54).

With his suggestion shortly afterward that Adelaida Epanchina should
paint the head of a condemned man a minute before his execution, Myshkin
demonstrates that he sees painting, too, as a way of appropriating for the
artist's own ends the uniqueness and otherness of another's life and feelings.
He justifies his choice of this subject heatedly (in the face of Adelaida's clear
doubts that this is a suitable topic for a painting) by referring to a similar
work that struck him in Basel. The irony here is that the painting to which
he refers is almost certainly an altarpiece painted in 1514 by the Swiss religious artist Han Fries, depicting the beheading of John the Baptist, a painting in which the religious content means that art is here serving the act
of bearing witness to biblical events—a key moment in the history of

Christianity—rather than supporting the voyeuristic and self-serving aims of the artist himself. There is implicit engagement here with the references elsewhere in the novel to Holbein's deposition, a painting in which, despite the apparently religious content, the aim appears to be not the affirmation of God's glory, but the indulgence of the artist's own imagination and "realism." The result, as Myshkin comments, is that it undermines faith, thus identifying itself as demonic rather than worshipful art. As he outlines his idea to Adelaida, Myshkin twice more compares the face of a condemned man to a sheet of white writing paper, reminding us that here too he is writing himself and his own feelings into the agony of another. The third Epanchin sister, Alexandra, senses that there is something disturbing in the nature of Myshkin's account of his choice of subject when she says that it is nothing like the "quietism" of which he has previously been accused. Moreover, Aglaia picks up on the fact that, as soon as he finishes his tale, Myshkin is immediately ashamed of what he has narrated (VIII, 56–57). It is Aglaia, too, who later comments on Myshkin's attitude toward Ippolit, saying "It is very gross to look on and judge a man's soul in the way that you judge Ippolit. You have no tenderness in you, only truth—and that's unjust" (VIII, 354).

Myshkin's various accounts of the condemned man contrast vividly with Lebedev's later tale of the execution of Madame Du Barry (VIII, 164–65). We have seen how for the former the condemned man is essentially narrative *material*, stripped of otherness and incorporated into his authoring of his tale. Indeed, Myshkin later applies the words "material" and "living material" to other human beings in the episode where he regales the Epanchins' guests with his view on utopianism, before breaking the china vase and falling into a fit. In that scene, too, he is guilty of writing his own expectations on to others in his misjudgment of the "benign" motives of Russian high society (VIII, 457–58). Lebedev, on the other hand (and despite the fact that he is a liar and a rogue), exhibits genuine empathy and compassion for the unhappy Du Barry, to the extent that Myshkin is "involuntarily" obliged to acknowledge him as a man "not without a heart" (V, 165). We should note also Lebedev's nephew's comment to the effect that his uncle "is extremely well-read" and that he "reads all kinds of books and memoirs." This is the crux of the matter: Lebedev is a *reader* of the lives of others, immersing himself in the desperate plight of Du Barry, whereas Myshkin approaches others as a would-be *writer*, authoring their plights into narratives serving his own purpose. He is thus guilty—admittedly in a far more benign way—of essentially the same selfish subjugation of others displayed by the Underground Man and the pawnbroker from *A Gentle Creature*. Moreover, he is aware of this tendency in himself, as he shows in his later thoughts on his attitude to Lebedev and his nephew: "In any case who was he to take it on himself to judge them so definitively and pronounce sentence on them, he who had only just arrived that morning? Lebedev had indeed given him a lesson that morning: Had he expected a Lebedev like that? Had he ever come across a Lebedev like that before? Lebedev and Du Barry, for goodness sake!" (VIII, 190). But Myshkin is slow to learn his lesson, and at the end of his account of the condemned man he goes on to insist that he can "read the faces" of the Epanchin sisters, too, even admitting that he might have his own motives for so doing (VIII, 57, 65). Later, General Epanchin is to round on Ippolit for the same tendency, saying: "It is not for you, young man, to judge the actions of Lizaveta Prokofevna, just as it is not for you to mention aloud and in my presence what is written in my face" (VIII, 243).

Myshkin's tendency is thus "to approach fellow characters as though he were their author,"[23] and the relationship between such potential authorship and diabolism is at the heart of Adam Weiner's analysis of the demonic novel, in which it is seen "to individualize the world, a process that may readily be (and often has been) perceived as an affront to one's human and divine surroundings."[24] We shall consider the fuller implications of this in our analysis of *The Brothers Karamazov* in chapter 5, for it is in that work that Dostoevsky most effectively exploits the demonism of highly individualized and self-serving narratives. Myshkin's "affront" to his human and divine surroundings may be seen in his relations with most of those with whom he comes in contact, and it culminates tragically in the way he "authors" the outcome of the Rogozhin-Nastasia Filippovna relationship. At one point, for example, he wonders whether he cannot use his good influence in order to "make something" out of the pugnacious, but good-hearted, Keller. His choice of vocabulary here is interesting, to say the least, as are the terms in which Keller responds, as he accuses Myshkin of looking at things with too "pastoral" a view and of understanding others in such a "Swiss way" (VIII, 257). Elsewhere Myshkin's tendency to author others takes the less benign form of attributing to them devious motives: He entertains the thought, for example, that Radomsky might be behind the "poor knight" joke at his expense (VIII, 208–10), and he later confesses to Keller his tendency to entertain "double thoughts" in which he is capable of "dark and base suspiciousness" (VIII, 252, 258).

In a scene that is as significant in its own right as it is rich in implications for his relationship with Nastasia Filippovna, Myshkin finds himself looking at Aglaia in a similarly authorial way: "Sometimes he would suddenly start to look at Aglaia, and for five minutes he would not take his eyes off her face. But his look was too strange: It seemed as though he were looking at her as if she were an object situated a mile or so away, or at her portrait, rather than at herself" (VIII, 287). By this act of objectification of a "beloved" woman we are reminded that Myshkin's first encounter with Nastasia Filippovna was with her portrait, onto which he mapped the outlines of his own expectations, expectations that were structured on the template of his Swiss relationship with Marie. Shortly after seeing that portrait, he begins his authoring of Nastasia's tragic destiny with his comment to Gania that Rogozhin would be capable of marrying such a woman, but equally capable of taking a knife to her a week later (VIII, 32). His first actual meeting with Nastasia is at the Ivolgin household, where she initially takes him for a "lackey" before learning he is a "prince," both terms traditionally applied to the devil. Myshkin "recognizes" her not only from her portrait, but also because he has in a sense "pre-scripted" her:

"How did you recognize me?"
  "From your portrait and. . . ."
  "And what else?"
  "And also because you're just as I imagined you. . . . I also seem to have seen you somewhere."
  "Where? Where?"
  "It's as though I've seen your eyes somewhere . . . but that cannot be! I'm just . . . I've never been here before. Perhaps in a dream . . ." (VIII, 90)

Moreover, within just a few pages it is not only her appearance he recognizes. In his reproach that she is not the sort of person she makes herself out to be, Myshkin shows that he also has an identity already mapped out for Nastasia Filippovna (VIII, 99). When he then starts to enact that identity by saying that Nastasia is innocent and that he would be prepared to take her as she is, the response of others draws attention to the authorial role Myshkin has thus assumed. General Epanchin murmurs, "Well, that's a new twist to the story!" (Literally: "Well, that's a new anecdote!"), while Nastasia herself responds, "But that's . . . straight out of novels! It's old-fashioned fantasy, my dear Prince, but nowadays the world has grown wiser and all that is nonsense" (VIII, 138).

Myshkin's authorship of the fates of Nastasia Filippovna and Rogozhin consists not only in his matching them to a pre-existing narrative template and in his insisting that he "foresaw" everything on his return to Petersburg, but also in the way he unconsciously draws attention to the very knife with which Rogozhin will finally murder Nastasia. On his visit to Rogozhin's mausoleum-like house, in which Nastasia will eventually die, Myshkin keeps picking up—to his host's obvious annoyance—a brand new gardening knife (VIII, 180–81). Twice Rogozhin takes it from his hand, and twice he asks him to leave it alone before we learn that this knife is used for cutting the pages of new books. This information could hardly send out a clearer signal: The knife is the instrument for bringing to light already-written, but as yet unenacted narratives. It is as though Myshkin is implicitly inviting Rogozhin to "open the pages" of the tragic narrative and denouement that he has already scripted for these characters. His assumption of authorship over the behavior of Rogozhin and the fate of Nastasia Filippovna is explicitly demonized in the scene after the visit to Rogozhin's house. Myshkin decides to test his suspicion that Rogozhin is following him—a suspicion that takes the form of Rogozhin's demon eyes appearing wherever Myshkin walks—by visiting Nastasia Filippovna's home even though he knows she is not there. When his suspicions begin to dissipate, and he reaches the more charitable conclusion that perhaps Rogozhin is capable of light as well as darkness, Myshkin rejoices at the thought that his "demon is vanquished." But within seconds his doubts return and "he once again believed in his demon. [. . .] A strange and terrible demon had attached itself to him for good and did not mean to leave him from now on" (VIII, 191–93). As in the scene at the Epanchin soiree, this demonic possession soon translates into the semiotically charged form of the epileptic fit that overcomes him at the moment he sees Rogozhin and *that* knife emerging from the staircase.

Different though it is in its malicious intent and overt offensiveness, Keller's newspaper article in book 2, purporting to reveal Myshkin's disregard for the worth and fate of "Pavlishchev's son," Burdovsky, in essence, does to Myshkin what Myshkin does throughout in his attitude to others: It incorporates him into a narrative not of his making, snaring his person and forcing him to act out an unbecoming role in another's fiction. Once again the "authorial" nature of such snatching of another's soul for one's own purposes is made abundantly clear through Keller's excessive authorial pride in the way he has scripted Myshkin (VIII, 242). The same use of false narratives and misappropriated souls informs General Ivolgin's tale of how he served as Napoleon's page. He claims in his anecdote to be bearing witness to great historical events, but in reality he has merely incorporated historical figures into a self-aggrandizing narrative. He is blithely insensitive to the irony of the inscription that, he claims, Napoleon wrote in his sister's album: "Ne mentez jamais!" (VIII, 417).

The presence of Myshkin's demon—his tendency "to approach fellow characters as though he were their author"—cripples all his attempts to relate effectively to those he meets in Russia. It thus compromises his naive dreams of human brotherhood, love, compassion, and the resurrection of the wronged and humiliated woman; and it renders inevitable his eventual return to the pathological Swiss self-absorption and isolation that was the source of his behavioral and narrative templates in the first place. As Radomsky says to him toward the end of the novel: "You, a young man, longed in Switzerland for your native country, and you charged into Russia like an unknown but promised land; you read a great many books about Russia, fine books, perhaps, but for you they were harmful" (VIII, 481). The result, according to Radomsky, was that in reality Myshkin probably loved neither Aglaia nor Nastasia Filippovna, but only his own imagined preconceptions. During his final vigil with Rogozhin over the denouement he himself has authored, Myshkin finally realizes "that for a long time he had not been saying what he should have been saying, not doing what he should have been doing" (VIII, 506). More than that, he has been looking at things in the wrong way. This, of course returns us to the discussion with the Epanchin family shortly after Myshkin's arrival, when the question of how to look is raised in the context of Adelaida's quest for a subject for her painting (VIII, 50). "I don't understand anything about this," says Myshkin. "It seems to me that you simply look and paint." Adelaida's response that she "does not know how to look" goes straight to the heart of Myshkin's shortcomings and anticipates his future inability to break free from his own narrative templates and see through to the otherness of others. Moreover, Mrs. Epanchina's retort to Adelaida to the effect that if she does not know how to look here in Russia, she certainly won't learn abroad, frames and ironizes Adelaida's remark that "the Prince learned to look while he was abroad" (VIII, 50).

Myshkin's flawed and ultimately demonic way of looking at others is thus a symptom of his contamination by that very same Western Europe that Mrs. Epanchina believes to be responsible for reducing Russians to phantoms. As we have seen in chapter 1, the malign effect of Western Europe on Russia's native spirituality is a theme that consistently attracts demonic motifs and symbolism in Dostoevsky's fiction. And nowhere is this more evident than in the most explicitly demonic of his novels, *The Devils*.

Chapter Four

A Devil's Vaudeville: *The Devils*

> "Devils undoubtedly exist, but our under-
> standing of them can vary considerably."
> —Tikhon to Stavrogin, "At Tikhon's"

THE DEVILS, serialized in *Russkii vestnik* between January 1871 and December 1872, is a political novel that outgrew itself. Conceived during Dostoevsky's protracted and painful stay in Western Europe, during which he dreamed of earning enough to pay off his Russian creditors and thus return home, it was designed as a "pamphlet novel," a polemical catharsis in which he would have his say about the spread of "nihilism," that is, revolutionary activity, in Russia, as well as warning of the dangers inherent in the Russian liberal intelligentsia's apparently unconditional love affair with Western European ideas and civilization. By the time he began work on the novel in late 1869, his own earlier liberal sympathies had all but disappeared and his political views had hardened into an uncompromising religious nationalism and an intolerant aversion to Westernism in both its liberal and radical embodiments. In a letter to his friend A. N. Maikov (October 9, 1870), he recalls with distaste his own past association with the Petrashevsky circle, remembering how he was then "under the strong ferment of the mangy Russian liberalism preached by turd-eaters such as the dung-beetle Belinsky and his ilk" (XXIX/1, 145). This loss of respect for his erstwhile mentor of the 1840s goes hand in hand with contempt for the generation of monstrous radicals that had followed in the 1860s. Citing to Maikov the parable of the Gadarene swine that was to serve as one of the epigraphs to *The Devils,* Dostoevsky concludes his vituperative account of the Russian revolutionary movement with the observation: "The devils have departed from the Russian man and entered into the herd of swine, that is into the Nechaevs" (XXIX/1, 145). The reference is, of course, to the infamous "Nechaev affair" of November 1869, when the student Ivanov was suspected of informing and was murdered by members of a group of conspirators led by Sergei Nechaev, an event dramatized by Dostoevsky in the Shatov-Petr Verkhovensky plot line of *The Devils*.[1] The Nechaev affair provided a focus for Dostoevsky's antiradicalism and gave impetus to the polemical purpose of his novel. "The nihilists and Western-izers need a decisive thrashing," he wrote to his friend Nikolai Strakhov. "You're far too soft on them. With them you must write with a whip in your hand" (XXIX/1, 113).

We need not rehearse here the creative process by which *The Devils* outgrew its original, narrowly polemical design. Suffice to say that while it retained its political immediacy and reliance on events of the Nechaev affair, the emergence of Stavrogin as primary hero brought with it an enlargement of the novel's philosophical grasp that enabled it to transcend its origins in polemics of the 1860s and to retain its impact on the imagination of suc-ceeding generations of readers. Its enduring vitality is suggested by the fact that it has been translated into English on several occasions, the most recent being in 1994.[2] Interestingly though, the translators of the various English versions have not established a canonical version of the novel's title. Constance Garnett's original English translation was called *The Possessed;* subsequent versions have used *The Devils*, simply *Devils,* and *Demons.* Even the presence or absence of the definite article slightly shifts the semantic weighting, and the range of titles is suggestive of conceptual uncertainty on the part of Dostoevsky's translators. We may apply Tikhon's warning to our reading of the novel: Devils certainly exist in this work, but they are likely to mean different things to different people. Dostoevsky's Russian title— *Besy*—is neutral to the degree that it creates uncertainty even among inter-preters drawing on the same cultural tradition and discourse; and the prob-lem is unmanageably enlarged when we ask ourselves not only whether *besy* semantically carries the same import as the English words "devils" or "pos-sessed," but also how, if at all, these correspond to those implicit in the German *dämonen,* the Spanish *demonios,* or the French *possédés* (all found in the titles of translated versions of *The Devils*). Pursuit of this line of in-quiry is akin to the traveler's pursuit of the *besy* in the poem by Pushkin also used by Dostoevsky as an epigraph to this novel: We shall end up in a dark field, going round in circles. Instead, the present chapter seeks to discuss some of the cultural traditions and discourses on which Dostoevsky appears to have drawn in his treatment of the demonic in *The Devils.* We shall see how some of these, particularly those employed in the depiction of the ac-tivities of Petr Verkhovensky and his followers, are drawn from carnival tra-ditions, such as folklore, the Russian puppet theater, and the cultural-historical phenomenon of imposture and role-play, traditions that are structured on the breakdown or inversion of established hierarchies. Other discourses, however, drawn from Romantic and Christian traditions, surround the tragedy of Stavrogin and serve to establish an apocalyptic and re-demptive purpose that forms the core of the novel's ideological design.

The place to start might appear to be with the two epigraphs already mentioned. The tradition of epigraph as coded signifier, or clue, is well es-tablished in literature. Unfortunately, so is the tradition of epigraph as red herring. As interpretational signposts, the epigraphs to *The Devils* appear to point in different directions: Pushkin's poem, with its references to house sprites and witches, toward the pagan world of popular superstition and folk tradition, and St. Luke's story of the Gadarene swine toward a biblical para-ble of demonic possession and redemption through Christ. Moreover, we must at least acknowledge the possibility that Dostoevsky intended his epigraphs to be read only at a superficial level, and that their references to de-monic possession and enticement by devils merely introduce a conveniently "diabolical" rhetoric for the expression of a straightforwardly political point on Dostoevsky's part: that Russian Westernized liberals and radicals are "pos-sessed" by evil ideologies and that they have used these to entice Russia from its proper path. This is the interpretation that Stepan Trofimovich Verkhoven-sky attaches to the parable of the Gadarene swine in the novel's closing pages. Moreover, the nihilists had themselves used demonic rhetoric to express their opposition to the established order and instill fear in their opponents: For ex-ample, the student Dmitry Karakozov, who attempted the assassination of Tsar Alexander II in 1866, belonged to an organization that termed itself "Hell."[3] Equally, as Harriet Murav has pointed out, the tradition of the anti-nihilist novel, to which *The Devils* contributes, had attempted to demonize the radicals by attaching to them diabolical symbolism.[4]

Dostoevsky's employment of demonic motifs certainly serves such a directly metaphorical function in *The Devils,* but this function alone is not enough to account for the complex cultural and ideological implications with which he invests his "devils," and which are perhaps signaled in the epigraphs; nor indeed does it explain what appears to be the literal, as op-posed to merely figurative, presence of the demonic in the novel. Tikhon's warning holds true again: devils *do* exist in this work. The Russian provincial town, whose topographical and social credentials the narrator seeks so ea-gerly to establish in part I, is soon transformed into a fissure in the Russian earth, a turnstile to hell through which pass sundry demons, great and small. As befits a sociopolitical novel, the characters in *The Devils* possess social and ideological identities, and they articulate positions in the polemical ex-changes of their time. Stepan Trofimovich Verkhovensky is invested with the generalized characteristics of a liberal Westernizer of the 1840s; his son Petr caricatures the revolutionary nihilist of the 1860s; Stavrogin, somewhat anachronistically, suggests the Byronic nobleman of the 1820s[5]; Shatov is a messianic Slavophile; his neighbor Kirillov is a Westernizer; and so on. But all these sociopolitical identities vie with the demonic physical characteristics manifested by the majority of the novel's characters. Attention is consistently drawn, for example, to the bestiality that breaks through Stavrogin's aristocratic veneer. He is described as possessing the mask-like face, supernatural strength, predatory instincts, and death-like demeanor of a vampire; his very presence arouses supernatural alarm in children; and one description of him alone in his room conveys the impression of an "undead" ghoul who arouses dread in his mother:

> Seeing that Nicholas was sitting somehow unnaturally still, she cautiously approached his divan with a beating heart. It was as though she were struck by how quickly he had fallen asleep and how he could sleep thus, sitting upright and so motionless; even his breathing was hardly perceptible. His face was pale and stern, but immobile as though it had completely frozen; his brows were slightly drawn together and frowning; he looked decidedly like a soulless wax figure. She stood over him for about three minutes, hardly drawing breath, and suddenly she was seized with terror. She withdrew on tiptoe, stopped in the doorway, hurriedly made the sign of the cross over him, and went away unobserved, her heart heavy with a new despair. (X, 182)

The passage leaves little doubt that we are approaching the realm of the supernatural, and Varvara Petrovna's apparent blessing of her son—the sign of the cross—must also be seen as a traditional response to the presence of evil, a ritual popularly believed to immobilize or trap the devil.[6]

The initial description of Petr Verkhovensky, when he arrives in town to begin the process of luring the unwary into his schemes, is also physically suggestive of the demonic. It occurs in a chapter appropriately titled "The Wise Serpent," and it is remarkable for its elusiveness, as though we were witnessing some intangible and diabolical mirage. It is littered with contradictions and imprecision, as well as with the sort of evasive particles, phrases, and adjectival suffixes that dissolve all semantic certainty:

> At first glance it was as though [kak budto] he were sort of stooped and rather awkward [sutulovatyi i meshkovatyi], but, however, not at all stooped and even free-and-easy. It was as though [kak budto] he were some sort of [kakoi-to] eccentric, but, on the other hand, we all then found his manners entirely becoming, and his conversation always to the point.
>
> No one will say that he was ugly, but nobody liked his face. His head was elongated at the back and as though [kak by] flattened at the sides, so that his face seemed pointed. His forehead was high and narrow, but his facial features were small. His eyes were sharp, his nose small and pointed, his lips long and thin.

The description—so reminiscent in its evasiveness of that of another collector of souls, Gogol's Chichikov—continues in this vein until the demon reveals his distinctive trademark:

> His speech was remarkably clearly articulated; his words tumbled out like large, smooth grains, always well chosen and always at your service. At first you found this appealing, but then it became repulsive, precisely because of that too clearly articulated speech and those pearls of ever-ready wisdom. Somehow or other, you began to imagine the tongue in his mouth as being surely of a special sort of shape, somehow unusually long and thin, terribly red and exceedingly pointed, with a tip that flickered constantly and involuntarily. (X, 143)

We thus find ourselves suddenly confronted not just by a Nechaev-intriguer who has arrived in town to begin his political machinations, but also by the Serpent-tempter and Father of Lies, about to embark on the gathering of souls and the dissemination of destruction. In this role Petr is helped by his circle of dupes, some of whom also bear the devil's mark. There is something ghoulish, for example, about the ears possessed by Shigalev, the group's theoretician: They are "of an unnatural size, long, broad and thick, and somehow sticking out in a peculiar way," like the ears of a beast. The narrator is further struck by the "ominous impression" Shigalev makes (X, 110). The same motif of concealed bestiality, with all its diabolical connotations, attaches also to Liamshin, who in the aftermath of Shatov's murder lets loose an "unbelievable scream" and displays classic symptoms of demonic possession, such as speaking in tongues, bulging eyes, and uncontrollable convulsions:

> There are extreme moments of alarm when a man, for example, suddenly starts to cry out in a voice that is not his own, the sort of voice no one could have suspected he possessed beforehand, and this can sometimes be very frightening. Liamshin started to scream in a voice that was not human, but somehow animal. Squeezing Virginsky from behind with his arms ever tighter in a convulsive fit, he screamed without pausing or stopping, staring at everyone with his eyes popping out of his head, his mouth hanging open extremely wide, and his feet tapping lightly on the ground, as if beating out a drum rhythm. (X, 461)

Kirillov too appears to lose his humanity and undergo an analogous process of bestial transformation in the scene leading up to his suicide. The hideously possessed engineer frightens even the usually imperturbable Petr Verkhovensky, almost severing his finger with his teeth (X, 476). What is more, there is a strange and general irritability distributed among many of the characters we encounter: The narrator is at a loss to account for the "strange irritability" (*strannaia razdrazhitel'nost'*) displayed by Kirillov, while in the same scene Shatov is also described by Stepan Trofimovich as "notre irascible ami" (X, 76). Liputin refers to Captain Lebiadkin as "an irritable fellow" (*chelovek razdrazhitel'nyi* [X, 79]), Stavrogin is described as the victim of "a kind of constant anxiety" (*nekotoroe postoiannoe bespokoistvo* [X, 81]), while the initial description of Lizaveta Nikolaevna emphasizes her "constant, morbid, nervous anxiety" (*boleznennoe, nervnoe, bespreryvnoe bespokoistvo*), which gives the impression that "everything within her was as if permanently seeking its level and was unable to find it, everything was in chaos, agitated and anxious" (X, 88–89). The same pattern, so suggestive of possession of some kind, is emphasized in several other characters.

This all contributes to the creation of an implicitly diabolic matrix against which the action of *The Devils* unfolds. It is reinforced by the verbal texture of the novel: constant and apparently casual references to the devil assume a menacing and incantatory value by the frequency of their repetition. Linguistically formulaic expressions such as "the devil only knows what" (*chert znaet chto*), "the devil take" (*chert voz'mi*, or, on Stepan Trofimovich's lips, *au diable*), and "go to the devil" (*k chertu*) acquire a more than conventional resonance against the novel's demonic background. The same is true when Stavrogin refers to Fedka the convict as a "little devil" (*besenok*) immediately after confessing to Dasha Shatova that he sees visions of the devil (X, 230); when we learn that the Governor's morose assistant Blum has red hair, popularly regarded as a sinister characteristic; and when we are told that the Governor himself courted popularity at school by his ability to play the overture to Daniel Auber's comic opera *Fra Diavolo* through his nose, an orifice with diabolical connotations in Russian folklore (X, 242). When Stavrogin undertakes his pilgrimage about the town in the chapters entitled "Night," Fedka offers to guide him through the maze of alleys, adding that the town is so confusing "just as though the devil had carried it around in a basket and shaken it all up" (X, 206). We cannot expect conscious literary references from Fedka, but the reader will surely sense an oblique echo here of the image in Gogol's story "Nevsky Prospect" of a world presided over by the devil, "some sort of demon" who has "crumbled up the world into pieces and mixed them all together without rhyme or reason".[7] In his final conversation with Petr Verkhovensky, Kirillov raises such a prospect of a world abandoned by God, in which "the very laws of the planet are a lie and a devil's vaudeville" (*diavolov vodevil'* [X, 471]). The carefully constructed matrix of demonic references in *The Devils* sets the scene for the novel's own account of a contemporary Russia in which all tradition has been sacrificed, all authority has broken down, and all sense is lost in the devil's vaudeville that has overwhelmed it.

The ability of *The Devils* to function as a sociopolitical novel while simultaneously accommodating a "devil's vaudeville" points to the sort of generic enrichment that Leonid Grossman saw as characteristic of the "adventure novel" (*avantiurnyi roman*). It was, according to Grossman, Dostoevsky's debt to the tradition of the adventure novel that permitted his art to express "the impulse to introduce the extraordinary into the very thick of the commonplace, to fuse into one, according to Romantic principles, the sublime with the grotesque, and by an imperceptible process of conversion to push images and phenomena of everyday reality to the limits of the fantastic."[8] Bakhtin, however, has shown how the adventure novel in turn can be seen as only one branch of the generic tradition of the seriocomic, a tradition reaching deep into the past and characterized by a folkloric carnival "sense of the world" that encourages the breakdown of generic boundaries.[9] Each new contribution to the generic tradition represents a "contemporization" (*osovremenenie*) that "lives in the present, but always *remembers* its past"[10] in the sense of addressing the present while renewing archaic elements of the genre. In considering the credentials of *The Devils* as a contemporization of the seriocomic genre we shall seek to examine how it "remembers" past tradition and how such remembering contributes to its depiction of the demonic.

At the risk of rehearsing the already over-familiar, we might begin by testing *The Devils* against the primary generic characteristics of the seriocomic identified by Bakhtin. These are, first, a starting point in "the living present [. . .] without any epic or tragic distance" and a presentation that is consequently provisional and reliant on experience, rather than one validated by time and distance. The presentation of *The Devils* as a contemporary chronicle narrated by a participating and often bemused "chronicler," who only occasionally resorts to devices of the "as we later found out" sort, is clearly important in this respect (although it is arguable that a more "distanced" and authoritative set of values is introduced into the novel by its ultimately tragic form and its pervasive religious symbolism). Second, Bakhtin draws attention to "the deliberately multi-styled and hetero-voiced nature" of the seriocomic genres:

> Characteristic of these genres are a multi-toned narration, the mixing of high and low, serious and comic; they make wide use of inserted genres—letters, found manuscripts, retold dialogues, parodies on the high genres, parodically reinterpreted citations; in some of them we observe a mixing of prosaic and poetic speech, living dialects and jargons (and in the Roman stage, direct bilingualism as well) are introduced, and various authorial masks make their appearance.[11]

Of these features we recognize in *The Devils* the mixture of the serious and comic, the reliance on inserted genres (most notably, Stavrogin's letter and the manuscript of his confession), parodies of high genres (Lebiadkin's poetry, Karmazinov's "Merci"), and a variety of speech characteristics (including, in Stepan Trofimovich's constant recourse to French, the bilingualism referred to by Bakhtin).

The Devils exhibits in a much more overt way than Dostoevsky's other great novels those folkloric-carnival features that Bakhtin held to be characteristic of the seriocomic genre. Space does not permit—nor, indeed, necessity demand—rehearsal of Bakhtin's analysis of carnival and carnivalized literature.[12] What is appropriate here is discussion of those carnival elements "remembered" in The Devils and that underpin the novel's presentation of the demonic. The primary characteristic of carnival—its setting in a "public square" that permits familiarity and intermingling, with a consequent suspension of normal hierarchical barriers—is met most obviously in The Devils in the drawing-room scandal scenes and the culminating grand scene of the fete organized by the Governor's wife Yulia von Lembke, a fete significantly designed to be nonexclusive and open to all. It is this "openness" that transforms what Yulia intends to be a dignified affair into a public spectacle, where people let their hair down, where respect and distance between the classes is broken down, and where all kinds of eccentric and inappropriate behavior take place. But the spirit of carnival is not confined to such scenes.

The novel suggests what Bakhtin terms "life drawn out of its usual rut" (zhizn', vyvedennaia iz svoei obychnoi kolei) and "life turned inside out" (zhizn' naiznanku)[13] in a much more fundamental way through its preoccupation with social breakdown and revolutionary ideas and activity. Indeed, in a sense revolution is carnival in its most concentrated form, resulting in social clashes and inversions, the relativizing of moral and social principles and ideologies, destruction and renewal, and the crowning and decrowning of kings, described by Bakhtin as the primary carnivalistic act. This act is particularly prominent in The Devils through the destruction of administrative authority in the figures of the Governor and his wife, as well as through Petr Verkhovensky's plan to install Stavrogin in power as "Ivan the Crown-Prince" (Ivan-Tsarevich) and Maria Lebiadkina's subsequent decrowning of Stavrogin as "Grishka Otrepev," a pretender to the Russian throne during the Time of Troubles in the early seventeenth century. Further echoes of carnival tradition may be discerned in the novel's use of parodistic doubles (for example, the relationship of Lebiadkin to Karmazinov and that of Kirillov and Shatov to Stavrogin), its preoccupation with masks, role-play and disguises (Stavrogin's mask-like face, the "masks" worn by the narrator-chronicler, the role of civic martyr played by Stepan Trofimovich, and the figures in the literary quadrille), its references to the profanation of the sacred (a desecrated icon and an abused Bible seller), and the function of Petr Verkhovensky as carnival jester.

The discussion of carnival features in *The Devils* could be extended, but what is important for our purposes is that the carnivalized world of the novel provides an ideal breeding ground for the demonic. The breakdown of social hierarchies leads to the sort of erosion of order that the Devil traditionally exploits, while the suspension of generic boundaries permits the intrusion of the paraphernalia of the supernatural into the world of the nineteenth-century sociopolitical novel. These features of carnival were seen by Bakhtin as essentially positive, promoting an atmosphere of "joyful relativity" (*veselaia otnositel'nost'*), "a mighty life-creating and transforming power, an indestructible vitality."[14] Recently, however, Harriet Murav has argued that the carnivalized world of *The Devils* is designed instead to promote a "frightening chaos" and thus to serve its author's polemical aim of alerting his readership to the dangers of nihilism.[15] The role played by laughter in the novel is the clearest confirmation of this inversion of emphasis. It is the kind of destructive and noninfectious laughter that Lotman and Uspensky have linked to the blasphemous and demonic.[16] Such noninfectious laughter (noninfectious, that is, outside the circle of the possessed) is widespread in *The Devils*, and it contributes a distinctively hysterical quality to the novel's mood. It originates primarily in the demon-jester Petr Verkhovensky, who even refers to himself as a clown (*shut* [X, 408]). "Il rit. Il rit beaucoup, il rit trop. . . . Il rit toujours," complains Stepan Trofimovich of his son (X, 171), while elsewhere we note that the book under which Stepan Trofimovich hides a letter from Mrs. Stavrogina is Victor Hugo's *L'homme qui rit* (X, 73). Lizaveta Nikolaevna is disposed to a malignant form of laughter particularly suggestive of loss of self-control and hysteria:

> From the moment that the Captain went out and collided in the doorway with Nikolai Vsevolodovich, Liza had suddenly started to laugh—at first quietly and intermittently, but then her laughter grew ever greater, becoming louder and more distinct. Her face turned red. The contrast with her gloomy mood of a short time ago was extraordinary. . . . She was visibly trying to regain control of herself and put her handkerchief to her mouth. (X, 156)

Destructive laughter becomes symptomatic of Petr's growing hold over the town and of the breakdown of propriety and social and moral values. In the build-up to the fete, a carnival mood prevails in the town, but it is a mood in which frivolity is tempered by the threateningly unpleasant:

> The state of mind among people at that time was strange. Particularly in female society a certain frivolous attitude manifested itself, and it cannot be said that it appeared gradually. It was as though certain extremely free-and-easy notions were carried on the wind. A mood of light-heartedness and mer-

riment set in, but I cannot say that it was always pleasant. Some sort of mental disarray was in vogue. Afterwards, when everything was over, the blame was attached to Yulia Mikhailovna, her circle and her influence. But all this could hardly have been the fault of Yulia Mikhailovna alone. (X, 249)

Yulia's circle of intimates, reflecting the hold Petr has over their patroness, resorts to a behavioral pattern structured on the sort of pranks and practical jokes that arouse an exclusive form of laughter based on the discomfiture of those outside the circle. The laughter arises from a carnivalistic and blasphemous disregard for established institutions and moral codes: A Bible seller is compromised when obscene photographs are introduced into her bag of holy books; a poor but worthy lieutenant's wife is acutely embarrassed when her debts are disclosed to her violent husband; a newly married couple is hounded and mocked when it emerges that the young wife was not a virgin on her wedding night; and the room where a young man has taken his own life after a final meal of cutlet and Château d'Yquem is invaded by irreverential scoffers (surely a world ruled by the inappropriate when a bottle of sweet Bordeaux is deemed suitable accompaniment for a cutlet!). All these events remind us that in Russian folklore the devil traditionally plays the role of prankster.

Bakhtin is careful to point out that the carnival elements in Dostoevsky's novels entered his work indirectly and unconsciously, not through the influence of carnival itself, which had diminished in importance as a public spectacle in Dostoevsky's day and of which he had little personal experience, but through the tradition of carnivalized literature. Bakhtin's discussion of this tradition is illustrated by references primarily to high culture (he cites, for example, Cervantes' *Don Quixote* and the works of Rabelais).[17] Dostoevsky's depiction of demons and demonism in *The Devils* is, however, inscribed with formulae derived also from low cultural forms such as folk literature, popular theater, and historical legend; and it is in this regard that the significance of the Pushkin epigraph begins to emerge. His presentation of the demonic is, for example, deeply indebted to the typology of the devil, and of the devil's world, as established by Russian folk tradition. We must leave aside the conventional physical form of the devil as shaggy with horns and a tail; such characteristics can have no place in a nineteenth-century novel with pretensions to realism (except, of course, in dreams and hallucinations, such as those experienced by Stavrogin—even here, though, the devil assumes a more modest and down-at-heel guise). Other features of the folk tradition are, however, embraced in *The Devils:* folk belief that it is dangerous to mention the devil by name for fear of summoning up his presence is, as we have seen, suggested in the consequences that follow his repeated invocation in the novel. Lameness is another characteristic popularly attributed to Satan, the result apparently of his fall from grace. Linda J. Ivanits has drawn our attention to Dostoevsky's extensive use of the motif of lameness in *The Brothers Karamazov*,[18] but the same motif is equally prominent in *The Devils*. The venomous schoolmaster in Petr's circle is lame; Stavrogin's wife, Maria Lebiadkina, is a cripple (*khromonozhka*); Lizaveta Nikolaevna hysterically anticipates breaking her legs in a fall from her horse and becoming a *khromonozhka*; and Captain Lebiadkin dedicates to her a poem on the theme of lameness. Mental disturbances, such as the hysteria and uncontrollable laughter displayed by Lizaveta and the members of Yulia von Lembke's intimate circle, are also ascribed in folklore to the work of the devil, as is the epilepsy attributed to Kirillov. Further behavior typical of popular conceptions of the devil and discernible in *The Devils* includes the seduction of other men's wives (compare Stavrogin), the abduction of young children from their parents (suggestive of Stavrogin's seduction of Matresha), a predilection for hooks with which to snare souls (compare the metaphorical hooks with which Petr Verkhovensky captures the von Lembkes), and responsibility for suicides, another motif common in the novel. We have already referred to the death of the young man who takes his life after a meal of cutlet and wine, but suicide is also a particular preoccupation of Kirillov, who however sees it not as a sign of the devil, but as the means of man's deification. His own terrifying demonic transformation in the minutes before his death suggests that he is wrong and that folk tradition is right.

As we have seen, Felix J. Oinas has drawn attention to the importance of the magic circle in folk belief about the devil, arguing that *chert*, the most commonly used word to denote the devil in Russian, is derived from the word family that includes *cherta* ("line" or "limit"), as well as the verb *chertit'* ("to draw"), and that this denotes an origin in the ritual of drawing a circle to protect oneself from the devil.[19] It is just conceivable that this notion has a tangential relevance to the two "circles" (*kruzhki*) we encounter in *The Devils*: the *exclusive* social circle gathered around Yulia von Lembke and the *inclusive* political circle managed by Petr Verkhovensky, from which Shatov is unable to detach himself.

"Petrusha," the affectionate diminutive form of "Petr" that Stepan Trofimovich sentimentally addresses to his son, is morphologically adjacent to "Petrushka," the name of the hero of the Russian carnival folk theater, the equivalent of Punch and Judy. This suggests the possibility of another cultural inscription carried by this jester-demon, one equally deeply embedded in popular tradition. As Catriona Kelly has shown, Petrushka was largely a nineteenth-century Russian adaptation of the Italian Pulcinella tradition, and it enjoyed great popularity from about the 1830s onward.[20] It was initially performed by foreigners, usually German and Italian puppeteers whose command of Russian—and therefore that of their puppets—was imperfect. (We might remember at this point Kirillov's stilted use of Russian, as well as Stavrogin's stylistic and grammatical inadequacies in his letter to Dasha, although both of these devices were primarily intended to serve Dostoevsky's polemic against the Westernized nobleman-intellectual.) Dostoevsky knew and enjoyed puppet shows from childhood, and this early familiarity almost certainly included the Pulcinella (in Russian: *Pul'chinel'*) text in which the figure of Petrushka appeared initially as a clown, a secondary figure.[21] Later the Petrushka figure acquired greater prominence and developed "an aggressive and unpleasant character."[22] Between the 1840s and 1870s the names Pul'chinel' and Petrushka became interchangeable and denoted the play's central character. The two figures are still distinct, however, in Dostoevsky's draft for his *Diary of a Writer* for 1876, where he writes:

> What a character, what a complete artistic character! I am speaking of Pul'chinel'. He is something like Don Quixote, and at the same time Don Juan. How trusting he is, how merry and straightforward; how angry he gets and how he is unwilling to believe evil and deceit. How quickly he gets worked up and sets about injustice with his stick, and how triumphant he is when he thrashes someone with that stick. But what a scoundrel that Petrushka, his constant companion, is. How he deceives him and makes fun of him, and Pul'chinel' never notices. Petrushka is like a Sancho Panza or Leporello, but completely Russianized, a folk character. (XXII, 180)

One is tempted to discern in this description echoes of the trustingly Quixotic Stepan Trofimovich, defending his values in the face of nihilism, and his deceitful scoundrel of a son, Petr.

Petrushka reflected the suspension of hierarchies characteristic of carnival. The hero triumphs over and outwits his superiors, even murdering some of them, and in some versions he even escapes the retribution symbolized in the final appearance of the devil. As Kelly has pointed out, this "subversive" quality encouraged some members of the radical intelligentsia in the 1860s to discern in the spectacle a reflection of the potential for popular rebellion in Russia.[23] Kelly concedes that, in its depiction of violence without retribution, Petrushka indeed expressed, and perhaps encouraged, "a fragmented sense of morality,"[24] and she cites descriptions of this "entertainment for hooligans by hooligans" that recoil from its antisocial and subversive implications, including a reference of 1908 by M. Braunschweig to "the Petrushka theater with its ugly, mangled, caricature figures, violent gestures, absurd squeaking, which can communicate nothing but crude foolery."[25] These are qualities that we also find in *The Devils*, with its recounting of social disruption, political murders, and gross caricatures of revolutionary figures. The primary function of Petrushka was to make people laugh, but the kind of laughter it sought to evoke was the same disruptive laughter, challenging all social and moral conventions, that fills Dostoevsky's novel. In other words, the disruptive carnival mood invited collusion: It passed beyond the puppet booth and infected the audience, just as Petr Verkhovensky's "pranks" extend beyond the immediate circle of his activities and infect the townsfolk with destructive laughter.

There is no canonical version of Petrushka, but despite textual variations the play always begins with the arrival of Petrushka, who launches immediately into a wordy monologue, often with his legs dangling from the booth in a gesture of familiarity with the crowd. We remember the arrival of Petr Verkhovensky and his breathless and verbally hypnotic ensnarement of his audience: "His speech was remarkably clearly articulated; his words tumbled out like large, smooth grains, always well chosen and always at your service." Petr's sugary over-familiarity with his superiors is a persistent feature of his behavior throughout the novel, and at times it is conveyed through reference to his tendency to curl his legs up on a sofa. See, for example, the following scene with his father:

> Stepan Trofimovich sat stretched out on the sofa. Since last Thursday he had grown thin and sallow. Petr Stepanovich settled down alongside him in a most familiar manner, unceremoniously tucking his legs below him and occupying much more of the sofa that respect for his father demanded. (X, 238)

And, in the presence of the Governor: "Petr Stepanovich sprawled out on the sofa, and in a flash drew his legs up under him" (X, 272). Certain physical and moral characteristics of Petrushka appear to have passed, with varying degrees of modification, into the figure of Petr Verkhovensky. For example, the puppet's deformed physical appearance—he is hunchbacked, with an unattractive physiognomy that includes pointed nose and chin and button eyes—is suggested in the initial evasive physical description of Petr, which alludes to the impression of round-shoulderedness he conveys, his sharp eyes, and his pointed nose. His movements are hurried and jerky, like those of a puppet, a feature that acquires additional resonance in light of comments Dostoevsky makes in the draft for *Diary of a Writer*, referred to above. Here he considers the possibility of translating Petrushka to the conventional theater using human actors who would retain the "wooden and doll-like" movements of the original (XXII, 180). Petrushka's moral characteristics coincide quite strikingly with those manifested by Petr. As Elizabeth Warner has written:

> In many cases Petrushka is no more than a bully and a hooligan, using violence for its own sake or to get out of an awkward situation. [. . .] Petrushka is violently disposed towards anyone in authority, whether civil, military or ec-

clesiastic. Although keen enough to belabor those weaker than himself, Petrushka is at heart a coward and sometimes his bravado and effrontery break down. . . . But in spite of his cowardice, his greed and his dishonesty Petrushka has a very high opinion of himself and is inordinately vain and cocksure.[26]

This description could be applied without modification to Petr, even the reference to greed and gluttony (which Kelly also mentions). Greed may well be a general and familiar human trait and thus in itself not carry a particular semiotic charge, but on several occasions this feature of Petr's behavior is given a surprising prominence: We recall the scene where he demands a cutlet, wine, and coffee during a morning visit to Karmazinov, much to his host's surprise and displeasure (X, 285); he insensitively finishes off the supper Kirillov has left as the latter contemplates the hour of his suicide; and on his way to convince Liputin of the willingness of Kirillov to take responsibility for the murder of Shatov he still finds time to call into a tavern, where he consumes steak with a gusto that repels Liputin (X, 423).

Many critics have commented on the use made in *The Devils* of the motif of *samozvanstvo* ("pretendership" or "royal imposture"). It is a motif Dostoevsky exploits for its demonic connotations. Bakhtin, for example, remarks that in the novel "all life that is penetrated by devils is portrayed as a carnival nether world. The entire novel is thoroughly permeated by the theme of crowning-decrowning and pretendership," and he cites the examples of Stavrogin's exposure as a Grishka Otrepev by Maria Lebiadkina and Petr's plan to crown him as "Ivan the Crown Prince," a later pretender to the Russian throne who appeared in 1845.[27] More recently, Murav has devoted an entire essay to the theme, claiming that the novel "is permeated with a vision of the past. Its vision of the political upheaval of late nineteenth-century Russia is refracted through the prism of the early seventeenth century, a period known as the 'Time of Troubles,' when the Ryurikid dynasty came to an end and a series of pretenders took the throne, most notably False Dmitry, believed by historians to be Grishka Otrep'ev, a runaway monk."[28]

Apart from such overt references to Grishka Otrepev and other historical pretenders, *The Devils* seeks to alert its readership to the presence of this theme through a network of motifs and incidents that focus attention on the cognate ideas of pretense, role-play, masquerade, imitation, and imposture. In the opening passage we are told that Stepan Trofimovich has always played a "civic role," that of a martyr to the liberal cause, but later we are warned that "to tell the truth, he was merely an imitator [*podrazhatel'*] of such figures" (X, 12). "Captain" Lebiadkin turns out to be not a staff captain, as he claims, but rather a villain once caught up in an incident involving *counterfeit* banknotes (X, 29, 79). The virtuoso Liamshin imitates animals at the piano (X, 30–31). Petr Verkhovensky's deception of the von Lembkes and others is repeatedly referred to as "role-play." The fete includes a literary quadrille, danced in masks and costumes, in which participants *pretend* to be literary journals. And the "silver" chin-setting of St. Nikolai the Miracle-Worker (note the coincidence of name with that of Stavrogin), stolen from a church by Fedka, turns out to be a fake (*similerovyi* [X, 220]). The implication carried by this final detail—that Stavrogin himself might turn out to be a comparable "fake"—is encouraged by passages in *The Devils* that appear to align him with Danila Filippov, the false god of the heretical sect of Castrates,[29] as well as with that paradigm of imposture in nineteenth-century Russian literature, Khlestakov in Gogol's *The Government Inspector*. The notebooks for *The Devils* refer to Khlestakov by name, but in connection with the arrival of Petr Verkhovensky; in the novel itself it is left to the narrator-chronicler to suggest indirectly a link with Stavrogin. He dutifully reports rumors in the town to the effect that Stavrogin is secretly a government official who has arrived incognito on a secret mission and who reports back to Petersburg (X, 168). The motif is taken up later when Petr and Stavrogin discuss whether or not the latter is secretly an inspector (*revizor*), albeit one working for the revolutionary movement (X, 299). In neither case do the participants appear to be alert to the literary resonance of the role ascribed to Stavrogin, but the novel's readership surely is. The same readership might also recall that the theme of imposture carries a demonic charge in Gogol's comedy too.

The more specific historical motif of royal imposture is also sustained by similar supporting references. The madness that follows the fete is described by the chronicler as "our time of troubles" (*nashe smutnoe vremia*), using the same linguistic formula applied to the historical interregnum (X, 354). And Mrs. Stavrogina dresses Stepan Trofimovich in the fashion of the poet and dramatist N. V. Kukolnik, whose portrait, we are told, is one of her most cherished possessions (X, 19). Kukolnik was a contemporary of Dostoevsky and the author of a historical drama about the Time of Troubles.[30]

The significance for our purposes of the theme of imposture and, in particular, royal imposture is suggested by Boris Uspensky, who has argued that it is a phenomenon carrying a particular cultural-historical significance in Russia, one that is popularly associated with the demonic. Recollection of the fete in *The Devils* is evoked by the following observation:

> It should be borne in mind that any kind of masquerade or dressing up was inevitably thought of in early Russia as *anti-behavior*: i.e. a sinister, black-magic significance was attributed to it in principle. This is quite plain from the example of the mummers of Yuletide, Shrovetide, St. John's Night and other festivals, who, it was assumed (by participants in the masquerade as well as spectators!) depicted devils, or unclean spirits; correspondingly, the

dressing up was accompanied by extremes of disorderly behavior, often of an overtly blasphemous character.[31]

The most extreme form of this antibehavior was to masquerade as Tsar. Citing the historian Kliuchevsky, Uspensky points out that royal imposture was a "chronic malady" of the Russian state, with hardly a single reign before the mid-nineteenth century not throwing up a pretender. Clearly, how such pretenders were viewed by Russians is inextricably bound up with Russian attitudes to royal power, for they represent an inversion of such power. As Uspensky writes:

> If true Tsars receive power from God, then false Tsars receive it from the Devil. Even the church rite of sacred coronation and anointing do not confer grace on a false Tsar, for these actions are no more than outward appearances; in reality the false Tsar is crowned and anointed by demons acting on the orders of the Devil himself. It follows therefore that if the real Tsar may be likened to Christ (i.e. a creation of God, not man) and perceived as an image of God, a living icon, then a pretender may be regarded as a false icon, i.e. an *idol*.[32]

This passage provides a particularly graphic template, allowing us to recognize several of the cultural symbols surrounding Stavrogin and his relationship with Petr Verkhovensky. First of all, of course, it serves to clarify the demonic resonances in both characters: Stavrogin is the false Tsar—in Maria Lebiadkina's terms "Grishka Otrepev" masquerading as a "Prince"—who derives his power from Satan, and Petr is the demon that anoints him. The presence of the demonic is suggested during Maria's final interview with Stavrogin by the supernatural terror that overcomes her on his entrance, by her attempts to protect herself by holding up her arms, and by her unwillingness to look Stavrogin in the face. Her fate is perhaps sealed by the symbolic gesture of inviting him into her *circle:* "'I would ask you, Prince, to get up and come in,' she said suddenly in a firm and insistent voice. 'What do you mean, *come in?*' [Stavrogin replied]. 'Come in where?'" (X, 217). Petr's complementary role emerges in the chapter "Ivan the Crown-Prince," during which he confesses that he is a rogue rather than a socialist, before unfolding his plan to reap the harvest of the moral disorder that afflicts contemporary Russia:

> "Then, sir, the troubles [*smuta*] will begin. There'll be an upheaval such as the world has never seen. . . . Rus' will be shrouded in mist, and the earth will cry out for its old gods. . . . Well, sir, then we'll unleash . . . do you know who?"
> "Who?"

"Ivan the Crown-Prince."

"Who?"

"Ivan the Crown-Prince; you, you!"

Stavrogin was silent for a moment.

"A Pretender?" he asked suddenly, staring in astonishment at the madman. "Ah, so that's your plan in the end." (X, 325)

Stavrogin is central to Petr's design as a usurper, a *false icon* attracting the worship of a morally confused populace, and this iconic imagery is also rich in meaning. For a start, it amplifies the significance of the desecration of real church icons by Fedka, another of Stavrogin's demon doubles. It also allows Petr to reveal the nature of his own aesthetic stance, one founded on blasphemy and the sin of *idolatry:*

"Stavrogin. you're beautiful!" Petr Stepanovich cried, almost in ecstasy. "Don't you know that you're beautiful! [. . .] I love beauty. I'm a nihilist, but I love beauty. Do nihilists really not love beauty? It's only idols they don't love, but I even love idols! You are my idol! [. . .] You're just what I need. I particularly need someone like you. I know of no one like you. You are my leader, my sun, and I am your worm . . ."

He suddenly kissed Stavrogin's hand. A chill ran down Stavrogin's spine, and he tore his hand away in alarm. They stopped.

"You're mad!" whispered Stavrogin. (X, 323–24)

We are here close to the core of Dostoevsky's own polemic with the aesthetic views of the nihilists, who had largely rejected the value of beauty in favor of an uncompromising utilitarianism. As early as 1861, Dostoevsky had addressed the issue in his article "Mr. -bov and the Question of Art" ("Gospodin -bov i vopros ob iskusstve"), where he defended ideal beauty from the attacks of the radical critic Nikolai Dobroliubov (Mr. -bov) in terms similar to those employed by Stepan Trofimovich Verkhovensky, when in his outburst at the fete he insists that Shakespeare and Raphael are more important for man's development than petroleum or a good pair of boots:

Don't you see, mankind can still get by without the Englishman, without Germany, and certainly without the Russian. It can survive without science, without bread. Only it can't survive without beauty, for then there would be absolutely no purpose to its existence on earth! The whole secret lies in this, the whole of history! Science itself would not last a minute without beauty— it would turn into loutishness; you wouldn't be able to invent a nail! (X, 373)

For Dostoevsky it was man's sense of ideal beauty that elevated him above bestiality and gave spiritual purpose to his existence, and the primary image of such beauty was that of Christ.[33] He did, however, recognize that in times of moral confusion man's instinct for ideal beauty, which comes from God, could be compromised by corrupt aesthetic instincts deriving from the Devil. In "Mr. -bov and the Question of Art" he wrote:

> We have seen examples where man, having achieved the ideal of his desires and not knowing what else to aim for, being totally satiated, has fallen into a kind of anguish, has even exacerbated this anguish within himself, has sought out another ideal in life, and out of extreme surfeit has not only ceased to value that which he enjoys but has even consciously turned away from the straight path, and has fomented in himself strange, unhealthy, sharp, inharmonious, sometimes even monstrous tastes, losing measure and aesthetic feeling for healthy beauty and demanding instead of it exceptions. (XVIII, 94)

It is Dmitry who, in *The Brothers Karamazov*, links such aesthetic confusion to the influence of the devil, an influence that encourages the illusion that evil can be beautiful. Dmitry admits to possessing an equal receptiveness to both "the beauty of the Madonna" and "the beauty of Sodom," and he concludes that beauty is a terrible mystery: "Here God and the Devil struggle for mastery, and the battlefield is the heart of man" (XIV, 100). The "beauty of Sodom," intoxication with the aesthetics of evil, was for Dostoevsky a characteristic of the late-Romantic, Byronic temperament, and it is therefore understandable that we should witness such confusion in *The Devils* in the person of Stavrogin, himself a Byronic figure gone to seed who deliberately marries the crippled Maria Lebiadkina partly in order to revive his perverted but flagging aesthetic sense. Shatov recognizes this when he confronts Stavrogin in the chapter "Night":

> "Is it true you claimed that you saw no aesthetic difference between some voluptuous, bestial prank and any kind of heroic feat, even the sacrifice of one's own life for mankind? Is it true that you found identical beauty, the same pleasure, in both extremes? [. . .] I don't know either why evil is squalid and good is beautiful, but I do know why the sense of distinction between them is erased and lost in gentlemen like Stavrogin!" (X, 261)

The loss of the same sense of distinction afflicts Petr too and allows him to mistake the sterile, mask-like countenance of Stavrogin for beauty, and to present this demon of nonbeing as a false icon, a focus for idolatry. The terms in which Petr couches his idolatry—"You are my leader, my sun [*solntse*], and I am your worm"—are also significant, for Uspensky reveals that the description "sun of righteousness" (*pravednoe solntse*), applied to Christ in liturgical texts, was also used of the False Dmitry.[34] The term is repeated elsewhere, for example in Stavrogin's description of his relationship with Shatov—"'Forgive me,' Nikolai Vsevolodovich said with genuine surprise, 'but you appear to look on me as some sort of sun [*solntse*] and yourself as some sort of insect in comparison'" (X, 193)— and in Lebiadkin's admission to Stavrogin that he has been waiting for him "as one awaits the sun" (X, 210). This use of "sun" to link Stavrogin with the theme of imposture and with the False Dmitry in particular is supported by other verbal and thematic symbols, such as the cross. The sign of the cross was the most common of the "royal signs" popularly held to be found on the body of a true (that is, divinely ordained) Tsar.[35] Stavrogin's name conceals the Greek word for "cross" (*stavros*), but he is a false Tsar and the fact that this "royal sign" fails to penetrate beyond his name emerges most clearly in the chapter "At Tikhon's," and in its draft and variant material. This chapter was, of course, excluded from the published version of the novel when Dostoevsky proved unable to tone down its shocking content to the censor's satisfaction. As a result, there is no truly canonical version, although the editors of the Academy edition have sought to establish one (XI, 5–30). In one variant of the chapter, the narrator refers to Stavrogin's written confession as driven by "the need for punishment, the need for a cross to bear," but goes on to point out that this need for a cross is manifested by a man "who does not believe in the cross" (XII, 108). Tikhon does urge Stavrogin to take up the "cross of shame" (XI, 26) and to seek redemption, significantly by entering a monastery (Grishka Otrepev was a runaway monk); but Stavrogin refuses to bear this cross and leaves, the variants describing how he accidentally breaks Tikhon's crucifix before storming out of his cell (XII, 114).

The accusation of antibehavior and imposture was frequently leveled at Peter the Great by those who saw in the Westernization of Russia begun in his reign a demonic reversal of true Russian tradition. Dostoevsky himself saw the subsequent absorption of Western culture by Russia's educated classes as a form of demonic possession, and this encourages us to recognize that while *The Devils* employs traditional Russian cultural symbols and discourses to alert us to the *presence* of the demonic, it seeks to suggest its *nature* through discourses derived from both Western European secular sources and biblical narrative. Moreover, this new cluster of cultural inscriptions pivots primarily on the figure of Stavrogin, confirming his centrality in the novel's compositional and ideological design. Stavrogin's eventual role as the compositional center of *The Devils* was recognized by Dostoevsky in the drafts for the novel, where he described the "Prince," the draft character from whom Stavrogin evolved, as the point around which all the rest turns "as in a kaleidoscope" (XI, 136). Elsewhere in the notebooks he wrote: "Everything is contained in the character of Stavrogin. Stavrogin is *everything*" (XI, 207). In the novel this centrality is suggested in the way that Stavrogin serves as both the source and the object of the emotional, psychological, or ideological aspirations of the other characters. Admittedly, at first he seems to have little bearing on the novel's initial polemical purpose as a "whip" with which to lash the nihilists, in that he actively has little to do with the political machinations of Petr and his group, and in any case he enters the flow of events at quite a late point. When he does appear, however, it soon becomes clear that he is a major player in this vaudeville of devils and that he is a figure of genuinely tragic stature when seen against the activities of the lesser prankster-devils. Stavrogin is, of course, also guilty of prank playing—he bites the old Governor's ear, pulls Gaganov's father by the nose, and subjects Liputin's wife to a minor sexual assault. But these are joyless acts disguising an inner inertia and lack of purpose. Ultimately, there is a bleakness about Stavrogin, a spiritual desolation, a death-like stillness at the core of his being that sets him apart from the "enthusiasm" of Petr, the mad conviction of Kirillov, or Shatov's desperate fanaticism. His "demonism" derives from the spirit of nonbeing that has consumed him, and it is articulated primarily through the symbols of European Romantic tradition that are attributed to him.

E. Loginovskaia has made a distinction in this respect between the notions in Russian literature of *devil* (*bes*) and *demon*. She argues that the former, usually envisaged in the plural as a collective horde and derived from biblical origins (for example, the devils in the parable of the Gadarene swine), have been conventionally used in a negative sense to denote the forces of evil that possess man and distort his spiritual makeup; however, this negative function has prevented their becoming symbols capable of giving expression to "man's rich and complex nature." The figure of the *demon*, however, draws on a literary tradition stretching through Milton's Satan and Byron's Lucifer, in order to provide, in works such as Lermontov's poem *The Demon* (*Demon*), a symbolic expression of "man's complex individualism, in conflict and tragically fated, but filled with force and grandeur."[36] Loginovskaia is perhaps wrong to imply that this distinction may be reduced to one of vocabulary, for in Russian Orthodox and folk tradition the terms *bes* and *demon* are often used interchangeably. What she does draw attention to, however, is a duality in the literary depiction of the demonic that emerges clearly in nineteenth-century Russian literature and that may be illustrated by comparing the anonymous and mischievous collection of spirits in Pushkin's "Devils" ("Besy," 1830) with the seductively rebellious individualism and irony of the "malignant spirit" in the same poet's "Demon" ("Demon," 1823).

The spirits tempting and deceiving the traveler in Pushkin's "Devils" are the anonymous and multitudinous petty devils of folkloric and Orthodox tradition. As Simon Franklin has argued, hagiographic tradition played down the depiction of *the* Devil in favor of devils, and its demonology gave little emphasis to "a towering figure of Satan in splendor."[37] This tradition of depicting devils is absorbed in the work of Gogol. What we see in Pushkin's "Demon," however, is an attempt to "psychologize" the devil/demon, to treat him as an allegory, an externalization of Romantic revolt and individualism. In this form he transcends the pedestrian nastiness, and indeed perceived cosmological *objectivity,* of the traditional petty devil (remember Tikhon again: "devils undoubtedly exist"); he becomes instead an aesthetically potent, *subjective* projection of man's rebelliousness.

As we have already seen, a typology of the demon in this incarnation is provided in the "hero" of Lermontov's narrative poem *The Demon* and in his human equivalent Pechorin. In *The Devils,* as many critics have pointed out,[38] a consistent system of both overt and oblique references point to Lermontov and Pechorin as yardsticks against which we must measure the demonism of Stavrogin. Apart from similarities in the spiritual and psychological makeup of the respective heroes, and a certain overlapping of plot motifs (for example, dueling and seduction), the novel offers a lengthy discourse on Stavrogin as an inheritor of Lermontovian malice (X, 165), as well as references to him as a "Pechorin ladykiller" (X, 84) and a "vampire," a term Pechorin applies to himself (X, 401). Other similarly suggestive details include the attribution of his behavior to "the demon of irony" and mention of a book he is reading called *The Women of Balzac* (X, 180), the latter recalling a description of Pechorin as "like a thirty-year-old Balzacian coquette after a particularly exhausting dance."[39] Such implied comparisons are intriguing, but we must approach them circumspectly. Like so much else in the relativistic world of Dostoevsky's polyphonic narrative, these details lack authority: they are contaminated by what Gary Saul Morson has termed "the irony of origins," in that they arise not from direct authorial discourse but from the voices of other characters.[40] The reference to the "demon of irony" is by Stepan Trofimovich, and it points as much to his own penchant for inflated Romantic rhetoric and desire to win favor with Stavrogin's mother as to any objective assessment of Stavrogin himself. The description "Pechorin ladykiller" is offered sarcastically by Liputin, whose wife Stavrogin has assaulted, and the vampire motif is the product of the inflamed passions of a local lady smitten by the hero. Even the extended discussion of Stavrogin's place in the gallery of Romantic heroes is offered by a narrator-chronicler whose partiality and perceptual lacunae are well documented. Stavrogin's own description of the demon that possesses him contributes to the process of compromising Romantic expectations. The spirit that visits him is a far cry from Lermontov's Demon, "shining with an unearthly beauty": He confesses to Dasha that it is "a petty, repulsive, scrofulous little devil (*besenok*) with a runny nose" (X, 231). Thus is Stavrogin's demonism subverted, and we are alerted to the possibility that this proud spirit of Romantic revolt might be only a deflated demon, a Lucifer with the air let out.

The presentation of Stavrogin's "demonism" through the accumulation and simultaneous subversion of Romantic motifs is not ideologically neutral. It coincides with views Dostoevsky expresses elsewhere to the effect that the "evil" represented by figures like Stavrogin is one not indigenous to Russian culture, but was imported along with the cult of Byron and "Byronism" during the 1820s. As we saw in the introduction to this volume, Dostoevsky acknowledged Byron and the mood of Romantic despair that attended his popularity as legitimate responses to the cultural and spiritual collapse that overtook Western Europe in the wake of the French Revolution, when "the old idols lay shattered" and the poet articulated "the dreadful anguish, disillusionment and despair" of his age (XXVI, 113–14). But the cult of Byron among Europeanized Russian noblemen, and the assimilation by them of the same spirit of despair and revolt, carried no such legitimacy, for it symptomized the alienation of the Russian upper classes from native tradition and the rupture of the organic unity of Russian society. The results were the estrangement of the Westernized intellectual from Orthodox spiritual culture in favor of rational Western civilization; the gulf that opened between such men and the Russian masses, still steeped in the traditions of pre-Petrine Russia; and the emergence in Russia of social and political disharmony, as the absorption of Western skepticism led to the questioning of the traditional Russian order. The phenomenon of the Russian educated man thus cut off from his own national identity was referred to by Dostoevsky as that of the *obshchechelovek*. This word, as we have seen in chapter 1, translates conventionally as "universal man," but the translation carries a positive charge that Dostoevsky did not intend. His *obshchechelovek* was a wraith-like being, a ghost drifting without the anchor of national identity, in whom the erosion of nationality had led to the erosion of personality.[41]

The concept of the *obshchechelovek* was central to Dostoevsky's conception of *The Devils* and to the demonism of its hero, Stavrogin. To Maikov in 1870 he wrote: "a man who loses his people and his national roots also loses the faith of his forefathers and his God. Well, if you really want to know, this is essentially the theme of my novel. It is called *The Devils*, and it describes how the devils entered the herd of swine" (XXIX/1, 145). The long discussion with Shatov in "Night" reveals the extent to which Stavrogin has lost his own national roots, and in the working drafts for the novel Dostoevsky refers to the Stavrogin-Prince character as an *obshchechelovek* whose very being has disintegrated along with his Russianness (XI, 134–35). The point to grasp is that for Dostoevsky Russianness was inseparable from Orthodoxy. Being Russian was not merely a matter of jingoistic national pride, it also meant being part of the only true God-bearing nation. Alienation from Russian national identity meant alienation from God. The tragedy of Stavrogin the *obshchechelovek* is thus not confined to his psychological and national estrangement: It is a religious tragedy transcending the sociopolitical. It is thus appropriate that our attempts to decode the demonic in *The Devils* should conclude with discussion of a pattern of symbolic inscriptions that enlarge the scale of Stavrogin's demonism and reveal its true significance by setting it in the context of the most potent biblical account of the struggle between good and evil—the Book of Revelation.

The apocalyptic patterning of *The Devils* is clear to the attentive reader, and its detail has been drawn out in the critical literature: Karmazinov compares the collapse of Europe to the fall of Babylon; Kirillov reads the Apocalypse at night to Fedka and cites its prophecy that "there will be time no more"; the Stavrogin estate, from which so much evil emanates, is called Skvoreshniki, a name derived from *skvorechnik*, a wooden bird box, suggesting an analogy with Revelation's description of Babylon as "a cage for every unclean and hateful bird," an analogy further implied by several references to the members of Petr's circle as "birds about to flee the nest" and by characters whose names are derived from birds (Lebiadkin, Gaganov, Drozdov); Stavrogin's indifference is described as being "neither cold nor hot," the formula used in Revelation to describe the Church of the Laodiceans; the novel's account of outbreaks of incendiarism and cholera in the district recall the scourges of fire and plague that accompany the Last Judgment; and so on.[42]

Dostoevsky's heavily annotated copy of the New Testament makes clear just how inspirational and suggestive he found the evocative but elusive imagery of the Revelation of St. John. His annotations to chapter 13 of Revelation suggest a particular interest in the predicted advent of a "beast," whose name is Mystery, and who will rule over the earth with supreme power. Revelation describes how the way is paved for this beast by a false prophet, a lesser devil with two horns and a dragon's tongue, who "exerciseth all the power of the first beast before him, and causeth the earth and them which dwell therein to worship the first beast" (Revelation 13:12). The false prophet, moreover, "maketh fire come down from heaven on the earth in the sight of men," "deceiveth them that dwell on the earth," and causes "that as many as would not worship the image of the beast should be killed." It is not extravagant to discern behind these devils the figures of the mysterious "wild beast" Stavrogin and the serpent-tongued deceiver Petr Verkhovensky. Petr's first appearance in the novel is when he comes on ahead to announce the advent of Stavrogin, whom he plans to make men worship. On the night of the fete he too makes fire come down to earth by organizing the incendiarism that claims the lives of the Lebiadkins. He practices the systematic deception of the Governor's wife and members of his own circle. And he arranges the murder of Shatov when the latter ceases to believe his fabrications.

Alongside a passage in Revelation 17:11 referring again to "the beast that was, and is not," Dostoevsky has written the single word *obshcheche-*

lovek,[43] a concept closely related, as we have seen, to his critique of the Westernized Russian intellectual and to his notebook conception of Stavrogin. In this way the devil's vaudeville of *The Devils* gives way to an apocalyptic warning of the dangers facing Russian society in its unnatural espousal of Western European values and a prophecy of the salvation to be found only through that society's rediscovery of native Orthodox culture.

This duality at the heart of the novel returns us neatly to the point from which we started: the two epigraphs, pointing in different directions in their implied interpretations of the demonic. It is clear now that the Pushkin epigraph anticipates the carnival strand of the novel and corresponds to the revolutionary activities of Petr Verkhovensky and his circle as they seek to lure Russia from its proper track. The discourses through which Dostoevsky approaches this aspect of the novel, with their gleefully disruptive disregard for conventions, a disregard drawn from carnival tradition, perfectly match Dostoevsky's own ambiguous attitude to Petr and what he represents. He is a demon, certainly, but what he creates dissolves into vaudeville. In a letter to Katkov, dated October 8, 1870, Dostoevsky referred to Petr as a "pitiful freak" who, despite his monstrous criminality, was emerging as a half-comic figure "unworthy of literature" and incapable of carrying the weight of the novel's import (XXIX/1, 141). Petr is caught in the same demonic trap as his victims: The breakdown of order he orchestrates offers the freedom only to go around in circles in a dark field. Like the travelers in Pushkin's poem, who cannot see where they are going (*sbilis' my*), the Russian revolutionary has no inkling of what lies ahead. As Dostoevsky remarked in 1873 to Varvara Timofeeva, his co-worker on the journal *Grazhdanin,* following a discussion about the penetration of European influences into Russia: "They don't suspect that soon it will be the end of everything, of all their 'progress' and idle chatter. They have no inkling that the Antichrist has already been born . . . and *he is coming!* . . . The Antichrist is coming among us! And the end of the world is close—closer than people think!"[44]

The epigraph from St. Luke, however, anticipates the apocalyptic or redemptive theme with which Dostoevsky overlays the carnival strand of the novel. It clearly points to the tragedy of Stavrogin, sick with the devils that have laid low several generations of Europeanized Russians who have lost the anchor of salvation offered by their nationality. It also prefigures the "cleansing" of the liberal Westernizer Stepan Trofimovich Verkhovensky, who at the end of the novel and shortly before his death revives the redemptive theme through espousal of those native Russian values that elude the *obshchechelovek* Stavrogin.

Chapter Five

The Father of the Lie:

The Brothers Karamazov

IN ADDITION to its core themes of familial discord and the breakdown of relations between fathers and their children, *The Brothers Karamazov* clearly foregrounds three further preoccupations: those of lying, telling a tale, and devils. All three emerge almost from the start, and they recur with a persistence and regularity that suggest they form an important component of the thematic and structural integrity of the novel. Moreover, it will turn out to be the case that these three preoccupations are inextricably linked, not only to each other, but also to the central condition of parricide and its demonic implications in the novel.

It is the eventual victim of parricide, old Fedor Pavlovich Karamazov, who first unwittingly signals the linkage of lying, telling a tale, and the demonic when, following a particularly extravagant exercise of his capacity for narrative fabrication, he declares to the company assembled in the monastic cell of the elder (*starets*) Zosima that: "I am the lie and the father of the lie" (XIV, 41). Fedor Pavlovich's anecdote has turned on a false narrative concerning the French philosopher Diderot's supposed religious conversion during his visit to the court of Catherine the Great, a conversion that, according to Fedor Pavlovich, resulted in his baptism with Princess Dashkova as his godmother and Catherine's favorite Potemkin as his godfather. Old Karamazov knows only too well that he is lying—"All my life I've had a feeling that it wasn't true!"—but he is unable to resist the role of "jester" (*shut*), a role often assumed by the devil in Russian folklore. Indeed, the chapter in which this passage occurs is entitled "The Old Jester" ("Staryi shut"). Moreover, the label he applies to himself—"the lie and the father of the lie"—is, of course, a close paraphrase of Christ's description of the devil in St. John:

> Ye are of your father the devil, and the lusts of your father ye will do. He was a murderer from the beginning, and abode not in the truth, for there is no truth in him. When he speaketh a lie, he speaketh of his own: for he is a liar, and the father of it. (John 8:44)

Fedor Pavlovich's reference to St. John is in turn rich in implications for the novel that is about to unfold, and it is characteristic of Dostoevsky's technique that major themes should be introduced in a minor key so early in his work. For a start, Fedor Pavlovich has just introduced himself as a diabolical figure, not only in his willing assumption of the roles of jester and liar, but also in his direct admission that he serves the "unclean force": "I won't deny that an unclean spirit might well reside within me, though it is of small caliber" (XIV, 39). Here the folk incarnation of evil in the form of the "petty demon" begins to emerge, a form to be assumed most prominently later in the novel by Ivan Karamazov's nocturnal "visitor," the rather seedy rheumatic sponger-devil who baits him on the night of the servant Smerdiakov's suicide. There are, moreover, further veiled references to Ivan in old Karamazov's description of himself as not only the lie, but "the father of the lie," and in Christ's words: "Ye are of your father the devil, and the lusts of your father ye will do." Ivan will turn out to be the most significant source of the demonism rife throughout *The Brothers Karamazov,* and we shall also eventually learn that he is the Karamazov son who, according to Smerdiakov, is most like his corrupt and depraved father.

Any temptation we may feel as readers to dismiss Fedor Pavlovich's lying at this early point in the novel as harmlessly entertaining self-display is quickly dispelled when the same theme is taken up by the holy man Zosima and invested with a profound seriousness by his warning to old Karamazov: "You yourself have long known what you must do, you have intelligence enough: don't give yourself over to drunkenness and verbal incontinence. [. . .] And the main thing, the very main thing—don't lie" (XIV, 41). Zosima's phrase "verbal incontinence" (*slovesnoe nevozderzhanie*) might be more accurately, if less elegantly, paraphrased as "lack of self-restraint in the use of the word for literary purposes," and we shall see in the course of this chapter how in this guise his advice will resonate throughout the novel and in contexts other than Fedor Pavlovich's baroque anecdotes. His warning that the *main thing* is not to lie because lying is a demonic condition, is taken up again in various modulations throughout the novel. Zosima himself returns to it shortly after the encounter with Fedor Pavlovich described above, when he offers identical advice to the "lady of little faith," Mrs. Khokhlakova: "The main thing is avoid the lie, any lie, and in particular the lie to yourself. Keep an eye out for your lies and look into them, every hour, every minute" (XIV, 54). Kolia Krasotkin, the schoolboy who enters the novel as an immature parody of Ivan Karamazov's philosophical positivism and ends it as one of the saintly Alesha's twelve disciples, also advises his schoolfriend Smurov, in words that pompously echo those of Zosima to Khokhlakova: "Schoolboy, abhor the lie, that's the first thing; even if it's in a good cause, that's the second" (XIV, 472). (As we shall see in due course, though, Kolia's pompous advice is not always applied to his own behavior.)

Accusations of lying fly throughout the novel. In the same early scenes in the elder's cell, Dmitry Karamazov dismisses his father's protestations of paternal concern as those of "one who is shameless and a hypocrite": "All this is a lie! From outside it looks like the truth, but inside it's a lie!" (XIV, 67). On the other hand, at the very end of the novel, as he prepares to embark on penal servitude, Dmitry confides that he has always loved his brother Alesha because the latter has always told the truth (XV, 186). The attentive reader will remember that Alesha has recently received a similar accolade from the "little demon" Liza Khokhlakova: "You won't believe how I respect you, Alesha, for the fact that you never lie" (XV, 23). Dmitry in turn is accused of lying by the drunken timber merchant Liagavyi, with whom he tries to strike a financial deal (XIV, 341). The accusation is unfounded in this case, but Dmitry does confess to his accusers to having fabricated a lie about the amount of money spent on his orgies at Mokroe, a lie that others take up as the truth and that eventually contributes to Dmitry's downfall and conviction. As he contemplates the consequences of his lie, Dmitry's speech begins to attract demonic rhetoric:

> "It doesn't mean anything. I lied, and after me everyone began to lie."
>
> "Yes, but why did you find it so necessary to 'lie,' as you put it?"
>
> "The devil knows. Out of boastfulness, perhaps . . . that I'd squandered so much money. . . . Perhaps in order to forget the money I'd sewn away . . . yes, that was the real reason . . . devil take it . . . how many times are you going to ask that question? So, I lied, and that's the end of it. I lied on one occasion and afterwards didn't feel like correcting myself. Why does a man lie on occasions?"
>
> "That's a very difficult question to answer, Dmitry Fedorovich, why a man lies." (XIV, 447)

The resignation sensed in this response of the Procurator to Dmitry's question is apparently shared by Liza Khokhlakova, who confides to Alesha her belief that the world is based on a universally accepted falsehood: "It is as though everyone at some point agreed to lie, and since that moment everyone has been lying. Everyone says that they hate what is nasty, but in their hearts they all love it" (XV, 23). This is a refrain taken up shortly afterward by her mentor Ivan and applied to the triangular relationship among himself, Katerina Ivanovna, and Dmitry: "Here everything is falsehood, lie upon lie!" (XV, 39)—a view of that relationship that acquires more authority when underwritten by the narrator: "Here, of course, there was indeed much falsehood" (XV, 49).

For many of the characters in the novel, lying is essentially an aesthetic device to which they resort for rhetorical effect. This will turn out to be an important consideration as the work unfolds, and once again it is remarkable how Dostoevsky introduces it early on in the minor key of Fedor Pavlovich's "verbal incontinence." In the early scene in Zosima's cell, where so much of later importance is insinuated, the incisive human understanding of the elder allows him to see straight to the heart of Karamazov's lying:

> The main thing is do not lie to yourself. He who lies to himself and listens to his own lie reaches the point where he can no longer distinguish the truth either in himself or around him, and consequently he loses respect for himself and others. Having no respect for anyone, he ceases to love, and in order to occupy and distract himself in the absence of love, he succumbs to his passions and coarse pleasures, reaching a state of complete bestiality in his vices, and all because of constant lying to other people and himself. He who lies to himself may take offence more readily than others. For it's sometimes very pleasant to take offence, isn't it? And yet that man knows that no one has offended him, that he has invented the offence himself and has lied for the beauty of it, that he has exaggerated in order to create an effect, that he has fastened on to a word and made a mountain out of a molehill. He knows all this himself, but nevertheless he is the first to take offence, to the point where it becomes pleasant and he derives great pleasure from it. (XIV, 41)

Fedor Pavlovich at once acknowledges Zosima's insight, conceding:

> It is indeed pleasant to take offence. You've put that very well, better than I've ever heard before. Yes indeed, my whole life I've been taking offence for the pleasure of it, for aesthetic reasons, for it's not only pleasant, but sometimes even beautiful to be offended—that's something you've overlooked, great elder: it can also be beautiful! I must make a note of that! I've lied and I've lied my whole life long, every day and every hour. (XIV, 41)

I have quoted from this passage at length, not only for the light it sheds on the false and self-humiliating posturing of such earlier Dostoevsky heroes as Marmeladov, but also because it provides a template for mapping the behavior of others in *The Brothers Karamazov*. The ridiculous and impoverished "landowner" Maksimov, for instance, turns out to be another compulsive liar who fabricates tall stories solely for effect, for "aesthetic" purposes. After Dmitry's flight to Mokroe to be with Grushenka and her Polish former lover, Maksimov entertains the assembled company with extravagant false narratives about the predilection of Polish women for Russian cavalry officers; about his own wife's lameness, which he initially ascribed to high-spirited hopping about; and ending with the outrageous (and chronologically impossible) claim that Gogol based a character in *Dead Souls* on him. Maksimov counters the skepticism of his audience with the assertion that they must not take Gogol literally, since "in Gogol all this is only in an allegorical form" (XIV, 381).

The mention of Gogol is highly significant, for it invites us to recontextualize our reading of Maksimov and his lies. Taken in conjunction with the assertion of Kalganov, a young distant relative of the Karamazovs also present in Mokroe, that "if he [Maksimov] lies—and he often lies—then he lies solely in order to give pleasure to others" (XIV, 281), it begins to suggest a linkage between lying and the practice of secular narrative fiction—a linkage on which, as we shall see, *The Brothers Karamazov* turns. The association of lying and fiction is further encouraged by Miusov's description of Fedor Pavlovich as a "Pierrot" and an "Aesop," to describe his clowning and lying respectively (XIV, 78). The name "Aesop"—that of a renowned writer of fables—becomes a persistent label for old Karamazov's lying when it is subsequently applied to him also by Ivan (XIV, 129) and Dmitry (XIV, 132; XV, 99).

The implication of Kalganov's defense of Maksimov is that lying, or fiction, serves the function of giving pleasure to others. This, of course, is hardly the whole story and the novel's account of Kolia Krasotkin's lying—referred to in passing above—serves to remind us that a false narrative may have adverse consequences and serve demonic purposes. Notwithstanding his advice to Smurov to "shun the lie" even when it is well intended, Krasotkin cannot resist the aesthetic effects with which he embellishes his pretense that the dog, Zhuchka, died after swallowing a pin fed to it by Iliusha Snegirev. To all intents and purposes, Krasotkin "novelizes" this event, suppressing the mundane reality (that Zhuchka spat out the pin at once) in favor of a more sensational narrative that culminates in the "resurrection" of the dog, presumed dead by all, in the form of the highly trained Perezvon. Like Maksimov, and like the writer of narrative fiction, Krasotin does this in order to maximize aesthetic impact and "give pleasure to others," especially the dying Iliusha; but Alesha Karamazov is quick to recognize the adverse effects of this deception on Iliusha's frail health (XIV, 491).

Several critics have commented on the way in which *The Brothers Karamazov* thematizes the art of fiction, but none has offered a sustained exploration of the demonic implications of this.[1] Most remarked on is the fact that the novel contains several interpolated narratives; less obvious is that these function as a set of variations on the theme of the narrative construct that bears false witness by sacrificing truth to effect. These variations will culminate in Ivan's narrative, "The Grand Inquisitor"—which attempts to write the dominant figure of Christ out of church history by foregrounding instead that of the devil (and which Malcolm Jones sees as a "more sophisticated version" of the tall stories told by Fedor Pavlovich and Maksimov)—as well as in the false accounts and interpretations of events given by both the prosecution and the defense at Dmitry's trial.[2] But the novel's earliest warning of the dangers and deceptions that attend the acts of telling a tale and bearing witness to events emerges from the author-narrator's apologia of an introduction, in which he both confronts and evades the appropriateness of his choice of Alesha Karamazov as the "hero" of his story. After skirting around the issue of whether it is likely to be to the reader's advantage to spend his time reading about such an "eccentric," the narrator concludes:

> Quite at a loss to resolve these questions, I have decided to leave them without any answer. Of course, the perspicacious reader will long ago have guessed that that is what I have been inclined toward all along, and will just be vexed at me for wasting words fruitlessly along with precious time. I shall offer a direct answer to this: I wasted fruitless words and valuable time firstly out of courtesy, and secondly out of cunning [*iz khitrosti*]: I have, so to speak, warned you in advance. (XIV, 6)

We have indeed been warned: warned from the start that we are in the hands of a narrator who is cunning, ambiguous, evasive, and fully prepared to use the rhetorical tricks of his trade against the reader when it serves his aims. His priority is not the integrity of "actual" events, but the integrity of his own narrative of those events, and he will turn out to be less concerned with chronicling the "truth" than with persuading the reader of the claims to truthfulness of his own account. As Jones among others has remarked, even the identity of this narrator is inconstant, "varying between an anonymous local resident who is a realist and skeptic and an omniscient narrator who is an idealist and believer."[3]

Victor Terras's analysis extends this inconstancy into the narrator's voice, noting the various qualifying devices he uses in order to evade categorical certainties, to hedge, or to gloss over holes in his account.[4] Terras's detailed textual commentary precludes the need for full illustration of the narrator's tricks here, but we should identify some of the forms they take. For a start he is not averse to validating his narrative by establishing his own credentials as a witness: He is willing to shift at a moment's notice from the impersonal role of omniscient narrator to that of local resident-in-the-know in order to vouch personally for the truth of his account and to invest it with a sense of immediacy. The reader can almost sense the narrator's arm confidingly around his shoulder as he approaches his account of the unseemly odor of corruption emanating from the recently deceased Zosima's corpse: "Here I shall add from my own part personally that I find it almost repulsive to recall that trivial and seductive event, in reality one of the utmost insignificance and naturalness, and I would of course have omitted it from my account without mentioning it at all, had it not been for the powerful effect it came to have on the heart and soul of my main, *but future* hero, Alesha" (XIV, 297). Similarly, he is careful to locate himself in a prominent position in the audience at the start of Dmitry's trial, but he is also prepared to own up to the possibility of gaps in his account in order to win the reader's confidence in the accuracy of what he does report (XV, 89, 92). This scene will be the object of our fuller attention later.

There are times when the narrator's contrived protestations of ignorance are tantamount to a refusal to accept responsibility for his own narrative—another way of persuading the reader of its "objective truth." For example, he gives up on an account of Alesha's feelings following Zosima's death and unseemly decomposition, saying: "Nevertheless, I admit openly that I myself would find it very difficult now to convey clearly the precise significance of that strange and ill-defined moment in the life of the [. . .] hero of my tale" (XIV, 305). Later, we see through such contrivances when, as Dmitry flees to Mokroe to be with Grushenka, the narrator refuses recourse to omniscience to confirm his suspicion that this might be the very same moment as Alesha's spiritual resurrection, while happily taking advantage of such omniscience to narrate all the details of Dmitry's inner turmoil (XIV, 369). Occasionally, such protestation of narrative incompetence results in his handing over narrative responsibility, overtly or covertly, to someone apparently more able, a device clearly designed to establish and reinforce the authority of that someone. The chapter in book 1 devoted to the Russian monastic institution of the elder provides an outstanding early example of this technique. The narrator starts from his position of ignorance: "It is necessary here to say a few words about what 'elders' generally are in our monasteries, and here it's a shame that I don't feel sufficiently competent or secure on this matter. I shall try, however, to give a superficial account of it in a few words" (XIV, 26). Within a few lines, however, we hear a rather different voice—one that is supremely confident and authoritative:

> What then is an elder? An elder is someone who takes your soul and your will into his own soul and his own will. On choosing an elder you renounce your own will and yield it to him in complete submission and with complete self-abnegation. This novitiate, this terrible school is accepted voluntarily by the man who consecrates himself to this life in the hope that after a long novitiate he will achieve such a degree of self-mastery and self-control that he will at last, through a life of obedience, achieve complete freedom, that is to say, freedom from himself, and so escape the fate of those who have lived their whole lives without finding themselves within themselves. (XIV, 26)

This does not sound like the voice of our narrator. Whose voice is it? And on what is its authority based? The recognizable and realistic voice of our narrator does return shortly afterward to warn us that the institution of the elder can sometimes lead not to humility and freedom, but to "satanic pride" and to slavery, but then it retreats once more in favor of Alesha's reported consciousness as the figure of Zosima himself is discussed. Phrases such as "Alesha almost always observed," "Alesha was especially struck by," "Alesha well understood that," and "Alesha knew that" serve to indicate that the author has now entrusted the account of the elder to his hero, who "knows" him so much better and who is likely to gain our approval of that account (XIV, 28–29).

A similar device introduces the account of Dmitry's trial. As we have seen, the narrator starts by warning us of the inadequacies of his own narrative: "I might have taken what was only of secondary importance to be the most important thing, even omitting altogether the most glaring and essential facts" (XV, 89); "there was much that I could not make out, some things I could not grasp the significance of, and others I forgot to commit to memory" (XV, 92). To get around the problem the narrator proposes to hand over responsibility for the narrative to others:

> I repeat, I do not intend to describe in full the examination of the witnesses. Besides, my description would turn out to be partly superfluous, since in the speeches of the public prosecutor and the defense, when they came to sum up, the whole course and meaning of the facts and testimony that had been heard were brought, as it were, into focus with clear and characteristic illumination, and those two speeches I took down in full, at least parts of them, and I shall quote them in due course. (XV, 95)

The irony here, of course, is that the narrator is about to cede his responsibilities to others whose own narratives are false in that they are driven by the desire, not to chronicle an objective truth, but to create through rhetoric a subjectively desired outcome. We shall need to recall this tendency of the narrator on another occasion when he seeks narrative validation by resorting to an apparently more authoritative voice: the account of Father Zosima's life and discourses in book 6, "A Russian Monk." But this is a problem for later.

The narrator's lead in drawing our attention to the novel's preoccupation with the creation of fictions and the bearing of false witness is soon followed by others. We have already observed Fedor Pavlovich's hyperbolically inventive narrative capabilities, but it is worth noting in particular that he too contributes a false narrative about Zosima, foreshadowing what we shall later see to be the creatively false elements in the narrated account of Zosima's life. Ironically, in light of what we later learn about Zosima's past, Fedor Pavlovich presents him as a sensualist and nonbeliever, a cross between Mephistopheles and Lermontov's Pechorin, in whose presence one should lock up one's wife and daughters (XIV, 124). Elsewhere, on introducing his sons Ivan and Dmitry to Zosima, the same Fedor Pavlovich embellishes his own squalid character and existence by embedding them in the fictional frame of Schiller's *The Robbers:* "This is my son, flesh of my flesh, my own most beloved flesh! He is my most respectful Karl Moor, so to speak, while that son who's just come in, Dmitry Fedorovich, and against whom I am seeking justice from you, that is my most disrespectful Franz Moor— both from Schiller's *The Robbers*—and I, I in that case am the *Regierender Graf von Moor!*" (XIV, 66). Katerina Ivanovna is also guilty of authoring her own future life and "love" for Dmitry when she outlines to Alesha her plans to sacrifice that future to the man who has rejected her:

> I shall be his God, to whom he will pray. [. . .] And let him see throughout his entire life that I shall be true to him my whole life long and to the word I once gave him, despite the fact that he has been unfaithful and betrayed me. I shall be. . . . I shall turn myself into nothing more than the means of his happiness, or (how can I put this) the instrument, the engine of his happiness, and this for the whole of my life." (XIV, 172)

Alesha quickly sees that this self-sacrifice and love are in fact based on a monstrous and (in its oblique reference to God's love of humanity) blasphemous pride, that the entire scenario is a theatrical and self-serving attempt to make Dmitry into a character in her own fiction, and that Katerina "loves falsely" (XIV, 175).

In his fine study of the demonic novel in Russia, to which we made reference in our introduction, Adam Weiner cites an interesting passage in which Denis de Rougemont seeks to identify the thirst for authorship with the original emergence of evil and the devil:

> Jacob Boehme tells a story to the effect that Satan when asked, "Why did you leave Paradise?" answered, "I wanted to become an author.". . . The Author of all things . . . authorizes himself to infinity in his unfolded Creation. . . . The Devil also wished to create his own Work. . . . In truth the will to create, the need to write, simply, coincides deep down with the Luciferian temptation: to become like God, to make oneself an author, to authorize oneself in an autonomous world. It is inevitable that the Devil should take a hand in it and that the best should see themselves more tempted than others to accept the advice of that Prompter of genius.[5]

We can extend the kind of authorship here described to also include the creation of unwritten fictions such as that generated by Katerina's pride. In all such cases authorship is defined by the fact that it is self-serving, and it stands in contrast, as Weiner has observed, to the case of the religious chronicler, for whom the purpose of narrative is not to "authorize oneself in an autonomous world," but to bear witness to events and to the glory of God's. *The Brothers Karamazov* offers an incisive perspective on the conflict between these two approaches to narrative, first in the scene where Dmitry confronts his accusers and tries to make his statement, and second in the testimonies offered during the trial itself. Shortly before his departure for Mokroe and his arrest, Dmitry has said goodbye to his friend Perkhotin by inaccurately quoting the chronicler-monk Pimen's famous lines from Push-kin's *Boris Godunov:* "Just one more final tale/And my chronicle is done" ("Eshche odno, poslednee skazanie/I letopis' okonchena moia"). Dmitry cites only the first line, and its meaning remains unclear in the context of his chaotic departure, loaded down with champagne and delicacies for a final orgy. It acquires, however, an emphatic resonance once his interrogation begins, and it immediately becomes clear that Dmitry is determined to nar-rate his story straight, *like a chronicler,* without any embellishments, in the correct chronological order, and with the important given precedence over the unimportant. The technique of his interrogators, however, has much more in common with that of the writer of secular fiction, in that narrative is seen primarily, not as a means of bearing witness, but as a snare and a means of entrapment. Their tricks, violations of chronology, and insistence on giving prominence to details Dmitry considers secondary drive him to distraction. He remarks, significantly, that to include all such details would require a novel—"you wouldn't get it all into three volumes, you'd need an epilogue as well!"—before he unwittingly points to the demonic nature of such narratives: "But the tiny trivia, gentlemen, let's do away with all these tiny, pettifogging trivia—otherwise the devil only knows what will come out of it" (XIV, 421).

The devil is indeed in the details (*chertochki*) with which the authori-ties insist Dmitry's account be embellished (XIV, 421–22). Left to his own devices, Dmitry does manipulate his narrative by leaving gaps in it, but he does so not for effect, not in order to deceive, but for a noble and selfless reason: to protect Katerina Ivanovna. This prompts us to recall another oc-casion when he resorts to narrative embellishment: his ecstatic use of verse in the service of self-revelation to his brother Alesha in book 3, chapter 3. But here too he exploits literary form not for the sake of its artifice, but for the way it permits him to articulate an emotional immediacy beyond his own expressive abilities. The authorities, on the other hand, create a narrative— the written record of their interrogation of Dmitry—that distorts his con-fession by allowing the wrong inferences to be drawn from his narrative si-lences and gaps: "But once again our duty consists in bringing to your atten-tion and making clear the harm which you yourself are doing to your cause by refusing to give a particular bit of testimony" (XIV, 422). Dmitry is referred to as the "narrator" (*rasskazchik*) of the account being taken down, but the "cunning" (*khitrost'*) of his interlocutors puts "devils" (we recall the subliminally demonic suggestion contained in the diminutive form *chertochki*) into his narrative and his motives until he eventually protests: "Gentlemen, this would infuriate (*vzbesit*) the Lord God Himself!" (XIV, 422). The demonic implications of Dmitry's outburst are clear only in the Russian text, where the verb not only means to enrage or infuriate but is constructed from the root *bes* (devil). Dmitry's dawning recognition of the "devils" entering his confession through the narrative "cunning" of those writing down his words with the wrong inflection leads him to take refuge in further poetic quotation: this time an inaccurate version of lines from Fedor Tiutchev's famous lyric "Silentium," a poem that returns us to the idea of demonic narrative through its insistence that "An uttered thought is a lie" (*mysl' izrechennaia est' lozh'*). Once again Dmitry's speech begins to resort to irritated invocation of the devil, until he finally exclaims: "O, the devil, pah! Gentlemen, it is literally impossible to talk to you!" (XIV, 424).

The titles given to the three chapters describing Dmitry's interrogation are highly significant: The first is called "The Journey of a Soul through Ordeals: The First Ordeal"; the second and third are entitled "The Second Ordeal" and "The Third Ordeal." In all three cases the word for "ordeal" is *mytarstvo,* which, as Terras remarks, contains echoes of Orthodox eschatology and its teaching that after death the human soul on its way to heaven is subjected to twenty trials (*mytarstva*) by evil spirits.[6] It is also conceivable that the chapter titles have hagiographical implications and point to the thematic preoccupation of medieval *vitae* with how the man of God endures and resists temptation by devils assuming various forms. The "devils" that are insinuated into Dmitry's confession represent a similar ordeal for him, as what he intended as a chronicle of how he resisted demonic temptation on the night of his father's murder is read instead as a deceitful demonic fiction.

The scene of Dmitry's interrogation prepares the ground for the trial itself, and together these episodes amount to an implied meditation on the nature of testimony, the bearing of false witness, and the theory and practice of the art of fictional narrative. The narrator's excuses as he approaches his account of the trial alert us to the fact that the whole of this book, entitled "A Miscarriage of Justice" ("Sudebnaia oshibka"), is to turn on the clash of fabricated and falsified narratives, as the spokesmen for the prosecution and the defense in turn "novelize" the facts at their disposal in order to fit their predetermined ends. Even before the trial begins, the town buzzes with rumors, exaggerations, downright lies, and "remarkable anecdotes" about the participants (XV, 90), many of them no doubt fed by earlier lies and false narratives written by the malicious Rakitin for the sensationalist newspaper

Rumors (*Slukhi*) (XV, 14–15). In a splendid piece of irony even the Procurator and Fetiukovich, the defense lawyer—the primary authors of false narratives about Dmitry—are themselves the subjects of outlandish rumors and anecdotes (XV, 91). The narrator even draws attention to the "devices" (*priemy*) used by Fetiukovich for falsifying a testimony by predetermining how it will be "read": "Later, people gladly told of how he managed to 'put on the spot' all the prosecution's witnesses in the most timely way, distracting them insofar as he could, and smearing their moral reputations and consequently their testimony itself. It was assumed, incidentally, that he did this for the most part for the fun of it, for the sake, so to speak, of demonstrating a certain juridical brilliance, and so that nothing should be forgotten of the devices used to serve his advocacy" (XV, 96).

If the mention of such devices for manipulating testimony suggests an analogy with the writing of fiction, so surely does the Procurator's description of his own speech as his *chef d'oeuvre,* a term more appropriately applied to a work of art (XV, 123). The Procurator is a decent man, and what he has to say in his speech is not contemptible, coinciding in many important respects with Dostoevsky's own views on the breakdown of moral order, society, and the family in contemporary Russia; but his speech is driven by personal vanity and the desire to display his own worth, and in serving that end it negates the truth and promotes a miscarriage of justice. He is, moreover, guilty of hubris in the way "he claims command of the workings of a human being's mind."[7] Throughout his speech the Procurator resorts to various rhetorical devices to embellish his fiction—something recognized by the public at the trial and commented on as they leave the courtroom at the end: "It was very clever indeed. [. . .] But there was a great deal of rhetoric and long phrases" (XV, 152). Most remarked on, by both audience and the narrator, is his reliance on "psychology"—an essential component in the construction of a novel—and the care with which he chooses his order of exposition in order to create the most powerful effect (XV, 143). At all times the Procurator seeks to turn Dmitry's accurate factual chronicle of events into a fiction—"Don't believe him," he keeps saying to his audience—while constantly maintaining that his own fictional interpretation is fact. With unwitting irony he dismisses Dmitry's account as the "the most implausible contrivance" of "a novelist" (XV, 149):

> The main thing here is that it's possible to trip up and reduce the exultant novelist to dust by means of details, those very details with which reality is always so replete, and which these unfortunate and unwilling storytellers always ignore as completely insignificant and unnecessary—indeed, they never even enter their heads. O, they have no time for these details at such a moment, their mind is concerned only with the creation of a grandiose whole—

and suddenly someone dares to raise such a trivial detail! But that's the way they get caught! (XV, 149)

As Terras has pointed out, there is an implicit discussion going on here about the role of naturalistic detail and of verisimilitude in the creation of realistic fiction, a discussion that mirrors Dostoevsky's own claim to be "a realist in a higher sense," one who, like Dmitry, sacrifices the devices of conventional surface naturalism—the appearance of reality—in favor of a narrative that uncovers the deep structures of truth.[8] Writing to his friend Nikolai Strakhov in 1869, Dostoevsky made the following well-known statement on the nature of his own art:

> I have my own view of reality (in art), and what most people regard as fantastic and exceptional is sometimes for me the very essence of reality. Everyday trivialities and a conventional view of them, in my opinion, not only fall short of realism, but are even contrary to it. (XXIX/1, 19)

The Prosecutor, on the other hand, is arguing from the point of view of the kind of "realist" whom Dostoevsky dismissed in 1868 in a letter to another friend, A. N. Maikov:

> I have entirely different notions of reality and realism from our realists and critics. [. . .] With their kind of realism you cannot explain so much as a hundredth part of the real facts that have actually occurred. But with our idealism we have even prophesied facts. (XXVIII/2, 329)

We must resist the temptation to dwell further on Dostoevsky's views on the nature of realism, for this is a complex and distinct topic that has been well explored by others.[9] We should simply note that, like Dmitry, Dostoevsky believed that it was the power of vision that best bore witness to the truth, and not the "little details" or "little devils" (*chertochki*) whose presence often signaled the sacrifice of truth in favor of the mere appearance of truth.

When his turn comes to respond, Fetiukovich too lays the charge of "artistic creation" (*khudozhestvennoe tvorchestvo*) and "novel writing" at the Procurator's door, comparing his flights of fancy to those of the Gothic novelist, Ann Radcliffe, and the figure of Dmitry he has described to a fictional character: "You have created a novel and in it a completely different person. That's the point, you've created a different person!" (XV, 158–59). But Fetiukovich's discourse makes plain his own mastery of the art of fiction, and the Procurator in turn accuses him of falsifying his narrative, of distorting his facts, and, in his justification of the murder of an unworthy father by a son, of rejecting divine law in favor of rational humanism and thus setting forth a false image of Christ:

> The Gospel and religion are corrected: that is all mysticism, we are told, and ours, you see, is the only true Christianity, one that has already passed the test of analysis by reason and sound ideas. And so they set before us a false image of Christ! "With what measure ye mete, it shall be measured to you again," cries the counsel for the defense, and at the same moment he concludes that Christ taught you to mete out as it is measured to you—and that from the tribune of truth and sound ideas! We peek into the Gospels only on the eve of making our speeches in order to impress with our knowledge of what is after all a fairly original composition, which can come in useful and serve to create a certain effect as and when required! But that is precisely what Christ commands us not to do, but to beware of doing that because that is what the world of evil does, while we ought to forgive, turn the other cheek, and not mete out in the same measure as our persecutors mete out to us. That's what our God taught us, and not that it's a prejudice to forbid children to murder their fathers. And we shouldn't be correcting from the tribune of truth and sound ideas the Gospel of our God, whom the counsel for the defense sees fit to call merely "the crucified lover of mankind," in opposition to the whole of Orthodox Russia which calls upon him "For Thou art the Lord our God." (XV, 174–75)

This passage merits such lengthy quotation for the light it also sheds on the rational humanism of Ivan Karamazov, on his rejection of an "unworthy father"—God himself—and on the false image of Christ that he creates in his own demonic narrative "The Grand Inquisitor," where the figure of the Son of God, by virtue of the kiss he plants on the Inquisitor's "bloodless lips," is intended implicitly to condone the latter's rejection of divine justice in favor of man's. It is in Ivan's revolt that the theme of false and demonic narratives comes to a head, for in a very real sense that revolt turns on a disputed claim to authorship, this time the most fundamental authorship of all: that of Creation. Ivan "returns his ticket of admission" to paradise, not because of a lack of faith in the existence of God, but because he does not agree with the way God has scripted the narrative of Creation: "It's not God I don't accept, you understand, it's the world he has created, the world of God, that I don't accept and can never agree to accept" (XIV, 214). Although he is prepared to recognize the inevitability of God's narrative resolution, or *dénouement*—one of universal reconciliation, when the lion will lay down with the lamb and the victim with the victimizer—Ivan does not like the "narrative devices," the *khitrosti,* the mysterious ways employed by God in the service of that resolution. This is because they seem to him to be an affront to the intelligence of God's "readership," one consisting of rational human beings with Euclidean minds, beings such as Ivan himself who, like the Prosecutor with Dmitry, demand that God make transparent all the "little details" of His grand design, especially those relating to how the sufferings of little children can possibly be necessary for the attainment of that design. We recall the Prosecutor's words about the "novelist-criminal"—"O, they have no time for these details at such a moment, their mind is concerned only with the creation of a grandiose whole—and suddenly someone dares to raise such a trivial detail!"—and we now sense in them a travesty of the logic of Ivan's revolt.

The "authorial" nature of Ivan's dispute with God begins to emerge during his discussion with Alesha in book 5, "Pro and Contra." Here, in quoting Voltaire's famous dictum, Ivan raises the possibility that it is man who is the author not only of how the world is made, but also of God himself:

> There was one old sinner in the eighteenth century who spake, saying that if God did not exist, then it would be necessary to invent him, *s'il n'existait pas Dieu il faudrait l'inventer.* And indeed man created God. But what is so strange and marvelous is not so much the idea that God might actually exist, but that such a thought—the idea of the necessity of God—should have crept into the head of so savage and wicked a creature as man; so holy is it, so touching and so wise, and so much does it redound to man's honor. But, as far as I am concerned, I've long ago decided to give up thinking about whether it was man that created God, or God man. (XIV, 214)

Instead, Ivan concentrates his own revolt on his insistence that he would write the narrative of Creation *better* than God, that is to say, in a more transparently humane and rational way. It is at this point that he advances, not an argument, but "little anecdotes" (*anekdotiki*) designed to torpedo God's larger narrative, stories of cruelty to children that he has gathered from newspapers and other sources with that specific purpose in mind. In using narratives in this way, in order to challenge the authority of the Creator, Ivan is of course investing them with demonic intent, and in the course of his conversation with Alesha these little anecdotes become little demons, tempting and undermining the novice's faith and pushing him into his own demonic assumption of divine power when he passes judgment on the evil victimizer in one of Ivan's tales with the words "Shoot him!," an outburst that prompts from Ivan the highly significant response, "So that's the sort of little devil [*besenok*] you've got sitting in your heart, Aleshka Karamazov!" (XIV, 221).

These little anecdotes prepare the reader for "The Grand Inquisitor," the very heart of Ivan's revolt and his most significant demonic narrative, setting out as it does to displace God and Christ from the authorship of creation in favor of those projections of Ivan's own demonic pride, the Inquisitor and his master, the devil.[10] This displacement is evident from the moment the Inquisitor confronts the arrested Christ in his cell and does not allow him to speak: "The old man remarks to him that he has no right at all to add to what he has already said in the past" (XIV, 228). Here we see just how intent the Catholic church is on "correcting" Christ's insistence on erecting His ministry on the principle of freedom of faith: It now takes His word and narrative away from Him. The Inquisitor and his kind will write the future of the Christian church, erecting it on unfreedom and the three pillars of miracle, mystery, and authority.

Although "The Grand Inquisitor" is a narrative contrivance of Ivan's, it is not one, we are told, he has ever gotten around to writing. Notwithstanding this, the narrative he relates to Alesha is one in which his sense of his own authorial role is ever present, and one that constantly draws attention to its own artifice and falseness. Ivan starts half apologetically, seeking to justify his "poem" by embedding it in established literary tradition and practices:

> "You see, here too it's impossible to begin without a foreword, that is a literary foreword—oh, dear," Ivan laughed, "what sort of a writer am I! You see, the action of my poem takes place in the sixteenth century, at a time when, as you ought to know from your classes, it was the custom in poetical works to bring divine powers down to earth. Leaving aside Dante, in France judicial clerks as well as monks in monasteries put on entire productions in which they introduced on to the stage the Madonna, angels, the saints, Christ, and even God himself." (XIV, 224)

Ivan goes on to say that similar poems and plays were composed at that time in Russian monasteries, before concluding: "Well, that's the sort of thing my poem would have been if it had appeared at that time." The irony here, of course, is that the tradition in which Ivan seeks legitimacy for his "poem" is a tradition that used its rhetorical devices in the affirmation of God's glory, not in order to undermine it; so right from this opening gambit at self-justification Ivan's demonic narrative is contaminated with the ideas of falsehood and pretendership. There is also evidence of authorial pride on Ivan's part, as he describes to Alesha how Christ's appearance amid the autos-da-fé of the Spanish Inquisition, and the instant recognition he inspires in all, "could have been one of the best passages in the poem" (XIV, 226). But Ivan is not a very good poet and, as Terras has shown, "The Grand Inquisitor" is "an exercise in self-delusion," something suggested by the masquerade and melodrama on which it relies for its effect: "a twenty-three-year-old Russian student lets a ninety-year-old Spanish cardinal—'tall and erect' and 'fiery-eyed'—express his innermost thoughts. [. . .] 'The Grand Inquisitor' is not a very good poem, and when everything is said and done, not very good rhetoric either."[11] Its artificiality and lack of truth shine through in its tacky Gothic romanticism, its sentimental and corny imagery, its overblown rhetorical flourishes, and its self-conscious (and inexact) use of quotation.[12] In it Ivan conceals himself behind all the rhetorical influences he has ever absorbed, as he presses them into the service of his demonic revolt; but his true purpose and his own voice constantly break through, revealing the self-serving nature of his narrative. His sixteenth-century Spanish cardinal begins to speak to Christ as a nineteenth-century Russian radical atheist would, indicating only too clearly that he has been narrated into being not for his own sake, but merely to serve the egoism of his creator:

> Don't you know that centuries will pass and mankind will proclaim from the lips of its own wisdom and science that there is no crime, and consequently no sin, but that there are only hungry people. "Feed them first, and then demand virtue of them!"—that's what they'll write on the banners that they'll raise against you and with which they'll destroy your church. (XIV, 230)

The editors of the Academy edition of Dostoevsky's complete works see fit to identify here a reference to Aleksandr Herzen's essay on the British socialist Robert Owen (XV, 559–60). Such reference may well have been intended, but more obvious is the connection between this statement and Ivan's own oft-proclaimed belief that, in the absence of God, there is no such thing as crime and "everything is permitted." Later, in the Inquisitor's reference to the "anthill" of a compliant and harmonious social order we sense a further anachronism, as this image was one that dominated Russian debates on socialism in the 1860s, the decade in which *The Brothers Karamazov* is set, and debates to which Dostoevsky himself contributed.

But the self-disclosure of "The Grand Inquisitor"—a process of which, as we have seen, Ivan is not always conscious—goes further than this. It ultimately reveals that what rules Ivan is not socialism, not atheism, but *demonism,* and that his vision of social reconstruction, as articulated by his creature the Inquisitor, is erected not on any love for suffering humanity—for which he has only contempt—but on his own boundless egoism and desire to displace God. He attributes ultimate wisdom to neither God nor man, but to the "terrible and wise spirit, the spirit of self-destruction and non-being," whose words in the wilderness as he tempted Christ represented the very pinnacle of intelligence:

> Just from those questions alone, just from the miracle of their appearance, you can see that what you are dealing with here is not the human transient

mind, but one that is eternal and absolute. For in those three questions the entire future history of mankind is, as it were, combined in one whole and anticipated, and three images are made manifest in which all the insoluble historical contradictions of human nature throughout the world will come together. At that time it could not be so clearly seen, for the future was still unknown, but now, when fifteen centuries have passed, we can see that in those three questions everything was so fully divined and predicted, and has been so completely vindicated, that nothing more may be added to them or subtracted from them. (XIV, 230)

"We are not with you, but with *him*, that's our secret!" says the Inquisitor to Christ, as instead of salvation through divine grace, he offers a profoundly demonic redemption of original sin, one in which he and other tyrants like him take on themselves "the curse of knowledge of good and evil," leaving the rest of mankind restored to a "paradise" of sheep-like equality and obedience (XIV, 234–36).

The demonism of the Inquisitor and his creator has been well signaled by an intensification in the placement of semiotic markers in this section of the text. In his discussion with Alesha in the approach to "The Grand Inquisitor" Ivan's speech has been particularly densely punctuated by conventional invocations of the devil of the kind that we have seen elsewhere. After the narration of the "poem" Ivan insists that Alesha should depart to the right, while he himself goes off to the left, the devil's side, before referring to Zosima as *Pater Seraphicus,* an explicit reference to a personage in the final scene of Goethe's tale of diabolic temptation, *Faust.*[13] Finally, as Ivan departs, Alesha observes that there is something wrong with his brother's movements, a feature he has never noticed before and which Terras describes as "a very strong metonymic symbol."[14] Ivan is at that moment on his way to see one of the novel's most compelling incarnations of the devil, the repellent lackey Smerdiakov, who is sitting on a bench at the gate to the Karamazov house. Ivan's strange movements are symbolically explicable when we learn a page or two later that "the lackey Smerdiakov was also sitting in his soul, and it was precisely that person that his soul could not abide" (XIV, 242). We shall return to Smerdiakov in due course.

The sort of demonic markers deployed in this scene are also used effectively elsewhere to signal the all-pervasive presence of the devil in *The Brothers Karamazov.* Indeed, Terras has suggested that the novel might be read not just as it conventionally has been, as a "theodicy," that is, a vindication of God, but also as the opposite—a "diabolodicy"—on account of its persistent preoccupation with images of both hell and the devil.[15] The text is particularly rich in the sort of demonic markers drawn from folk tradition that Dostoevsky has employed before to set out the demonic patterning of his earlier novels. These include references to the shrieking sickness (*klikushestvo*), which was held to be a symptom of demonic possession: The mother of Alesha and Ivan was a sufferer (XIV, 13), and the narrator sees fit to devote an entire page to description and explanation of the condition (XIV, 44). There is further exploitation of the demonic significance of liminal spaces and conditions: The enemy of superstition, Miusov, is at odds with the monastery over a *boundary* dispute (XIV, 31); there are several occasions when the Karamazov brothers meet or part at *crossroads* (for example, XIV, 141–42; XV, 41); Fedor Pavlovich keeps all windows and doors closed—something widely believed to ward off the devil—while much is later made of the disagreement between Dmitry and the servant Grigory over whether the door into the house was open or closed, a disagreement that leads Dmitry to the conclusion that "the devil must have opened it" (XV, 42). We learn that Grigory's wife, Marfa Ignatevna, once gave birth to a "dragon-child" born with six fingers rather than five. Marfa's patronymic suggests "stillborn" (*ignatus*) and her deformed child is rich in significance: it anticipates the moral deformation that later affects the entire Karamazov family, while on the very day that the short-lived creature is buried, Marfa Ignatevna awakes in the night to the sound of a newborn's crying. This child turns out to be the demon-parricide Smerdiakov, whom the servants raise in place of their own lost child (XIV, 88–89). Moreover, such birth defects were held in popular superstition to be a sign that a child was a "demon child," a servant of the unclean force.

Finally by way of example, *The Brothers Karamazov* displays a preoccupation with folk beliefs about the demonic phenomenon of the "unclean dead" (*zalozhnye pokoiniki*), those victims of suicide or of violent, premature, or unseemly deaths whose souls are unable to find peace in the other world. The narrator tells of a novice monk who once broke his vow of obedience to his elder and whose body was subsequently rejected by consecrated ground, something often attributed to *zalozhnye pokoiniki* who were usually buried not on church land but in liminal spaces (XIV, 27). Little Iliusha's dying request to be buried under a large stone to which he and his father used to walk is denied because it would be unseemly to bury him "under an unclean stone like someone who has hanged himself" (XV, 191). After his death there is little or no odor of corruption from Iliusha's corpse, in strong contrast, of course, to the stench given off earlier by the deceased Zosima, which led to Alesha's temporary loss of faith. In Russian hagiographic tradition the failure of a corpse to decompose may be seen as a sign of sanctity, and this is what everyone expected from the holy elder, but it is worth recalling that Zosima's wisdom is more rooted in that of the Russian people than in established church tradition, and according to folk belief bodily decay was a prerequisite of the acceptance of the dead by Mother Earth, and a corpse that did not decompose was that of a *zalozhnyi pokoinik*, so that in those terms Zosima's fate is confirmation both of his acceptance by the Earth and of the fact that he is untouched by the unclean force.[16]

Similar signs drawn from both the folk and Orthodox cultural traditions attend in particular several key scenes of especial demonic content or significance for the novel: We have already seen the example of how Ivan's exposition of his revolt to Alesha attracts demonic rhetoric and motifs. Earlier, during the family visit to Zosima's cell, Fedor Pavlovich's shameless and insulting verbal attack on the monastery acquires a diabolical aspect through suggestions of his possession by a "stupid devil" and through use of the motif of casting oneself from a great height, a motif whose demonic import was examined in chapter 1 and which is used by several other characters in *The Brothers Karamazov*—for example, Dmitry (XIV, 97), Snegirev (XIV, 192), Perkhotin (XIV, 403), and Katerina (XV, 120)—both before and after its demonic meaning is disclosed in the second temptation of Christ in "The Grand Inquisitor." As Ivanits has pointed out, demonic markers such as lameness, tightly closed windows, drunkenness, and a quotation from Pushkin's "Demon" also inform the description of the "miniature hell" of the Snegirev household.[17] They are there in abundance, as one might expect, during the scene of Fedor Pavlovich's murder and of Dmitry's assault on Grigory, a scene in which much is made of boundary fences, doors, windows, mirrors, Grigory's lameness, and the presence of the bathhouse (XIV, 352–56).

But the most evocative example of how such scenes attract demonic signs derived from Russian cultural semiotics is provided by the episode in which Grushenka, the "infernal woman" (*infernal'nitsa*) and "queen of all infernal women" (XIV, 143), attempts to seduce the innocent novice Alesha. The attempt coincides with the moment of Alesha's own rebellion against his God, as Rakitin points out (XIV, 317). The scene is punctuated with oblique references to, and invocations of, the devil, of the kind with which we are now familiar, and indeed in a roundabout way Rakitin refers to himself as the Judas betraying Alesha (XIV, 325). But in its entirety the scene is surely designed to replicate, as in Myshkin's relationship with Nastasia Filippovna, the conventional motif from medieval hagiographical literature of "the demonized and harlotized female" attempting to seduce the ascetic man of God from the path of righteousness.[18] The name Alesha (Aleksei) means "man of God," and the semiotics of this scene thus serve to promote the positive identity intended for Alesha by both the narrator and the implied author.[19]

Apart from the sort of culturally significant semiotic markers we have examined so far, *The Brothers Karamazov* proclaims its preoccupation with the demonic through a persistent tendency among its characters to raise and discuss openly the nature of both hell and devils. This has been much remarked on by commentators, but we should at least identify here the major instances of its occurrence.[20] The early scene in Zosima's cell, which sets in motion so many of the novel's subsequent concerns, plays an important role here too, for it offers us Fedor Pavlovich's vision of hell, a vision that is both comic and replete with serious implications. The starting point for his conception is an image found both in Russian folk literature (in the genre of the "spiritual verses": *dukhovnye stikhi*) and in Orthodox iconography: that of devils dragging sinners down to hell with hooks[2]:[1]

> Why, it's not possible, thinks I, that the devils will forget to drag me down to their place with their hooks when I die. But then I get to thinking: hooks? But where do they get their hooks from? What are they made of? Iron? Where do they forge them? Have they got some sort of factory there, is that it? You see, there in the monastery the monks no doubt insist that hell, for example, has a ceiling. Now I'm quite prepared to believe in hell, but only if it has no ceiling—it makes things more refined, as it were, more enlightened, more Lutheran. But essentially isn't it all the same whether it has a ceiling or not? And yet the whole accursed question turns on that! For if there's no ceiling, there can be no hooks. But if there are no hooks, it means all the rest goes to pot and is unlikely: for who then will drag me down with hooks? And if they don't drag me down, then what will happen? Where would be the justice in the world? *Il faudrait les inventer*—the hooks, that is, just for me. (XIV, 23)

Fedor Pavlovich knows he is being ridiculous, but his comic inventiveness acquires a serious resonance in the novel, as his challenge to the way hell is ordered, his comically inappropriate references to justice, his quotation from Voltaire, and his mock dialectical reasoning all stand as a preemptive travesty of Ivan's later questioning of God's order. Fedor Pavlovich's grotesquely utilitarian, literal, and materialistic conception of hell is later to be counterbalanced by Zosima's belief that hell is "the suffering that comes from consciousness that one is no longer able to love" (XIV, 292). This figurative conception is derived from St. Isaac of Niniveh,[22] but it also reflects the notion of hell as human solitude explored by Dostoevsky in the works examined in chapter 1 of this study. A similar idea—that hell may be the consequence of self-centeredness—lies behind Grushenka's folk tale of the onion and the sinner who tries to save herself at the expense of others (XIV, 319), and, rather more obliquely, behind the view of Dmitry's coachman Andrei, on the road to Mokroe, that hell is for those such as grandees, rulers, judges, and rich folk, who ride roughshod over others and "give way to no one" (XIV, 371–72).

The novel supports a similar diversity of views on devils and demons—indeed, in no other novel of Dostoevsky's do devils appear so frequently and in so literal a guise. Both Dmitry and Fedor Pavlovich are referred to as "possessed" (XIV, 68), Zosima attributes the discord in the Karamazov family to devils that have been disturbed (XIV, 71), and Alesha tells Kolia Krasotkin that the devil, "literally the devil," has taken the form of vanity and crawled into the hearts of the present generation (XIV, 503). Alesha also confesses to having experienced the same vision of devils described by Liza Khokhlakova, one in which they advance when encouraged by blasphemy and retreat when confronted with the sign of the cross—a motif common to both folk and Orthodox demonology (XV, 23). Liza's dream of "devils everywhere, in every corner, under the table, and when the doors open and there's a crowd of them there too, behind the doors," recalls the experience of the ghoulish Father Ferapont, Zosima's rival, whose apparent humility and holiness is driven by pride, and who has paradoxically become a fanatical servant of those very devils he professes to despise, as Father Paisy shrewdly suggests (XIV, 303). Ferapont's devils are, like Liza's, the multitudinous and opportunistic petty demons of Russian folk and Orthodox tradition. There is nothing grand or Miltonic about them, and he sees them everywhere: "I went to the Father Superior's during holy Pentecost last year, and I haven't been back since. I saw one monk who had a devil sitting in his bosom, hiding under his cassock with only his horns poking out. Another had one peering out of his pocket, with such sharp eyes, and it was afraid of me. Another had one in his belly, in his unclean paunch, and yet another had one hanging around his neck" (XIV, 153). Ferapont then goes on to describe to the little monk visiting from Obdorsk, how he trapped a particularly fine specimen's tail in the door, made the sign of the cross, and watched him die: "I suppose by now he must have rotted away in the corner and is stinking the place out, but they can't see it." The verb used for "stinking" (*smerdit*) here serves the architectonics of the novel by establishing in the reader's mind at this early stage a link between devils and Smerdiakov. Later, when the deranged Ferapont sets about exorcising the deceased Zosima's cell, his own demonic credentials are established as he pauses on the threshold, and they are then confirmed by the petty demon-like appearance of the Obdorsk monk "peeping out from under his right arm with his sharp and curious little eyes" (XIV, 302). Ferapont is affronted by Zosima's disregard for the more ascetic aspects of monastic life and his apparently tolerant attitude to the unclean force. His accusation that Zosima did not believe in devils is unsubstantiated—the elder had rather offered a more figurative view of hell in place of the physical form conventionally envisaged—but it is true that his whole approach to evil, hell, and the devil is more "modern" than the medieval conceptions espoused by Ferapont. Zosima's recommendation of physical medicine in a case of demonic possession where conventional fasting and prayer had been ineffective is evidence of his willingness to entertain psychological and physiological causes for the apparently supernatural (XIV, 303).

As the architect of parricide in its ultimately metaphorical form—that of turning against the Heavenly Father—Ivan Karamazov is central to the novel's demonology. Described by his own brother Dmitry as "a grave" on account of his enigmatic demeanor, he is the would-be author of a universe governed by the abstract laws of Euclidean geometry—another "house of the dead" in which the devil, not God, reigns supreme and laughs at mankind (XIV, 124). Ivan also spawns a variety of demon doubles, and in the forms of the Inquisitor and his own nocturnal visitor-hallucination he also authors two very different embodiments of the demonic, the first consciously and willingly, the second unconsciously and unwillingly. Ivan's demon doubles consist of a cluster of figures who to a greater or lesser degree have been contaminated by his ideology, and who together consitute a graduated set of variations on that ideology's implied outcomes, ranging from the sotto voce skepticism of the immature Kolia Krasotkin to the emphatic and murderous demonism of Smerdiakov. Between these two extremes may be found the intermediate figures of the malicious Rakitin and the "little demon" Liza Khokhlakova, both of whom are unwillingly in thrall to Ivan. Rakitin outgrows the merely nasty and assumes a potentially demonic identity in the scene where he sets about tempting the gullible Dmitry with a materialism, a denial of the spiritual and the afterlife, and a consequent advocacy of moral nihilism that are clearly attributable to Ivan's influence. The scene is narrated by Dmitry to his brother Alesha, and it turns on Rakitin's earlier efforts to describe and advocate to Dmitry the physiological theories of the French naturalist Claude Bernard (1813–78), theories that make Dmitry "feel sorry for God" because of the way in which they have apparently displaced Him as creator and source of all human perception and morality in favor of the "little tails" of human nerve endings. Dmitry's stumbling attempts to convey the essentials of this to Alesha are contaminated by suggestively demonic exclamations and imagery:

> Imagine: it's there in the nerves, in the head, that is to say that in the brain there are these nerves (oh, the devil take it!) . . . there are some sort of little tails, the nerves have got these little tails, and, well, as soon as they begin to quiver . . . that is, see, I look at something with my eyes, like that, and they start to quiver, the little tails, I mean . . . and as soon as they start quivering then an image appears, not at once but after a moment, a second or so passes, and a sort of moment comes, that is, not a moment—the devil take the moment!—but rather an image, that is an object or event—well, the devil take it whatever it is!—and that's why I contemplate and then think . . . because of the little tails, and not at all because I've got a soul or am made in someone's image and likeness, that's all stupid. That, brother, is what Mikhail [Rakitin] explained to me yesterday, and it fired me up. It's wonderful, Alesha, this sci-

ence! A new man is coming, I understand that. . . . But nevertheless I feel sorry for God! (XV, 28)

Dmitry's adjacent references to Rakitin crawling through a crack, to his malicious laughter and his lying, as well as the description of him as a *smerd*—an obsolete Russian term for a serf or peasant, but one that also carries implications of "stench" and brings to mind Smerdiakov—all contrive to add to the demonic subtext of this scene.

Liza Khokhlakova, too, is possessed by Ivan and becomes another of his demonic projections. In the chapter entitled "The Little Demon" she displays both physical and moral characteristics of a devil: She has darting eyes, she rejects order and advocates destruction, and she displays a moral nihilism and perverted sensualism that come together in her strikingly demonic desire to watch a child's crucifixion while eating pineapple compote. This reference to a crucified child in turn picks up the thematic core of Ivan's own rebellion: the sufferings of innocent children. Liza is undergoing a crisis of faith akin to the one Alesha has just endured, and this adds significance to their shared dream of advancing devils. Moreover, it is the temptingly demonic ideas of Ivan that have brought about this crisis in both characters. The scene between the two, which sees Liza trying to exorcise one Karamazov brother by turning to another with the words "Save me!" (XV, 25), serves to prepare the ground for Ivan's own later visit from the devil.

The demonism of Smerdiakov, and his dependency on Ivan for the moral and ideological core of that demonism, culminate in the act of parricide that he perpetrates against his natural father, Fedor Pavlovich. There is little need to rehearse again here the oft-remarked parallelism between Ivan's "murder" of a God who will not justify Himself at Ivan's insistence and Smerdiakov's murder of a hateful and neglectful parent. Indeed, there are well-developed linkages between Smerdiakov and all three Karamazov brothers, linkages designed to suggest that he is the dark heart of this diseased family, disclosing its illegitimacy by implicating all its members in the demonic act of parricide.[23] He achieves this in a variety of ways: by standing as an indictment of the father's moral failure, by exploring and articulating the potential for parricide in the sons, and by travestying and deforming their "word," that is, what they stand for, say, and do. In his performance of these complex functions, Smerdiakov occupies a zone of ambiguity in the novel. Part person and part parody, part human and part demon, part servant and part master, he is both a son and not a son to Fedor Pavlovich, and both a brother and not a brother to the sons. Fittingly, in his behavior and speech, too, he is a master of his demonic craft of evasiveness and ambiguity, and nowhere is this more apparent than in his dialogues with Ivan in books 5 and 11. The effects of Smerdiakov's speech are cumulative, and they do not emerge in full from a single illustration, particularly in English translation where the verbal mannerisms are compromised. The following extracts from his conversation with Ivan over whether the latter should leave his father to his fate by taking off for Chermashnia contain characteristically ambiguous pauses, suggestive gestures, and implied double meanings:

> "He's still asleep, sir [the father]," Smerdiakov pronounced in an unhurried way. ("You were the first to speak, not I," he seemed to say.) "I'm surprised at you, sir," he added after a pause, lowering his eyes in an affected sort of way, putting his right foot forward and playing with the toe of his patent-leather boot. [. . .] "Why, sir, don't you go to Chermashnia, sir?" Smerdiakov said suddenly, looking up and smiling familiarly. ("And you ought to understand yourself why I'm smiling, if you're an intelligent man," his screwed-up left eye somehow seemed to be saying.)
>
> "Why should I go to Chermashnia?" Ivan asked in surprise. Smerdiakov was silent again.
>
> "Why, Fedor Pavlovich himself begged you to, sir," he pronounced at last, unhurriedly and as though not thinking much himself of his reply. ("I'm fobbing you off, as it were, with a third-rate reason, just for something to say," he appeared to be saying.)
>
> "Ah, you devil! Speak more clearly, what is it you want?" Ivan finally cried out angrily. (XIV, 244)

In Russian the constant repetition of the word *sudar'* (sir) and its common contraction, the hissing sibilant "-s" added as a suffix to the preceding word, suggests an improper conspiracy below the surface forms of respect, and the particles and ambiguous "sort of"s, "somehow"s, and "as though"s that litter Smerdiakov's speech serve to enhance its demonic suggestiveness. The whole effect is comparable to that achieved by Petr Verkhovensky's orotund discourse in *The Devils*. This kind of slipperiness provokes Ivan to the desperate insistence that Smerdiakov "speak more clearly," but the latter's ambiguousness is not the result of inadequate communicative skills. On the contrary, Smerdiakov is a skilful and conscious creator of what Morson calls "verbal pollution"[24]—the manipulation and abuse of language in order to create anomaly, destabilize meaning, and generate absurdity. In his own way, Smerdiakov too is a master of the demonic narrative and a "father of the lie."

Smerdiakov's demonic identity is further confirmed, during the scene we have just analyzed, in Ivan's realization that the lackey is "sitting in his soul" and that he finds "this creature" disgusting, with his sickly eunuch's complexion and particularly demonic characteristics of hair that stands on end (held in popular belief to be a physical characteristic of the devil), epilepsy, and a tendency to screw up his *left* eye (XIV, 243). Moreover, this servant to Ivan seems to have some supernatural and hypnotic power over what his master does, to the extent that the latter is momentarily scared of his own loss of control over his movements, a fear that translates into demonic verbal tics and motifs entering his speech. But Smerdiakov's demonism has been well established even before this crucial scene. Early in the novel Rakitin had remarked on the "smell" of crime in the Karamazov household in terms that evoked Smerdiakov, "smerdit u vas" (XIV, 73), while the description of Smerdiakov's birth is richly endowed with demonic markers. We have already commented on the conjunction of his birth and the death of Grigory's "demon child," but we also note that, having somehow scaled the liminal boundary of the Karamazov garden wall, Smerdiakov's mother gives birth to him in the Karamazov bathhouse. It emerged in the introduction to this volume that the bathhouse was a favorite place to give birth among Russian peasant women, but that it was also a dangerous location where the soul of the newborn infant was believed to be susceptible to appropriation by devils. Smerdiakov's birth is, moreover, clearly intended as a travesty of that of Christ: Christ was born in a manger, Smerdiakov in a bathhouse; Christ was immaculately conceived of God and a virgin, Smerdiakov is held in local rumor to be the result of an obscene sexual union between "the devil's son" (old Karamazov) and a "righteous woman" whose naive simplicity allows her to combine sexual abuse by locals with a virginal demeanor (XIV, 92). The travesty is sustained when we recall that Christ subsequently dies for his father, while Smerdiakov murders his.

Demonic significance also attaches to the details we are given about Smerdiakov in the chapter carrying his name (book 3, chapter 6). We learn that despite the sacrifices made on his behalf by Grigory and Marfa Ignatevna, the child grew up "without any gratitude" (XIV, 114). Quite the contrary, he resents his status as a lackey, and he later admits to his girlfriend, Maria Kondratevna, that Grigory has accused him of "rebelling against his birth" (XIV, 204). The word for "birth" used here is not the more usual *rozhdenie*, but the possibly significant *rozhdestvo*, the term used to denote Christ's birth, that is, "nativity" or "Christmas." Smerdiakov's monstrous nature emerges when we also learn that as a child he liked to hang cats and then bury them with full ceremony. We shall recall this hobby later, when we discover that it was he who taught little Iliusha the trick of feeding pins enclosed in bread to the local dogs (XIV, 480). Grigory constantly refers to him as a monster, claiming: "You're not a man, you appeared out of the bathhouse slime, that's what you are" (XIV, 114). In his intellectual posturing, too, Smerdiakov betrays not only his demonism, but also its source. His attempt to discredit God's creation with a logical conundrum is perversely similar to the admittedly much more sophisticated rational underpinnings of Ivan's revolt: "God created the world on the first day, but the sun, moon and stars only on the fourth day. Where then did the light come from on the first day?" (XIV, 114). Like Ivan, Smerdiakov is holding God to account and demanding clarification of His design. He subsequently parades his fashionable Europeanism in his insistence that he hates all things Russian, a travesty of beliefs expressed elsewhere by Fedor Pavlovich and implicitly held by Ivan (XIV, 204; XV, 164). We recall from our analysis in chapter 1 that such alienation from Russian nationality is often used by Dostoevsky to signal demonism.

The three interviews that Ivan has with Smerdiakov late in the novel are significant not only for the way they bring home the extent of Ivan's responsibility for the murder of his father, but also for the way they prepare for the immediately subsequent appearance of the devil during Ivan's nightmare. As a sort of precursor of that devil, Smerdiakov is enveloped in a particularly dense aggregation of demonic motifs during these scenes. Immediately before the first interview, Ivan has parted with Alesha at the crossroads and heard from Dmitry that it must have been "the devil" who opened the door into the Karamazov house on the night of the murder (XV, 42). During the subsequent interviews, it is re-emphasized that Smerdiakov's hair stands on end, that his left eye keeps winking, that his speech is deliberately ambiguous and evasive,[25] and that Ivan cannot address him without peppering his own speech with invocatory demonic formulae. Moreover, Ivan allows himself to be drawn into what is effectively an implicit pact with the devil as he takes his leave after the first interview:

> "Goodbye. By the way, I won't say anything about the fact that you know how to feign [a fit] . . . and I advise you to keep quiet too," Ivan suddenly said for some reason.
>
> "I quite understand, sir. And if you don't let slip about that then I, sir, shan't advertise everything about the conversation we had together that time at the gate." (XV, 47)

The settings for the second and third interviews are also suggestively dark: Throughout the second, which takes place in Smerdiakov's own room, there is the constant rustle of "a terrible quantity" of cockroaches crawling about in the cracks beneath the wallpaper, while the third meeting takes place during a blizzard (XV, 50, 57). There is something almost tangibly supernatural about Smerdiakov and his effect on Ivan during this last encounter. He uncannily reiterates Alesha's earlier reassurance to Ivan: "It wasn't you who killed him." He indirectly identifies the fact that Ivan is already suffering demonic hallucinations by suggesting the presence of a third party between them. It turns out he is referring to God, but Ivan's terrified look tells us that he is expecting to see the devil who has taken to visiting him at night. Ivan is thrown into "convulsive alarm" and "insane terror" as Smerdiakov appears to be about to remove his left stocking. "You frightened me . . . with that stocking," he says, and it is difficult to resist the conclusion that he is expecting to witness the emergence of a cloven hoof (XV, 60).[26] Finally, we later learn that after this meeting Smerdiakov commits the demonic act of suicide in his room in a house liminally located "at the edge of town" (XV, 126).

The following chapter is that in which the devil finally appears in his own right not only to Ivan, but also to us, an appearance that coincides exactly with the time of Smerdiakov's death. After all the expectations sown from the start by the novel's demonic subtext and Ivan's diabolical doubles, the devil—when he does finally put in an appearance—assumes the form not of the Prince of Darkness, not of Lucifer or the demon of Romantic revolt, but rather of the petty demon spawned by Russian demonological tradition. As Ivan later confesses to Alesha: "He is not Satan, he's lying there. He's a pretender. He's just a devil, a worthless petty devil. He visits the bathhouse. Undress him and you'll surely find a tail, long and smooth like that of a great dane" (XV, 86). In this unprepossessing, homegrown incarnation, his role is to travesty Ivan's diabolical intellectual revolt and to undermine its aesthetic dimension, both of which are drawn largely from European or Europeanized sources. In this regard, he serves the same function as Svidrigailov in *Crime and Punishment*, standing as a *reductio ad absurdum* both of the hero's earlier ideology and of the forms attributed to that ideology. Just as Svidrigailov discredits Raskolnikov's demonic ideal—that of unconstrained human freedom as embodied in the figure of Napoleon—so Ivan's devil debases the heroic demonism of the Grand Inquisitor. In the course of his nightmare Ivan is compelled to recognize this: "Everything that is stupid in my nature, everything that I've already lived through and hammered out in my mind long ago, everything I've thrown aside like so much carrion—all this you present to me like something new" (XV, 82). In recognizing that this devil is merely an embodiment of his own beliefs, Ivan concludes that there is nothing to be learned from him: "You are I, I myself, only with a different mug. You say exactly what I am already thinking . . . and it is not in your power to say anything new to me!" (XV, 73).

But Ivan is wrong: this devil dialogizes Ivan's beliefs not by countering their content, but by travestying their form. In this product authored by Ivan's unconscious, rather than conscious, self, the grandeur of the Inquisitor is stripped down to a rheumatic sponger in threadbare clothes and suffering from a cold in the head, leaving Ivan to wonder: "How could my soul have begotten a lackey such as you?" The devil represents, in Bakhtin's words, "someone else's voice whispering into the ear of the hero his own words with a displaced accent."[27] He mercilessly exploits all the intellectual weaknesses, false notes, inner contradictions, and empty rhetoric contained in Ivan's earlier attempts to articulate his ideological position. Yet immediately before this encounter, Ivan had recognized the need to "express his own word boldly and decisively, and 'to justify himself to himself'" (XV, 70). This is profoundly ironic, since Ivan's "word" as spoken by the devil is shown to be not his own at all. It is littered with quotations, direct and indirect, from the whole range of Ivan's reading: from Herzen, Turgenev, Belinsky, Voltaire, Schiller, Lermontov, Gogol, Griboedov, Descartes, Goethe, and others. The devil's foppish demeanor and penchant for progressive liberalism recall Turgenev[28]; his description of himself as "a sort of phantom of life who has lost all ends and beginnings" obliquely refers to the title of Herzen's essay of 1862–63, "Ends and Beginnings"[29]; his assertion that "Je pense, donc je suis" directly quotes Descartes' well-known aphorism; and so on.[30] In this way Ivan's originality is brought into question: His word is shown, to both the reader and himself, to be second-hand rhetoric, the borrowed word of others. In this way the devil's voice fails to justify Ivan to himself. Instead of reinforcing his ideas, it embarrasses him by revealing his own falseness, lack of originality, and naivety. As Bakhtin explains, "Ivan's words and the devil's replies do not differ in content but only in tone, only in accent. But this change of accent changes their entire ultimate meaning."[31] This formal rearrangement ultimately constitutes a "new word," and that new word marks the beginning of Ivan's reassessment of himself and of the possibility of his eventual escape from the cul-de-sac of reason.

Terras has carefully traced in Ivan's nightmare a detailed and progressive parody of Ivan's demonic narrative, "The Grand Inquisitor," so that illustration of that parody here may be confined to a single example. Toward the end of their meeting the devil presents to Ivan a highly subversive recapitulation of what is clearly one of his earlier versions of "The Grand Inquisitor," a project entitled "The Geological Upheaval." This compares in importance the moment in human history when man proclaims his independence from God with the onset of a new age in the Earth's geological evolution. At that moment "people will unite to seize from life all that it has to offer, but inevitably for the sake of happiness and joy in this world alone" (XV, 83). Man will then become the "man-God," uninhibited by superstition, freed from the yoke of religion, and confident in his own moral independence. We recognize here both the dream of rational, atheistic humanism and the particular inflection Ivan has given to this ideal in "The Grand Inquisitor." But the devil's voice continues:

> In this sense "all is permitted" to man. What is more, even if this period never comes to pass, then since there is still no God and no immortality, it follows that the new man is permitted to become the man-god, even though he

may be the only one in the whole world, and of course in this new role he may with impunity leap over every moral barrier that constrained the previous slave-man, if he so wishes. There is no law for a god! Where a god stands, that is his place. Wherever I stand will become the starting point—"all is permitted" and that's all there is to it! All this is very nice; only, if you want to behave like a scoundrel why bother with the sanction of truth? But that's our modern Russian man for you: he won't be a scoundrel unless he has the sanction of truth. That's how much the truth has come to mean for him. (XV, 84)

In this cynical argument, where moral freedom is reduced to the right to behave like a scoundrel, the elevated humanist rhetoric of "The Grand Inquisitor" is shown for what it really is: a shabby and hypocritical recipe for demonic self-indulgence. At this moment in Ivan's mind his own responsibility for the murder of his father becomes clear, and the aestheticized ideal of the rebellious Inquisitor must be replaced by the hideous features of the slippery parricide, Smerdiakov.

In the planning of *The Brothers Karamazov*, the refutation of Ivan's demonic revolt was not to be entrusted solely to the oblique form of travesty. Indeed, Dostoevsky appears to have sensed that there was a danger of the devil being left with the best tunes, at least on the level of ideas, and that Ivan's terrible vision required more direct confrontation. Dostoevsky's conservative friend Pobedonostsev also recognized this in a letter to the author dated August 16, 1879, as the novel appeared in serialized form in the journal *Russian Herald*: "Your 'Grand Inquisitor' has made a very strong impression on me. Rarely have I read anything so powerful. Only I have been waiting and wondering where the refutation, rejoinder and elucidation will come from." Dostoevsky always intended to provide such a refutation of Ivan's views, as he explained in a letter to his editor Liubimov on May 10, 1879: "My hero's blasphemy will be triumphantly refuted in the next (June) installment on which I am now working with fear, trepidation and awe, for I consider my task (the rout of anarchism) to be a civic feat" (XXX/1, 64). Like Pobedonostsev, however, he recognized that it would be no straightforward matter to counter Ivan's compelling and logically impeccable rebellion against divine order if he confronted his hero on his own terms. He wrote to Pobedonostsev on August 24, 1879, revealing the extent of his reservations: "In this lies all my concern and all my unease, for I have intended this sixth book, 'A Russian Monk,' which is due on August 31, to be a reply to this entire *negative side*. Therefore, I tremble for it, wondering if it will be a *sufficient* reply. The more so since it is an indirect reply, not one which takes up point by point propositions expressed earlier (in 'The Grand Inquisitor' and before); it is therefore oblique. It presents something diametrically opposed to the worldview expressed earlier—but once again, it is not presented point by point, but as an artistic picture, so to speak. This is what worries me: will I make myself clear and will I achieve even a small part of my aim" (XXX/1, 122).

Dostoevsky thus conceived of "A Russian Monk," which is made up of extracts from the life and teachings of the elder Zosima, as an oblique response to Ivan's rebellion, as an "artistic picture." Its very indirectness helps to explain why many commentators have found it not only inadequate as a response, but also out of place despite Dostoevsky's insistence that it formed the "culminating point" of his novel (XXX/1, 105). The aim he set himself in this book was a dauntingly difficult one: to counter his own all-too-realistic depiction of contemporary demonism with an example of Christian virtue that was simultaneously iconic and mimetic. The result is a clash of Orthodox and novelistic imperatives, as the desire to *bear witness* to the superiority of Zosima's Christian wisdom over Ivan's demonic rationalism confronts the novelist's requirement to *create* a fictional world that is convincing in its verisimilitude. Comments in Dostoevsky's letters show how anxious he was to create a figure capable of affirming Christian ideals without violating the conventions of what was acceptable and believable in a nineteenth-century novel. "Like it or not," he wrote to Pobedonostsev, "artistic considerations demand that I include in the biography of my monk even the most banal aspects, in order not to offend against artistic realism" (XXX/1, 122). Earlier he had written to Liubimov explaining that "A Russian Monk" would not be a sermon but "a tale of real life," merging moral idealism and artistic truth, and thus triumphantly demonstrating "that the pure, ideal Christian is not something abstract, but is concretely real and possible before our eyes" (XXX/1, 68).

Any discussion of whether Dostoevsky succeeds in this aim, and whether the inclusion of "A Russian Monk" within *The Brothers Karamazov* is appropriate, demands consideration of both the content and the form of this book. For the non-Orthodox reader it is perhaps the content of Zosima's biography and teachings that affords most difficulties. His biography appears to offer little more than several conventional, psychologically unsubstantiated parables of spiritual rebirth, while his teachings seem to mingle restatements of Orthodox doctrine with some decidedly non-Orthodox opinions on Mother Earth veneration, paradise on earth, divine elation, the cult of tears, and mutual forgiveness and responsibility. No matter how successfully dressed up in an "artistic picture," such ideas form a wholly indigestible course for the reader whose polemical appetite has been whetted by Ivan Karamazov's arguments. Indeed, in resorting to an "artistic picture" Dostoevsky seems already to have conceded the intellectual high ground to his creature, Ivan. The problem he faced in "A Russian Monk"—and the reason he shrank from a point-by-point refutation of Ivan—was the same one he faced in the epilogue to *Crime and Punishment:* how to depict in words the ineffable mystery of faith and salvation. He recognized that he could counter Ivan's Euclidean arguments against God's order only with the "non-Euclidean" answer of Zosima's life and teachings; the analysis of doubt is countered with an image of faith; intellect is refuted through mystery and emotion. The question is, though, whether such "non-Euclidean arguments" belong in the Euclidean world of the analytical, psychological novel: for those readers most likely to have been shaken by Ivan's demonism are also the least likely to be persuaded by the icon of Zosima. The gulf between unbelief and belief remains unbridged. For the skeptical intellect the affirmations of Zosima must seem, like Raskolnikov's conversion, to be little more than what Mochulsky calls a "pious lie," the barely concealed attempt of a religious zealot to nudge his reader into God's camp.[32]

In "A Russian Monk," then, Dostoevsky's religious purpose, his professed desire to show his readers "the way to the Church," is shipwrecked on the inadequacy of the realistic novel to the task of bearing effective witness to divine grace and religious conviction. The strengths of that genre lie in ideological and psychological analysis. The affirmation of faith and representation of an ideal require something rather different, as Dostoevsky discovered in his attempts to depict the ideal of the positively good man in *The Idiot.* Instead of analysis, "A Russian Monk" offers the synthesis of a poetic image, and as such it strains against the novelistic form that contains it, appearing, as Hackel argues, to be "segregated from the narration proper."[33] Ideas elsewhere in the novel are shown to be ideas that are held, embodied, and enacted by individuals, and as such they are presented as provisional and tested in the twin crucibles of conflicting discourses and psychological dynamism. Ivan's beliefs are required to hold their own against both the views of others and the weaknesses brought into his ideological system by his own personal failings and shortcomings. While there can be little doubt that Zosima indeed holds and lives by the ideas expressed in his discourse, that discourse is static and assertive, rather than dynamic and revelatory. In the rest of the novel truth about the characters and what they represent emerges from dramatic verbal, ideological, or psychological clashes, such as the scandalous early scene in Zosima's cell, where the personalities of all present are disclosed in their reactions to the encounter between the shameless Fedor Pavlovich and the saintly Zosima, or the marvelous meeting between Alesha and Ivan as the latter reveals the extent of his rebellion. The "truth" of "A Russian Monk" is, on the contrary, presented in the form of an indigestible and unqualified tract and parable, apparently untouched by those rhetorical and psychological "glitches" that have earlier relativized and undermined Ivan's position. In Bakhtin's terms, the presentation of Zosima's beliefs is monological rather than dialogized: Neither irony nor paradox is allowed to challenge the supremacy of the elder's voice or the authority of the views he expresses:

> He who does not believe in God will not believe in God's people. But he who has faith in God's people will also behold His glory, even though he had not believed in it hitherto. Only the common people and their coming spiritual power will convert our atheists, who have torn themselves away from their native soil. (XIV, 267)

The proximity of these words to views expressed elsewhere in Dostoevsky's journalism and personal correspondence also helps to suggest that we are now in the presence not so much of Zosima, a freestanding character in a work of narrative fiction, but of an ideological mouthpiece for an author who has temporarily sacrificed fictional imperatives to Orthodox ones. Dostoevsky appears to sense this himself in several semiapologetic passages from his correspondence at this time. For example, he confides to Pobedonostsev that "A Russian Monk" has been written "for *the few*," rather than for the many to whom the novel as a whole was presumably addressed (XXX/1, 105), while he later admits to the same correspondent that Zosima's discourses are "absurd in an everyday sense, but they seem justified in another, inner sense" (XXX/1, 122).

Bakhtin described this shift from fictional to Orthodox imperatives in terms of Dostoevsky's adoption in "A Russian Monk" of "hagiographical" rather than novelistic discourse. This goes right to the heart of the matter, for the whole question of the relationship of this book to the rest of *The Brothers Karamazov* turns essentially on the question of genre. What Bakhtin terms "hagiographical discourse" (*zhitiinoe slovo*) is that discourse appropriate to the Orthodox generic tradition of the "saint's life" (*zhitie*), a medieval literary form designed, unlike the novel, to bear witness to the greatness of God's creation rather than to showcase the creation of the author. The absence of psychological conviction, vitality, and dynamism that distinguishes Zosima's discourse from the way ideas are presented elsewhere in the novel is also explicable in these terms, in that what Morson calls a "psychological reading" of ideas—so necessary to the reading of a novel—is inappropriate to genres such as lives of saints or religious narratives of conversion:

> There are, in other words, works in which one will go wrong to "separate . . . ideas from those characters who carry the ideas" and those in which one will go wrong if one does *not* separate them. In novels or novelistic short stories one must understand ideas as *someone's* ideas; in utopias, saints' lives, certain philosophical parables (such as Voltaire's), or medieval dream-visions, one must not. *The question, in short, is one of genre.*[34]

To put matters at their simplest, if Dostoevsky is to get away with the "absurdity" of Zosima's discourse, he needs to leave behind the novelistic genre, with its insistence on a psychological reading, and take refuge in one more supportive of his Orthodox imperatives. We see this happening before our eyes in "A Russian Monk." Both Dostoevsky as novelist and his fictional narrator seem at first to drop out of the picture altogether in this book, as though they sense that they have no place here. Distance is created by the interposition of thick layers of narrative insulation between real author and the incidents described. Apart from the sudden introduction of an entirely different narrative form in the recreation of the traditional genre of the saint's life, a recreation that draws freely on the conventions of earlier models, we now find authorial responsibility handed over to someone else— Alesha Karamazov.

I say that Dostoevsky and his narrator *seem* to drop out of the picture because in reality a deception is being practiced here. For a start, although we are told that Alesha painstakingly transcribes from memory the words of Zosima himself, the narrator feels compelled to point out that Alesha's role is much more than that of mere scribe or chronicler: It is truly *authorial*. The young novice avails himself of such narrative stratagems as the disruption of chronological sequence, the reporting of speech out of context, and the weaving of uninterrupted narrative out of fragmentary recollections in order to tell Zosima's life as if it were "a story" (*povest'*) (XIV, 260). He makes full use of the paraphernalia of the saint's life, especially in the Church Slavonic titles given to his manuscript and its individual sections, as well as in his assumption of biblical diction, but he is surprisingly not averse to resorting also to the rhetorical devices of the novelist in order to create anticipation, suspense, and uncertainty. Indeed, in places there are enough "suddenlys," "unexpectedlys," and "somehows" to satisfy the taste of the most enthusiastic reader of Ann Radcliffe.[35] The act of bearing impartial witness in the chronicled life of a saint is compromised by devices borrowed from the demonic form of the novel. Moreover, Alesha's *zhitie* makes use of the inserted narratives of others: Zosima tells the story of his past and the spiritual rebirth of his brother Markel; the Mysterious Visitor recounts his own criminal past, as well as his path to enlightenment and contrition. We cannot help but feel that the real purpose of these various narrative layers is to allow Dostoevsky the opportunity to deny responsibility and appear to slip away unnoticed from the scene of that most heinous of the novelist's crimes—direct and overt moral idealism and didacticism.

Further doubt is cast on Alesha's trustworthiness as a true and impartial monk-chronicler of the events of Zosima's life and the content of his discourses when it becomes clear that *someone* is manipulating the account of those events and discourses in order to set up implicit situation, character, and thematic rhymes with incidents elsewhere in the novel, thus creating an impression of architectural coherence and integrity by implying that "A Russian Monk" is somehow bound to the rest of *The Brothers Karamazov.* These "rhymes," or echoes, are persistent enough to merit further exploration.

Alesha's "manuscript" is divided into two main sections, occupying chapters 2 and 3 of "A Russian Monk." Chapter 2 deals with Zosima's biography, chapter 3 with his teachings. Each of these chapters is in turn subdivided, and each of the subdivisions shows itself to be particularly relevant to the experience of one of the Karamazov brothers, although each also contains material that bears on the other brothers too. The first subdivision of chapter 2 is designed primarily to evoke Alesha and his experience. In it Zosima describes the life, religious transfiguration, and early death of his elder brother Markel, of whom, he remarks, Alesha is reminiscent. As is soon to be the case with Alesha after Zosima's death, Markel is rescued from the abyss of unbelief by means of an ecstatic, revelatory experience of the beauty and harmony of God's universe, and, like Alesha in his dealings with Snegirev, Markel also flirts with the heresy of utopianism—the belief that if we only wished it enough, paradise could be established on earth. Moreover, he expresses his sense of paradise and universal harmony in the same image Alesha associates with memories of his mother: the slanting rays of the setting sun, one of Dostoevsky's favorite and most recurrent images.[36] Markel's sense of paradise also aligns him with Dmitry, for he too is acutely aware of how his own imperfect existence dishonors the glory of God's creation. Furthermore, his own past history—he was once a freethinking rebel whose logic predisposed him against creation—clearly echoes Ivan's.

Ivan, though, is most clearly evoked in the second subdivision of chapter 2. Here Zosima's profession of admiration for the biblical story of Job provides a barely concealed counterpoint to Ivan's rebellion against divine justice. Job's faith withstands the tests imposed by God: the loss of his wealth, cattle, and children. The fact that the meaning of these tests remains unclear increases the greatness of the story, according to Zosima: "But it is great just because there is a mystery here: Eternal truth and its transient earthly image are brought together here. Before earthly justice the act of eternal justice is accomplished" (XIV, 265). Unlike Ivan, Job's love of God and creation is more important than his understanding of them, and the fact that his "tests" turn on the same pivot as Ivan's rebellion—the sufferings of innocent children, in Job's case his own—makes the linkage clearer, as does the echo of Ivan's article on ecclesiastical courts contained in Zosima's words. Ivan's dilemma, and Alesha's earlier advice that he should love life regardless of reason, are also to be discerned in Zosima's observation: "Every blade of grass, every tiny insect, ant, golden bee, all of them know so wondrously their path, without possessing reason" (XIV, 267).

The third subdivision of chapter 2, where Zosima recounts his experiences as an army officer, completes the symmetry by providing an oblique commentary on the life of Dmitry. Zosima's description of his younger self as a reckless, "almost savage creature," his predilection for drunkenness, debauchery, and dashing behavior, his inheritance of a sum of money, and his determination to plunge without restraint into the pleasures of life, all recall Dmitry. The young Zosima's love of books echoes Dmitry's intoxication with poetry, and both share a Schilleresque love of beauty. When Zosima describes his attachment to "a young and beautiful girl, intelligent and worthy, of noble and pure character, the daughter of a highly respected family," who is in fact in love with another, we see the outlines of Dmitry's relationship with Katerina Ivanovna. The young Zosima's assault on his servant Afanasy matches Dmitry's attack on Grigory, and when he subsequently seeks Afanasy's forgiveness by bowing to the ground before him, his chronologically later bow before Dmitry is grotesquely anticipated. Zosima's "conversion," as he prepares to shed blood in a duel, also parallels Dmitry's: Just as the latter is prevented by a feeling of shame and disgrace from carrying out the murder of his father, so Zosima is unable to go through with his duel. The beauty of the morning, the feeling that he alone impairs that beauty, and a sudden realization that every man is responsible for others, all accompany Zosima's change of heart, just as they do Dmitry's.

These variations on situations elsewhere in the novel continue in the fourth and final subdivision of Zosima's biography, the tale of the mysterious visitor who has murdered the woman he loved and who eventually confesses to the crime some fourteen years later. Not only does this tale explore such themes as those of guilt, isolation, the nature of brotherhood, and mutual responsibility—themes central to the novel as a whole—but in its description of the murder and its aftermath it echoes details from the Dmitry plot. The victim, to whom the mystery man is passionately drawn, refuses to marry him because she is pledged to another, an officer on active duty whom she expects to return soon. These details compare with Dmitry's passion for Grushenka and her faithfulness to her Pole. After the crime the true murderer escapes suspicion, but an innocent servant is apprehended, intoxicated, and covered in blood. This inverts Dmitry's eventual fate, when he is arrested though innocent, while the guilty servant Smerdiakov escapes suspicion. The fate of Ivan is also anticipated in the mysterious visitor's tale: He first refuses to confess and submit to God's justice on the grounds that it would involve the suffering of innocent children, those of his own family who would share his disgrace. Also like Ivan, he eventually tries to confess publicly to his crime and is not believed, whereupon he succumbs to brain fever and his actions are ascribed to mental breakdown.

The second part of Alesha's manuscript, consisting of Zosima's discourses on monasticism, brotherhood, love, equality, prayer, humility, mercy, judgment, and hell, also seeks to legitimate itself artistically by striking in the reader chords of recognition of events, themes, and characters in the novel as a whole. Thus Zosima's advocacy of the contemplative isolation of the monastic way of life, which is a form of worship of God's creation, is offered as a counterpoint to the novel's preoccupation with the godless, rebellious, and demonic isolation of contemporary man. His insistence that man's quest for freedom without God must lead to slavery affords an answer to Ivan's Inquisitor, as does his belief that man must love his brother even in his weakness and sinfulness. Indeed, despite Dostoevsky's protestations to the contrary, there are moments when Zosima's discourses appear to approach point-by-point refutation of the arguments consituting Ivan's rebellion. We hear a travesty of Ivan's voice in Zosima's protest against the exploitation of the young in factories: "There must be no more of this, monks, there must be no more torturing of children" (XIV, 286). We see Ivan also in Zosima's characterization of the educated classes: "Following science, they wish to erect a just life on the basis of their reason alone, but no longer with Christ as before, and they have already proclaimed that there is no such thing as crime, no such thing as sin. And they are right in their way, for if you don't have God then how can you have crime?" (XIV, 286). The novel's main theme of the illegitimacy of the Karamazov family, culminating in the act of parricide, is suggested in Zosima's words about servants: "Why should my servant not be like a relative of mine, so that I accept him finally into my family and rejoice at this?" (XIV, 288). Here we see not only an implied comment on Smerdiakov's position as the excluded bastard son through whom the Karamazov poisons seep, but we also sense a reference to Dmitry's relationship with Grigory. There are many more examples of such recapitulation in Zosima's discourses, far too many to explore fully here, but many have been identified in Terras's commentary.[37]

Who is responsible for such situation rhymes and the spurious sense of artistic legitimacy they confer on "A Russian Monk"? The fictional narrator has largely left the scene after his introductory preamble to this book, returning only at the conclusion of Alesha's narrative to recapitulate its qualities. Zosima himself is too unaware of the details of Karamazov family life to have contrived these rhymes himself, while Alesha, although party to many of those details, has no identifiable motive for the introduction of such devices. This leaves the author who, like all good suspects, has opportunity, means (in the form of appropriately detailed and omniscient knowledge), and pressing motives for trying to persuade us that his idealized Russian monk is properly integrated into his narrative. But "A Russian Monk" never really belongs. It remains a cuckoo in the nest, a piece of artistic sleight-of-hand, testifying to Dostoevsky's belief in an overriding divine order without ever becoming a satisfactory answer to the demonism posed by the rest of the novel. It is a contrived and compromised authorial device, designed to shoehorn one narrative form into a generically incompatible one. It is too loaded with the deceptions, deceits, and devices of secular narrative fiction to win our trust as a *vita,* and it sets out too emphatically to bear witness to sit comfortably in a nineteenth-century realist novel. In his attempts thus to square the circle, to pull the wool over the eyes of his readership, and to use the "demonic" form of the modern novel in the service of the Lord, it is perhaps Dostoevsky himself who emerges as the true "father of the lie" in *The Brothers Karamazov.*

The Kingdom of Devils

THE PURPOSES of the present volume have been two-fold: first, to show how demonic markers derived from a variety of cultural sources pollute the narrative terrain of Dostoevsky's major fiction, carried either through the voices of particular characters or through those of the narrator or implied author; and, second, to analyze how such markers function as a rhetoric through which that fiction mediates its most pressing ideological and artistic concerns. Our aim has not been to explore the nature or extent of Dostoevsky's own supernatural beliefs nor to evaluate the degree to which demonism occupied space in his own philosophical system. Dostoevsky's core Christian beliefs, and particularly his well-known meditation on the possibility of resurrection and an afterlife—written in the immediate wake of his first wife's death in 1864—clearly suggest his profound belief in "another world" beyond the physical (XX, 172–75).[1] But Dostoevskian metaphysics, as we remarked near the start of our study, represent a separate and extremely rich field of inquiry, one to which much critical attention has been and continues to be paid.[2] Yet while recognizing that this field lies beyond the scope of the present volume, we should perhaps not conclude our analysis of the demonic in Dostoevsky without paying some attention to the one occasion when the writer appears to have addressed directly his attitude to the "other world" of devils and spirits. I say "appears to have addressed directly," for the occasion in question is an entry in *The Diary of a Writer* for January 1876, and the voice we hear is that of the authorial persona assumed in that remarkable work, a voice contaminated by sly irony and combative polemicism and one that we cannot necessarily afford to take at face value.

The entry in question is entitled "Spiritualism. Something about Devils. The Extraordinary Cunning of Devils, that is if they really are Devils," and it appears to be almost an afterthought to the January issue, as Dostoevsky contemplates the various topics—the Balkan war, literature, the Decembrists—that he has failed to address and that will have to be deferred. Instead of these serious matters, Dostoevsky decides to conclude the January 1876 issue with discussion of something much more "cheerful"—the current Russian enthusiasm for spiritualism and interest in the other world. He cites as an example of this phenomenon the story related to him by V. S. Solovev of a young man at a Petersburg séance whose chair apparently galloped across the room; and he also refers to other contemporary instances of paranormal activity, such as the supernatural infestation of a provincial lady's house, and letters seemingly dictated to mediums in which the long-dead Gogol warns of the dangers of stirring up devils: "If at night you start to be troubled by nervous insomnia, don't become irritated [*ne zlis*'], but pray, for this is devils at work; cross yourself over your nightshirt and make a prayer" (XXII, 32).

In describing such incidents, Dostoevsky's tone is mock serious and archly ironic, but it is clear nevertheless that he is struck by the willingness of others to take seriously such manifestations of the unclean force, including warnings from churchmen of the dangers of engaging with the supernatural even in the spirit of proper scientific inquiry. As he wrote to N. P. Vagner on December 21, 1875: "In the end, I am decidedly unable to look upon spiritualism with equanimity" (XXIX/2, 68). As the editors of the Academy edition of Dostoevsky's works observe, interest in spiritualism and the supernatural had begun to spread in Russia from the early 1870s, encouraged by the activities of such advocates as A. N. Aksakov, A. M. Butlerov, and N. P. Vagner, who had organized a series of séances in the capital (XXII, 334). Even Tsar Alexander II had permitted the staging of séances in the Winter Palace and, following this imperial example, high society quickly adopted spiritualism as a new form of amusement. So firm a hold did it take that in 1875 the renowned chemist D. I. Mendeleev argued for the establishment of an official scientific Commission of Inquiry, with a view to testing the claims of the spiritualists. After consultation with leading advocates of spiritualism, the Commission, acting under the auspices of the Physical Society, invited practitioners and mediums to organized and controlled séances, and in December 1875 Mendeleev presented his preliminary findings in a public lecture. The experiments continued and were still in progress at the time of Dostoevsky's entry in the *Diary of a Writer*. It is clear from Dostoevsky's personal library and correspondence that he took a great interest in the activities of both the spiritualists and the Commission, the progress of which he followed in the press. He also corresponded with N. P. Vagner, meeting him personally in the summer of 1875, and apparently attended séances himself (see XXII, 335). Moreover, his interest is reflected in an ironic mention of spiritualism in *A Raw Youth,* on which he was working at the time (XIII, 424–25).

Yet, despite this interest in spiritualism and in the fact that "a terrible number of people who do not believe in God believe, however, in the devil, happily and readily," Dostoevsky finds himself admitting: "My whole problem is that there is no way I can bring myself to believe in devils myself."

This in turn poses a problem for him, for he reveals that the purpose of the January 1876 *Diary* entry is to develop his own "very clear and astonishing" theory about spiritualism, but a theory that is based entirely on the existence of devils: "Without them the whole of my theory collapses of itself" (XXII, 33). For the sake of this theory, therefore, the Dostoevsky of the *Diary* is prepared to concede—for the moment at least—the existence of spirits, even arguing that such spirits can only be devils, agents of the unclean force. He is even prepared to defend them from the charges of those opponents of spiritualism who claim that the spirits summoned at séances always turn out to be "stupid," incapable of achieving more than some minor rearrangement of furniture, giving silly answers to questions posed, and communicating in ungrammatical nonsense. They reveal nothing of the mysterious other world they inhabit, nor do they seek to win over followers by revealing what is beyond the current state of human knowledge or by showering man with revelations and discoveries that would allow him to overcome the material deprivations imposed by his current, imperfect understanding of his environment. Surely such largesse would quickly win over doubters; men would "eat, drink and be merry"; and the voice of mankind would be raised in a "common hymn": "Who can be likened unto this beast? Praise him, for he brings us fire from heaven!"

But, as Dostoevsky points out, this refusal of devils to pursue the ideal of material plenty, as advanced by the Russian socialists, or to perform the miracle of "stones turned into bread," as advocated by the Grand Inquisitor, is in fact a measure of their intelligence and insight into human nature. For mankind would quickly tire of such a life of material blessings, and, rather than entering a new era of sublime thoughts, righteousness, and universal concerns, would sink instead into despair:

> People would suddenly see that they had no more life left, that they had no freedom of spirit, no will or personality, that someone had stolen all this from them; they would see that their human image had disappeared and that the brutish image of a slave had emerged, the image of a beast, with the one difference that the beast does not know that it is a beast, whereas a human would realize that he has become a beast. And mankind would begin to decay; people would be covered in sores and would start to bite their tongues in torment, seeing that their lives had been taken away for the sake of bread, for the sake of "stones turned into bread." (XXII, 34)

Like the Underground Man, the devils have recognized that "happiness lies not in happiness, but only in the attempt to achieve it." The boredom that would follow the final realization of material sufficiency, when man had sated himself on earthly bread but was starved of the bread of heaven, would lead inevitably to despondency and mass suicide: "And then, perhaps, those who remained would cry out to God: 'Thou art right, O Lord; man does not live by bread alone!' Then they would rise up against the devils and abandon sorcery. . . . Oh, God would never have inflicted such torments on mankind! And the kingdom of devils would collapse!" (XXII, 34). But the devils are profound politicians, and they are not about to commit such a "grave political mistake." They have recognized that the key to the establishment of "the kingdom of devils" is to exploit discord and strife in human affairs. Such discord (*razdor*) began with Adam's prioritization of his own will over that of God, an act that alienated him from the rest of creation; it then continued through the turbulent history of human strife and bloodshed, through the processes of religious schism and fragmentation of belief, and it continued to manifest itself in an infinite variety of ways even in Dostoevsky's day, not least in the disagreements provoked by the emergence of spiritualism. It is a measure of the political cunning of devils that they are prepared to exploit even disagreements over the question of whether or not devils or spirits actually exist in order to "divide and rule." Let the official Commission of Inquiry find in favor of deception and trickery, let the believers in spiritualism be shamed and scorned, let offense be taken all round, let the desire for revenge creep like poison into the hearts of both sides, let intolerance and persecution "spread in an instant, like burning kerosene, and ignite everything" (XXII, 36)—in these ways discord will grow, and "in the final analysis the devils will take what is theirs, and they will crush humanity like a fly" (XXII, 35).

Dostoevsky ends his entry with the unsurprising revelation that he has been "joking and having a laugh from the first word to the last." But although the universal discord anticipated in the outcome of the debate over spiritualism, charted on a larger scale through the wider preoccupations of the *Diary of a Writer,* and exemplified in the characters and events of his major fiction, may not for Dostoevsky have been literally the work of those devils in whom he could not bring himself to believe, it was nevertheless a monumental evil threatening the human race, one fully deserving of the demonic rhetoric that accompanied its depiction in the works we have here considered.

Notes

INTRODUCTION

1. For more on the narrative irony of *Poor Folk* see my "Dostoevskii and Literature: Metafictional Strategies in the Works of the 1840s," in *The Cambridge Companion to Dostoevskii,* ed. W. J. Leatherbarrow (Cambridge: Cambridge University Press, 2002), pp. 47–65.

2. See, for example, N. K. Piksanov, "Dostoevskii i fol'klor," *Sovetskaia etnografiia,* nos. 1–2 (1934): 152–80, and Faith Wigzell, "Dostoevskii and the Russian Folk Heritage," in Leatherbarrow, *Cambridge Companion to Dostoevskii,* pp. 21–46.

3. A. M. Dostoevskii, *Vospominaniia Andreia Mikhailovicha Dostoevskogo* (Leningrad: Izd. pisatelei v Leningrade, 1930), pp. 44–45.

4. Joseph Frank, *Dostoevsky: The Seeds of Revolt, 1821–1849* (London: Robson Books, 1977), p. 11.

5. Wigzell, "Dostoevskii and the Russian Folk Heritage," p. 21.

6. For a recent study of Gogol's treatment of the demonic see Christopher Putney, *Russian Devils and Diabolic Conditionality in Nikolai Gogol's "Evenings on a Farm near Dikanka."* Middlebury Studies in Russian Language and Literature, 15 (New York: Peter Lang, 1999).

7. Faith Wigzell, "The Russian Folk Devil and His Literary Reflections," in *Russian Literature and its Demons,* ed. Pamela Davidson (New York and Oxford: Berghahn Books, 2000), p. 59.

8. Simon Franklin, "Nostalgia for Hell: Russian Literary Demonism and Orthodox Tradition," in Davidson, *Russian Literature and its Demons,* p. 35

9. Linda J. Ivanits, *Russian Folk Belief* (Armonk, New York, and London: M. E. Sharpe, 1989), p. 124.

10. Ibid., p. 41.

11. Iu. M. Lotman and B. A. Uspenskii, "The Role of Dual Models in the Dynamics of Russian Culture (Up to the End of the Eighteenth Century)," in Lotman, Iu., and B. A. Uspenskii, *The Semiotics of Russian Culture,* ed. Ann Shukman (Ann Arbor: Department of Slavic Languages and Literatures, University of Michigan, 1984), p. 4.

12. See, for instance, Wigzell, "Dostoevskii and the Russian Folk Tradition," p. 25.

13. Consider, for example, the popular belief that each individual has his or her own devil at the left shoulder and an angel at the right (Ivanits, *Russian Folk Belief*, p. 47) and the requirement in popular superstition to face east when casting good spells, for the west was the devil's side, possibly because it appeared to the left on maps with north at the top (see W. F. Ryan, *The Bathhouse at Midnight: An Historical Survey of Magic in Russia* [University Park, Penn.: Pennsylvania University Press, 1999], p. 54).

14. Ryan, *The Bathhouse at Midnight*, p. 56.

15. See Ivanits, *Russian Folk Belief* for a full treatment of such spirits. I have drawn much of the detail that follows from Ivanits's account.

16. Lotman and Uspenskii, "The Role of Dual Models," p. 9.

17. Ibid., p. 30, note 20.

18. Ivanits, *Russian Folk Belief*, p. 52.

19. Ibid., p. 38.

20. See, for example, E. Loginovskaia, "Motiv demonizma v *Besakh* Dostoevskogo. Tekstovye i vnetekstovye koordinaty," *Scando-Slavica* 26 (1980): 35–36.

21. Wigzell, "The Russian Folk Devil and his Literary Reflections," p. 64. See also Ivanits, *Russian Folk Belief*, p. 39.

22. Felix J. Oinas, *Essays on Russian Folklore and Mythology* (Columbus: Slavica, 1985), p. 98. Not all would concur with Oinas's etymology.

23. Ivanits, *Russian Folk Belief*, pp. 40, 44.

24. Simon Franklin, "Nostalgia for Hell," p. 38.

25. Ryan, *The Bathhouse at Midnight*, p. 54.

26. Ivanits, *Russian Folk Belief*, p. 105.

27. Ryan, *The Bathhouse at Midnight*, p. 46. Interestingly, Ryan excludes dusk from his list of especially dangerous liminal times, whereas the Russian scholar L. N. Vinogradova argues that dusk was regarded as a particularly demonic time. See her "Kalendarnye perekhody nechistoi sily vo vremeni i prostranstve," in *Kontsept dvizheniia v iazyke i kul'ture*, ed. T. A. Agapkina (Moscow: Indrik, 1996), pp. 166–67.

28. M. Bakhtin, "Forms of Time and Chronotope in the Novel," in *The Dialogic Imagination: Four Essays by M. M. Bakhtin*, ed. M. Holquist (Austin: University of Texas Press, 1992), p. 250.

29. Bakhtin, *Problems of Dostoevsky's Poetics*, ed. and trans. Caryl Emerson (Manchester: Manchester University Press, 1984), p. 170.

30. Bakhtin, *Rabelais and His World*, trans. Hélène Iswolsky (Bloomington: Indiana University Press, 1984), p. 7.

31. Ibid., pp. 39–40.

32. Ryan, *The Bathhouse at Midnight*, p. 39. Yuletide (a liminal time)

was the favorite time for the traditional folk practice of "mumming." Apart from the wearing of masks, the mummers also engaged in other potentially demonic behavior, such as cross-dressing, dressing up as animals, wearing clothes upside down or inside out (inversion), and parodying traditional Church rites (Ibid., p. 46).

33. Bakhtin, *Problems of Dostoevsky's Poetics,* p. 107.

34. Lotman and Uspenskii, "New Aspects in the Study of Early Russian Culture," in Lotman, Iu., and B. A. Uspenskii, *The Semiotics of Russian Culture,* ed. Ann Shukman (Ann Arbor: Department of Slavic Languages and Literature, University of Michigan, 1984), p. 40.

35. See Ivanits, *Russian Folk Belief,* pp. 106–9. For a recent study of *klikushestvo,* including an analysis of its treatment in Dostoevsky, see Christine D. Worobec, *Possessed: Women, Witches, and Demons in Imperial Russia* (DeKalb, Ill.: Northern Illinois University Press, 2001).

36. Linda J. Ivanits, "Folk Beliefs about the 'Unclean Force' in Dostoevskij's *The Brothers Karamazov,*" in *New Perspectives on Nineteenth-Century Russian Prose,* ed. George J. Gutsche and Lauren G. Leighton (Columbus: Slavica, 1982), p. 137.

37. See XXII, 246; and XXIV, 75, 82, 102, 133.

38. See Linda J. Ivanits, "Suicide and Folk Beliefs in Dostoevsky's *Crime and Punishment,*" in *The Golden Age of Russian Literature and Thought,* ed. D. Offord (London: St. Martin's Press, 1992), p. 139, and Oinas, *Essays on Russian Folklore and Mythology,* p. 99.

39. See the essay "Heretics as Vampires and Demons in Russia," in Oinas, *Essays on Russian Folklore and Mythology,* pp. 121–30.

40. Ryan, *The Bathhouse at Midnight,* p. 40.

41. On the cult of earth worship and its resonance in Dostoevsky's work see, for example, Wigzell, "Dostoevskii and the Russian Folk Heritage," pp. 28–32. More generally on Dostoevsky and religious heresy—in particular, Russian sectarianism—see Richard Peace, *Dostoyevsky: An Examination of the Major Novels* (Cambridge: Cambridge University Press, 1971), passim.

42. Lotman and Uspenskii, "The Role of Dual Models," p. 6.

43. Ibid., p. 10.

44. Franklin, "Nostalgia for Hell," p. 32. Putney, *Russian Devils and Diabolic Conditionality* offers a useful introductory survey (pp. 1–71) of the evolution of views of the devil in Christian tradition, as well as of the devil's subsequent depiction in Russian medieval literature and folklore.

45. Ibid., p. 34.

46. Ibid., p. 33.

47. Ibid., p. 52.

48. Ibid., p. 35.

49. Ibid., p. 33.

50. Valentin Boss, *Milton and the Rise of Russian Satanism* (Toronto: University of Toronto Press, 1991), p. xxii.

51. Bakhtin, *Rabelais and His World*, pp. 40–41.

52. Boss, *Milton and the Rise of Russian Satanism*, p. xxiii.

53. See Boss, *Milton and the Rise of Russian Satanism*, pp. 85, 136, and 159.

54. Ibid., p. 85.

55. Adam Weiner, *By Authors Possessed: The Demonic Novel in Russia* (Evanston: Northwestern University Press, 1998), p. 50.

56. Boss, *Milton and the Rise of Russian Satanism*, p. xxii.

57. The tendency of nineteenth-century Russian literature to "internalize" or "personalize" the demonic is a central theme of Julian W. Connolly's *The Intimate Stranger: Meetings with the Devil in Nineteenth-Century Russian Literature* (New York: Peter Lang, Middlebury Studies in Russian Language and Literature, 26, 2001). Connolly's study, which appeared after this volume was completed, offers analyses of the demonic in *The Devils* and *The Brothers Karamazov*.

58. M. Iu. Lermontov, *Polnoe sobranie sochinenii* (Moscow-Leningrad: Academia, 1937), vol. 5, p. 306.

59. Robert Louis Jackson, *Dostoevsky's Quest for Form: A Study of His Philosophy of Art* (New Haven and London: Yale University Press, 1966), p. 44.

60. Ibid., p. xi.

61. Peace, *Dostoyevsky*, p. 173.

62. Jackson, *Dostoevsky's Quest for Form*, p. 41.

63. O. Miller and N. N. Strakhov, *Biografiia, pis'ma i zametki iz zapisnoi knizhki F. M. Dostoevskogo* (St. Petersburg: A. G. Dostoevskaia, 1883), p. 372.

64. Weiner, *By Authors Possessed*, p. 2.

65. Ibid., pp. 14–20 and passim; Pamela Davidson, "Divine Service or Idol Worship? Russian Views of Art as Demonic," in Davidson, *Russian Literature and its Demons*, pp. 125–64.

66. James Billington, *The Icon and the Axe: An Interpretive History of Russian Culture* (New York: Vintage Books, 1970).

67. Weiner, *By Authors Possessed*, p. 39.

68. Davidson, *Russian Literature and its Demons*, p. 19.

69. Weiner, *By Authors Possessed*, p. 42.

70. Davidson, *Russian Literature and its Demons*, p. 141; Weiner, *By Authors Possessed*, p. 40.

71. Weiner, *By Authors Possessed*, p. 9.

72. Ibid., p. 18.

73. Ibid., p. 9.

74. Cited in Weiner, *By Authors Possessed,* p. 15.

75. For an excellent recent analysis of G-v's ambiguous narrative and a concise review of critical opinion on the subject, see Malcolm V. Jones, "The Narrator and Narrative Technique in Dostoevsky's *The Devils,*" in *Dostoevsky's* The Devils*: A Critical Companion,* ed. W. J. Leatherbarrow (Evanston: Northwestern University Press, 1999), pp. 100–18.

76. Weiner, *By Authors Possessed,* pp. 114–15 and passim.

77. Ibid., p. 95.

CHAPTER ONE

1. Recent examples include Liza Knapp, *The Annihilation of Inertia: Dostoevsky and Metaphysics,* Studies in Russian Literature and Theory (Evanston, Ill.: Northwestern University Press, 1996); Linda Kraeger and Joe Barnhart, *Dostoevsky on Evil and Atonement: The Ontology of Personalism in his Major Fiction* (Lewiston, N.Y.: Edwin Mellen Press, 1992).

2. Dostoevsky's views of the Russian people and their embodiment of Orthodox spirituality and Russian nationality in the face of the Westernization that had turned the educated classes from the true path, and of the need for those educated Russians to rediscover the native principles of Russian culture, are ideas of central importance for an informed reading of Dostoevsky's art, and they have been extensively treated in the critical literature. See, for example, Bruce K. Ward, *Dostoyevsky's Critique of the West: The Quest for the Earthly Paradise* (Waterloo, Ontario: Wilfried Laurier University Press, 1986); and Wayne C. Dowler, *Dostoevsky, Grigor'ev, and Native Soil Conservatism* (Toronto: Toronto University Press, 1982).

3. Robert Louis Jackson, *The Art of Dostoevsky: Deliriums and Nocturnes* (Princeton: Princeton University Press, 1981), p. xi and elsewhere.

4. A. I. Herzen, "Novaia faza v russkoi literature" in *Polnoe sobranie sochinenii v 30-i tomakh* (Moscow: Izd. Akademiia nauk, 1954–66), vol. 18, p. 219.

5. Comparisons between *Notes from the House of the Dead* and Dante's *Inferno* began with several of Dostoevsky's contemporaries, most notably Herzen and Turgenev. See Jackson, *The Art of Dostoevsky,* p. 353, note 9.

6. Konstantin Mochulsky, *Dostoevsky: His Life and Work,* trans. Michael Minihan (Princeton: Princeton University Press, 1967), p. 185.

7. Jackson, *The Art of Dostoevsky,* p. 9.

8. Ibid., p. 6.

9. Herzen, *PSS,* vol. 18, p. 219.

10. Jackson, *The Art of Dostoevsky,* p. 36.

11. This notebook has survived. See IV, 235–48.

12. Herzen, *PSS,* vol. 18, p. 219.

13. Such instances of anti-Semitism are an unpleasant but persistent fea-

ture of Dostoevsky's writings; see David Goldstein, *Dostoevsky and the Jews* (Austin and London: Texas University Press, 1981). Dostoevsky exploits the demonic significance ascribed to the Jewish race again in the scene of Svidrigailov's suicide in *Crime and Punishment*; see chapter 3 of this study.

14. Jackson, *The Art of Dostoevsky,* pp. 212–15.

15. Ibid., p. 14.

16. Ibid., p. 15.

17. Ibid., pp. 152–53.

18. Information given by the editors of the Academy edition of Dostoevsky's works (see V, 399).

19. Jackson, *The Art of Dostoevsky,* p. 209.

20. Ibid., p. 210.

21. In *The Idiot* the character Lebedev explicitly demonizes the railway network by identifying it with the star of wormwood cited in Revelation.

22. Jackson, *The Art of Dostoevsky,* p. 219 and passim.

23. The phrase "everything is permitted" as used here suggests the affinity between *The Gambler* and *The Brothers Karamazov*, where it is attributed to Ivan Karamazov and expresses a belief identical to Aleksei's that in a universe where God is not acknowledged moral standards are impossible and the individual is responsible for his own actions.

24. Jackson, *The Art of Dostoevsky,* p. 215.

25. Ibid., p. 211.

26. Ibid., p. 234.

27. Mochulsky, *Dostoevsky: His Life and Work,* p. 320.

28. See *Dostoevskii and Britain,* ed. W. J. Leatherbarrow (Oxford and Providence: Berg, 1995), pp. 3–6.

29. M. Iu. Lermontov, *Polnoe sobranie sochinenii* (Moscow-Leningrad: Academia, 1937), vol. 5, p. 248.

30. I. Kireevskii, *Izbrannye stat'i* (Moscow: Sovremennik, 1984), p. 201. The quotation is from Kireevsky's essay "On the Principles of Russian Culture and its Relation to European Culture."

31. A. D. Nuttall, *Dostoevsky's "Crime and Punishment": Murder as Philosophic Experiment* (Sussex: Sussex University Press, 1978), p. 22.

32. J. M. Holquist, *Dostoevsky and the Novel* (Princeton: Princeton University Press, 1977), p. 64.

33. Malcolm V. Jones, *Dostoyevsky after Bakhtin: Readings in Dostoyevsky's Fantastic Realism* (Cambridge: Cambridge University Press, 1990), pp. 66–67.

34. Weiner, *By Authors Possessed,* p. 101.

35. Jones, *Dostoyevsky after Bakhtin,* p. 60.

36. Bakhtin, *Problems of Dostoevsky's Poetics,* p. 52.

37. Knapp, *The Annihilation of Inertia,* p. 41. The metronome passage may be found in XXIV, 35.

38. Jackson, *The Art of Dostoevsky,* pp. 241–42.

39. Ibid., pp. 237–38.

40. A. L. Bem, "*Faust* v tvorchestve Dostoevskogo," in ed. A. L. Bem, *O Dostoevském: Sborník statí a materiálu* (Prague: Edice slovanské knihovny, 1972), pp. 183–220. See also Jackson, *The Art of Dostoevsky,* pp. 252–56.

41. A point made by the editors of the Academy edition of Dostoevsky's works, who also see in these words a reference to Pushkin's Silvio (XXIV, 386).

42. Jackson, *The Art of Dostoevsky,* p. 252. I can find no evidence that *chertochki* has been used as a diminutive of *chert,* but this does not necessarily weaken Jackson's point in that it does contain the morpheme "chert" and would subliminally evoke the notion of devils.

43. Christopher Pike, "Dostoevsky's 'Dream of a Ridiculous Man': Seeing is Believing," in *The Structural Analysis of Russian Narrative Fiction,* ed. J. Andrew and C. Pike (Keele: Essays in Poetics, 1984), p. 27.

44. Edward Wasiolek, *Dostoevsky: The Major Fiction* (Cambridge, Mass.: MIT Press, 1964), p. 145.

45. Gary Saul Morson, *The Boundaries of Genre: Dostoevsky's "Diary of a Writer" and the Traditions of Literary Utopia* (Austin: University of Texas Press, 1981), p. 180.

46. Ibid., p. 181.

47. Ibid., p. 177.

48. Ibid., p. 182.

CHAPTER TWO

1. Philip Rahv, "Dostoevsky in *Crime and Punishment,*" in *Dostoevsky: A Collection of Critical Essays,* ed. R. Wellek (Englewood Cliffs, NJ: Prentice Hall, 1962), p. 21.

2. See, for example, Joseph Frank, *Dostoevsky: The Stir of Liberation, 1860–1865* (Princeton and London: Princeton University Press, 1986); Derek Offord, "Dostoyevsky and Chernyshevsky," *Slavonic and East European Review* 57 (1979): 509–30; and Richard Peace, *Dostoyevsky: An Examination of the Major Novels* (Cambridge: Cambridge University Press, 1971).

3. M. Iu. Lermontov, *Polnoe sobranie sochinenii* (Moscow-Leningrad: Academia, 1937), vol. 5, p. 312.

4. See, for example, Malcolm V. Jones, *Dostoyevsky after Bakhtin: Readings in Dostoyevsky's Fantastic Realism* (Cambridge: Cambridge University Press, 1990), chap. 4; and Gary Rosenshield, *Crime and Punishment: The Techniques of the Omniscient Author* (Lisse: Peter de Ridder, 1978).

5. Faith Wigzell, "Dostoevskii and the Russian Folk Heritage," in *The Cambridge Companion to Dostoevskii,* ed. W. J. Leatherbarrow (Cambridge: Cambridge University Press, 2002), p. 32.

6. See Ryan, *The Bathhouse at Midnight.*

7. Bakhtin, *Problems of Dostoevsky's Poetics,* p. 170.

8. Sidney Monas, "Across the Threshold: *The Idiot* as a Petersburg Tale," in *New Essays on Dostoyevsky,* ed. Malcolm V. Jones and Garth M. Terry (Cambridge: Cambridge University Press, 1983), p. 69.

9. See Ivanits, "Suicide and Folk Beliefs in Dostoevsky's *Crime and Punishment.*"

10. The name suggests the biblical town of Capernaum, which was near Mary Magdalene's place of birth.

11. For a discussion of the demonic significance of the mouse in Russian folklore, see Wigzell, "Dostoevskii and the Russian Folk Heritage."

12. Ivanits, "Suicide and Folk Beliefs in Dostoevsky's *Crime and Punishment,*" p. 141.

13. Ibid., p. 144.

14. Ibid., p. 138.

15. Wigzell, "Dostoevskii and the Russian Folk Heritage," p. 33.

16. Bakhtin, *Problems of Dostoevsky's Poetics,* p. 168.

17. Pushkin, *Boris Godunov,* scene 5. I have quoted the translation and emphases as they appear in *Problems of Dostoevsky's Poetics* (p. 169), although I was tempted to italicize also the mention of an ant-hill, given the role of that image in *Crime and Punishment.*

18. The association of imposture with magic, sorcery, and heresy was, according to Maureen Perrie, characteristic not only of Russian culture, but was to be found elsewhere in early modern Europe. See Maureen Perrie, *Pretenders and Popular Monarchism in Early Modern Russia* (Cambridge: Cambridge University Press, 1995), p. 56.

19. B. A. Uspenskii, "Tsar and Pretender: *Samozvancestvo* or Royal Imposture in Russia as a Cultural-Historical Phenomenon," in Lotman, Iu., and B. A. Uspenskii, *The Semiotics of Russian Culture,* p. 261.

20. Bakhtin, *Problems of Dostoevsky's Poetics,* p. 167.

21. Monas, "Across the Threshold," p. 71.

22. Ibid., p. 70.

23. Ibid., p. 68.

24. Pamela Davidson, "Divine Service or Idol Worship? Russian Views of Art as Demonic," in Davidson, *Russian Literature and Its Demons,* pp. 144–47.

25. This quotation is from the end of Gogol's tale "Nevsky prospekt." For a recent treatment of this theme see Julian Graffy, "The Devil Is in the Detail: Demonic Features of Gogol's Petersburg," in Davidson, *Russian Literature and Its Demons,* pp. 241–77.

26. Davidson, "Divine Service or Idol Worship," p. 146.

27. See Stephen Lessing Baehr, *The Paradise Myth in Eighteenth-Century Russia: Utopian Patterns In Early Secular Russian Literature and Culture* (Stanford: Stanford University Press: 1991), p. 166.

28. N. A. Dobroliubov, *Izbrannye sochineniia* (Moscow, 1948), p. 103.

29. Mochulsky, *Dostoevsky: His Life and Work*, p 312.

30. V. Ia Kirpotin, *Razocharovanie i krushenie Rodiona Raskol'nikova: Kniga o romane "Prestuplenie i nakazanie"* (Moscow: Sovetskii pisatel', 1970), pp. 382, 385.

CHAPTER THREE

1. Actually a quotation from *Romeo and Juliet*, act 3, scene 8.

2. See Monas, "Across the Threshold: *The Idiot* as a Petersburg Tale," passim.

3. David Bethea, *The Shape of Apocalypse in Modern Russian Fiction* (Princeton: Princeton University Press, 1989), p. 64.

4. R. Hollander, "The Apocalyptic Framework of Dostoevsky's *The Idiot.*" *Mosaic* 7 (1974): 123–39. For a treatment of apocalyptic symbolism in Dostoevsky see also Geir Kjetsaa, *Fyodor Dostoyevsky: A Writer's Life* (London: Macmillan, 1988), pp. 253–61, and W. J. Leatherbarrow, "Apocalyptic Imagery in *The Idiot* and *The Devils*," *Dostoevsky Studies* 3 (1982): 43–52.

5. Michael C. Finke, *Metapoesis: The Russian Tradition from Pushkin to Chekhov* (Durham and London: Duke University Press, 1995), p. 186–87.

6. Bethea, *The Shape of Apocalypse*, p. 84

7. On the importance of sectarianism in this and Dostoevsky's other novels see Peace, *Dostoyevsky: An Examination of the Major Novels*.

8. Jostein Børtnes, "Dostoevskij's *Idiot* or the Poetics of Emptiness," *Scando-Slavica* 40 (1994): 13.

9. See, for example, Jones, *Dostoyevsky after Bakhtin*, pp. 113–45; Robin Feuer Miller, *Dostoevsky and "The Idiot": Author, Narrator, and Reader* (Cambridge, Mass: Harvard University Press, 1981), especially chapters 3–5; Harriet Murav, *Holy Foolishness: Dostoevsky's Novels and the Poetics of Cultural Critique* (Stanford: Stanford University Press, 1992), pp. 71–98; Peace, *Dostoyevsky: An Examination of the Major Novels*, chapters 4 and 5; and W. J. Leatherbarrow, "Misreading Myshkin and Stavrogin: The Presentation of the Hero in Dostoevskii's *Idiot* and *Besy*," *Slavonic and East European Review* 78 (2000): 1–19.

10. Margaret Ziolkowski, *Hagiography and Modern Russian Literature* (Princeton: Princeton University Press, 1988), p. 5.

11. L. P. Grossman, "Biblioteka Dostoevskogo," in *Seminarii po Dostoevskomu: Materialy, bibliografii i kommentarii* (Moscow and Petrograd: GIZ, 1922), p. 8.

12. Ziolkowski, *Hagiography and Modern Russian Literature*, p. 30. I have derived from Ziolkowski the description of *topoi* that follows, as well as from N. K. Gudzy, *History of Early Russian Literature*, trans. Susan Wilbur Jones (New York: Macmillan, 1949), p. 26.

13. Ziolkowski, *Hagiography and Modern Russian Literature,* p. 126.

14. Ibid., p. 145.

15. Ibid., pp. 128–29. See also John Fennell and Antony Stokes, *Early Russian Literature* (London: Faber, 1974), pp. 144–57; and J. Fennell, "The Attitude of the Josephians and the Trans-Volga Elders to the Heresy of the Judaizers," *Slavonic and East European Review* 29 (1951): 486–509.

16. See W. J. Leatherbarrow, *Fedor Dostoevsky* (Boston: G. K. Hall, 1981), pp. 111–17.

17. Christopher Putney, *Russian Devils and Diabolic Conditionality in Nikolai Gogol's "Evenings on a Farm near Dikanka,"* p. 43.

18. Robert Lord, "An Epileptic Mode of Being," in *Dostoevsky: Essays and Perspectives* (London: Chatto and Windus, 1970), pp. 81–101.

19. Finke, *Metapoesis,* p. 78.

20. Ibid., p. 78.

21. Ibid., p. 81–82.

22. Ibid., p. 98.

23. Ibid., p. 81.

24. Weiner, *By Authors Possessed,* p. 15.

CHAPTER FOUR

1. For a fuller account of the Nechaev affair see Joseph Frank, *Dostoevsky. The Miraculous Years, 1865–1871* (Princeton: Princeton University Press, 1995), chap. 23.

2. Fyodor Dostoevsky, *Demons,* trans. Richard Pevear and Larissa Volokhonsky (New York: Random House, 1994).

3. Franco Venturi, *Roots of Revolution,* trans. Francis Haskell (Chicago: University of Chicago Press, 1960), pp. 331–53.1

4. Murav, *Holy Foolishness. Dostoevsky's Novels and the Poetics of Cultural Critique,* p. 115.

5. For a discussion of Stavrogin's anachronism see Frank, *Dostoevsky: The Miraculous Years,* pp. 467–70, 478.

6. Oinas, *Essays on Russian Folklore and Mythology,* p. 101.

7. N. V. Gogol, *Sobranie sochinenii v semi tomakh* (Moscow: Khudozhestvennaia literatura, 1966–67), vol. 3, p. 21.

8. L. Grossman, *Poetika Dostoevskogo* (Moscow: Gosudarstvennaia Akademiia khudozhestvennykh nauk, 1925), pp. 61–62. Cited in Bakhtin, *Problems of Dostoevsky's Poetics,* p. 103.

9. Bakhtin, *Problems of Dostoevsky's Poetics,* p. 107.

10. Ibid., p. 106.

11. Ibid., p. 108.

12. See Bakhtin, *Problems of Dostoevsky's Poetics*, chap. 4, and *Rabelais and His World*.

13. Bakhtin, *Problems of Dostoevsky's Poetics*, p. 122.

14. Ibid., p. 107.

15. Murav, *Holy Foolishness*, p. 9.

16. Lotman and Uspenskii, "New Aspects in the Study of Russian Culture," p. 40.

17. Bakhtin, *Problems of Dostoevsky's Poetics*, p. 131.

18. Linda J. Ivanits, "Folk Beliefs About the 'Unclean Force' in Dostoevskij's *The Brothers Karamazov*," p. 137.

19. Oinas, *Essays on Russian Folklore and Mythology*, p. 98.

20. Catriona Kelly, *Petrushka: The Russian Carnival Puppet Theater* (Cambridge: Cambridge University Press, 1990).

21. James L. Rice, *Dostoevsky and the Healing Art: An Essay in Literary and Medical History* (Ann Arbor: Ardis, 1985), p. 75.

22. Kelly, *Petrushka*, pp. 48–49.

23. Ibid., p. 160.

24. Ibid., p. 90.

25. Ibid., p. 55.

26. Elizabeth A. Warner, *The Russian Folk Theater* (The Hague and Paris: Mouton, 1977), pp. 115–16.

27. Bakhtin, *Problems of Dostoevsky's Poetics*, p. 180.

28. Harriet Murav, "Representations of the Demonic: Seventeenth-Century Pretenders and *The Devils*," *Slavic and East European Journal* 35, no. 1 (1991): 56.

29. X, 326. See also Peace, *Dostoyevsky. An Examination of the Major Novels*, pp. 171 and 323.

30. Murav, "Representations of the Demonic," p. 59.

31. Lotman and Uspenskii, *The Semiotics of Russian Culture*, p. 272.

32. Ibid., p. 263.

33. I have developed these ideas more fully than is possible here in *Fedor Dostoevsky* (Boston: Twayne, 1981). For a further treatment of Dostoevsky's aesthetic views see Jackson, *Dostoevsky's Quest for Form*.

34. Lotman and Uspenskii, *The Semiotics of Russian Culture*, p. 261.

35. Ibid., pp. 264–65.

36. Loginovskaia, "Motiv demonizma v *Besakh* Dostoevskogo," 35–36.

37. Franklin, "Nostalgia for Hell," p. 35.

38. See, for example, Elisabeth Stenbock-Fermor, "Lermontov and Dostoevskij's Novel *The Devils*," *Slavic and East European Journal* 17 (1959): 215–30.

39. M. Iu. Lermontov, *Polnoe sobranie sochinenii v piati tomakh* (Moscow-Leningrad: Akademiia, 1936–37), vol. 5, p. 224.

40. Morson, *Boundaries of Genre*, p. 77.

41. For a fuller discussion of these ideas than is appropriate in the present essay see Frank, *Dostoevsky: The Miraculous Years*, chap. 21 and 24.

42. W. J. Leatherbarrow, "Apocalyptic Imagery in *The Idiot* and *The Devils*," *Dostoevsky Studies* 3 (1982): 43–52, and Geir Kjetsaa, *Fyodor Dostoyevsky: A Writer's Life* (London: Macmillan, 1988), pp. 253–61.

43. Geir Kjetsaa, *Dostoevsky and His New Testament* (Atlantic Highlands, N.J.: Humanities Press, 1984), p. 77.

44. *F. M. Dostoevskii v vospominaniiakh sovremennikov*, ed. A. Dolinin (Moscow: Gosudarstvennoe izdatel'stvo khudozhestvennoi literatury, 1964), vol. 2, p. 170.

CHAPTER FIVE

1. See, for example, Victor Terras, "The Art of Fiction as a Theme in *The Brothers Karamazov*," in *Dostoevsky: New Perspectives*, ed. R. L. Jackson (Englewood Cliffs, N.J.: Prentice Hall, 1984), pp. 193–205; Victor Terras, *A Karamazov Companion: Commentary on the Genesis, Language, and Style of Dostoevsky's Novel* (Madison: University of Wisconsin Press, 1981), passim; and Nina Perlina, *Varieties of Poetic Utterance: Quotation in "The Brothers Karamazov"* (Lanham, N.Y.: University Press of America, 1985).

2. Jones, *Dostoyevsky after Bakhtin*, p. 186.

3. Ibid., p. 185.

4. Terras, *A Karamazov Companion*, pp. 89–90.

5. Denis de Rougemont, *Talk of the Devil (La Part du Diable)*, trans. Kathleen Raine (London: Eyre & Spottiswood, 1945), p. 98. Cited in Weiner, *By Authors Possessed*, p. 15.

6. Terras, *A Karamazov Companion*, pp. 316–17.

7. Ibid., p. 419.

8. Ibid., pp. 417, 423.

9. See, for example, Sven Linnér, *Dostoevskij on Realism* (Stockholm: Almqvist & Wiksell, 1967) and Jackson, *Dostoevsky's Quest for Form*.

10. For a full treatment of "The Grand Inquisitor" see Ellis Sandoz, *Political Apocalypse: A Study of Dostoevsky's Grand Inquisitor* (Baton Rouge: Louisiana State University Press, 1971); and Robert L. Belknap, *The Genesis of "The Brothers Karamazov": The Aesthetics, Ideology, and Psychology of Making a Text* (Evanston, Ill.: Northwestern University Press, 1990), especially chap. 7 and 8.

11. Terras, *A Karamazov Companion*, p. 92.

12. See Perlina, *Varieties of Poetic Utterance*, passim.

13. See Ralph Matlaw, *The Brothers Karamazov: Novelistic Technique* (The Hague: Mouton, 1957), p. 17. Valentina Vetlovskaia, on the other hand, uses the reference to Pater Seraphicus in order to trace links between

Zosima and St. Francis of Assisi: see Valentina Vetlovskaia, "Pater Seraphicus," in *Dostoevskii: Materialy i issledovaniia*, ed. G. M. Fridlender (Leningrad: Nauka, 1983), vol. 5, pp. 163–78.

14. Terras, *A Karamazov Companion*, p. 239.

15. Ibid., p. 47.

16. See Ivanits, "Folk Beliefs about the 'Unclean Force' in Dostoevskij's *The Brothers Karamazov*," p. 142.

17. Ibid., p. 138.

18. Putney, *Russian Devils and Diabolic Conditionality*, p. 43.

19. See Valentina Vetlovskaia, "Literaturnye i fol'klornye istochniki *Brat'ev Karamazovykh*: Zhitie Alekseia cheloveka bozhiia i dukhovnye stikhi o nem," in *Dostoevskii i russkie pisateli: Traditsii, novatorstvo, masterstvo: Sbornik statei*, ed. V. Ia. Kirpotin (Moscow: Sovetskii pisatel', 1971), pp. 325–54.

20. Apart from works already cited, in particular those by Terras and Belknap, see also Valentina Vetlovskaia, *Poetika romana "Brat'ia Karamazovy"* (Leningrad: Nauka, 1977); A. S. Dolinin, *Poslednie romany Dostoevskogo: Kak sozdavalis' "Podrostok" i "Brat'ia Karamazovy"* (Moscow-Leningrad: Sovetskii pisatel', 1963); Stewart R. Sutherland, *Atheism and the Rejection of God: Contemporary Philosophy and "The Brothers Karamazov"* (Oxford: Blackwell, 1977).

21. See Terras, *A Karamazov Companion*, p. 136, and the editorial note in XV, 525.

22. See Terras, *A Karamazov Companion*, p. 260, and XV, 569–70.

23. On this parallelism see, for example, Richard Peace, *Dostoyevsky: An Examination of the Major Novels*, chap. 8. For a full discussion of Smerdiakov see W. J. Leatherbarrow, *Dostoyevsky: The Brothers Karamazov* (Cambridge: Cambridge University Press, 1992), pp. 33–42.

24. Gary Saul Morson, "Verbal Pollution in *The Brothers Karamazov*," *PTL: A Journal for Descriptive Poetics and Theory of Literature* 3 (1978): 223–33.

25. Terras's commentary identifies most examples of this evasiveness. See *A Karamazov Companion*, pp. 376–77.

26. See Terras, *A Karamazov Companion*, p. 382.

27. Bakhtin, *Problems of Dostoevsky's Poetics*, p. 222.

28. See Terras, "Turgenev and the Devil in *The Brothers Karamazov*," *Canadian-American Slavic Studies* 6 (1972): 265–71.

29. Nina Perlina, "Herzen in *The Brothers Karamazov*," *Canadian-American Slavic Studies* 17 (1983): 349–61.

30. The many instances of such quotation are analyzed in Perlina, *Varieties of Poetic Utterance*.

31. Bakhtin, *Problems of Dostoevsky's Poetics*, p. 222.

32. Mochulsky, *Dostoevsky: His Life and Work,* p. 312.

33. Sergei Hackel, "The Religious Dimension: Vision or Evasion? Zosima's Discourse in *The Brothers Karamazov,*" in *New Essays on Dostoyevsky,* ed. Malcolm V. Jones and Garth M. Terry (Cambridge: Cambridge University Press, 1983), p. 140.

34. Morson, *The Boundaries of Genre,* p. 181. See also the discussion of *Dream of a Ridiculous Man* in chap. 1 of the present study.

35. These devices are identified in Terras's commentary, *A Karamazov Companion.*

36. S. N. Durylin, "Ob odnom simvole u Dostoevskogo: Opyt tematicheskogo obzora," in *Dostoevskii: Sbornik statei* (Moscow: Gosudarstvennaia Akademiia khudozhestvennykh nauk, 1928), vol. 3, pp. 163–98.

37. Terras, *A Karamazov Companion,* pp. 255–61

CONCLUSION

1. This meditation forms part of Dostoevsky's notebook for 1863–64. It has been subjected to detailed analysis by Joseph Frank in the third volume of his biography, *Dostoevsky: The Stir of Liberation, 1860–1865,* pp. 296–309, and by Liza Knapp in *The Annihilation of Inertia: Dostoevsky and Metaphysics,* passim.

2. See James Scanlan, *Dostoevsky as Philosopher* (Ithaca: Cornell University Press, 2002).

Selected Bibliography

Arban, D. "Porog u Dostoevskogo (tema, motiv i poniatie)." Vol. 2 of *Dosto-evskii: Materialy i issledovaniia,* 19–29. Leningrad: Nauka, 1976.

Averintsev, S. S. "Bakhtin i russkoe otnoshenie k smekhu." In *Ot mifa k lit-erature: Sbornik v chest' 75-letiia Eleazara Moiseevicha Meletinskogo,* edited by S. Iu. Nekhliudov and E. S. Novik, 341–45. Moscow: Rossiiskii universitet, 1993.

Baehr, Stephen Lessing. *The Paradise Myth in Eighteenth-Century Russia: Utopian Patterns in Early Secular Russian Literature and Culture.* Stanford: Stanford University Press, 1991.

Bakhtin, M. M. *The Dialogic Imagination: Four Essays.* Translated by Caryl Emerson and Michael Holquist. Edited by Michael Holquist. Austin: University of Texas Press, 1981.

———. *Problems of Dostoevsky's Poetics.* Edited and translated by Caryl Emerson. Manchester: Manchester University Press, 1984.

———. *Rabelais and His World.* Translated by Hélène Iswolsky. Blooming-ton: Indiana University Press, 1984.

Balzer, Marjorie Mandelstam, ed. *Russian Traditional Culture: Religion, Gender, and Customary Law.* Armonk, N.Y.: M. E. Sharpe, 1992.

Belknap, Robert L. *The Genesis of "The Brothers Karamazov": The Aes-thetics, Ideology, and Psychology of Making a Text.* Evanston: North-western University Press, 1990.

———. *The Structure of "The Brothers Karamazov."* The Hague and Paris: Mouton, 1967.

Bem, A. L. "Faust v tvorchestve Dostoevskogo." In *O Dostojevskem: Sborník statí a materiálu,* 183–220. Prague: Edice slovanské knihovny, 1972.

Bethea, David M. *The Shape of Apocalypse in Modern Russian Fiction.* Princeton: Princeton University Press, 1989.

Billington, James. *The Icon and the Axe: An Interpretive History of Russian Culture.* New York: Vintage, 1970.

Børtnes, Jostein. "The Function of Hagiography in Dostoevskij's Novels." In

Critical Essays on Dostoevsky, edited by R. F. Miller, 188–93. Boston: G. K. Hall, 1986.

———. "The Last Delusion in an Infinite Series of Delusions: Stavrogin and the Symbolic Structure of *The Devils.*" *Dostoevsky Studies* 4 (1983): 53–67.

Boss, Valentin. *Milton and the Rise of Russian Satanism.* Toronto: Toronto University Press, 1991.

Brodsky, Patricia P. "The Demons of Lermontov and Vrubel'." *Slavic and East European Arts* 6, no 2 (1990): 16–32.

Catteau, Jacques. *Dostoyevsky and the Process of Literary Creation.* Translated by Audrey Littlewood. Cambridge: Cambridge University Press, 1989.

Clayton, J. Douglas. "Pushkin, Faust and the Demons." *Germano-Slavica* 3, no. 3 (1980): 165–87.

Connolly, Julian W. *The Intimate Stranger: Meetings with the Devil in Nineteenth-Century Russian Literature.* Middlebury Studies in Russian Language and Literature, 26. New York: Peter Lang, 2001.

Danow, D. K. "Subtexts of *The Brothers Karamazov.*" *Russian Literature* 11 (1982): 173–208.

Davidson, Pamela. "Divine Service or Idol Worship? Russian Views of Art as Demonic." In *Russian Literature and Its Demons,* edited by Pamela Davidson, 125–64. New York and Oxford: Berghahn, 2000.

———, ed. *Russian Literature and Its Demons.* New York and Oxford: Berghahn, 2000.

de Jonge, Alex. *Dostoevsky and the Age of Intensity.* London: Secker and Warburg, 1975.

Dolinin, A. S. *Poslednie romany Dostoevskogo: Kak sozdavalis' "Podrostok" i "Brat'ia Karamazovy."* Moscow-Leningrad: Sovetskii pisatel', 1963.

Dowler, Wayne C. *Dostoevsky, Grigor'ev, and Native Soil Conservatism.* Toronto: University of Toronto Press, 1982.

Emerson, Caryl. *Boris Godunov: Transpositions of a Russian Theme.* Bloomington: Indiana University Press, 1986.

Faletti, Heidi. "Elements of the Demonic in the Character of Pechorin in Lermontov's *Hero of Our Time.*" *Forum for Modern Language Studies* 14 (1978): 365–77.

Fanger, Donald. *Dostoevsky and Romantic Realism: A Study of Dostoevsky in Relation to Balzac, Dickens, and Gogol.* Cambridge, Mass.: Harvard University Press, 1967.

Fennell, John. "The Attitude of the Josephians and the Trans-Volga Elders to the Heresy of Judaism." *Slavonic and East European Review* 29 (1951): 486–509.

Fennell, John, and Anthony Stokes. *Early Russian Literature.* London: Faber, 1974.

Finke, Michael C. *Metapoesis: The Russian Tradition from Pushkin to Chekhov.* Durham and London: Duke University Press, 1995.

Follinus, Gabor. "Thus Speaks the Devil: *Crime and Punishment.*" *Studia Slavica* 37 (1991–92): 343–51.

Frank, Joseph. *Dostoevsky: The Seeds of Revolt, 1821–1849.* London: Robson Books, 1977.

———. *Dostoevsky: The Years of Ordeal, 1850–1859.* Princeton: Princeton University Press, 1983.

———. *Dostoevsky: The Stir of Liberation, 1860–1865.* Princeton: Princeton University Press, 1986.

———. *Dostoevsky: The Miraculous Years, 1865–1871.* Princeton: Princeton University Press, 1995.

———. *Dostoevsky: The Mantle of the Prophet, 1871–1881.* Princeton: Princeton University Press, 2002.

Franklin, Simon. "Nostalgia for Hell: Russian Literary Demonism and the Orthodox Tradition." In *Russian Literature and Its Demons,* edited by Pamela Davidson, 31–58. New York and Oxford: Berghahn, 2000.

Gibian, G. "Dostoevsky's Use of Russian Folklore." *Journal of American Folklore* 69 (1956): 239–53.

———. "Traditional Symbolism in *Crime and Punishment.*" *PMLA* 70 (1955): 979–96.

Gibson, A. Boyce. *The Religion of Dostoevsky.* London: SCM Press, 1973.

Goldstein, David. *Dostoevsky and the Jews.* Austin and London: Texas University Press, 1981.

Grossman, L. P. *Poetika Dostoevskogo.* Moscow: Gosudarstvennaia Akademiia khudozhestvennykh nauk, 1925.

———. "Stilistika Stavrogina." Vol. 2 of *F. M. Dostoevskii: Stat'i i materialy,* edited by A. S. Dolinin, 139–48. Leningrad: Mysl', 1924.

Hackel, Sergei. "The Religious Dimension: Vision or Evasion? Zosima's Discourse in *The Brothers Karamazov.*" In *New Essays on Dostoyevsky,* edited by Malcolm V. Jones and Garth M. Terry, 139–68. Cambridge: Cambridge University Press, 1983.

Heldt, Barbara. *Terrible Perfection: Women and Russian Literature.* Bloomington: Indiana University Press, 1987.

Hollander, R. "The Apocalyptic Framework of Dostoevsky's *The Idiot.*" *Mosaic* 7 (1974): 123–39.

Hollingsworth, Paul, ed. *The Hagiography of Kievan Rus'.* Harvard Library of Early Ukrainian Literature. Cambridge, Mass.: Harvard University Press, 1992.

Holquist, J. M. *Dostoevsky and the Novel.* Princeton: Princeton University Press, 1977.

Iampol'skii, Mikhail. *Demon i labirint: Diagrammy, deformatsii, mimesis.* Moscow: Novoe literaturnoe obozrenie, 1996.

Ivanits, Linda J. "Dostoevskij's Mar'ja Lebjadkina." *Slavic and East European Journal* 22 (1978): 127–40.

———. "Folk Beliefs about the 'Unclean Force' in Dostoevskij's *The Brothers Karamazov.*" In *New Perspectives on Russian Literature,* edited by George L. Gutsche and Lauren G. Leighton, 135–46. Columbus: Slavica, 1982.

———. *Russian Folk Belief.* Armonk, N.Y., and London: M. E. Sharpe, 1989.

———. "Suicide and Folk Beliefs in Dostoevsky's *Crime and Punishment.*" In *The Golden Age of Russian Literature and Thought,* edited by D. C. Offord, 138–48. London: St. Martin's Press, 1992.

Ivanov, Viacheslav. *Freedom and the Tragic Life: A Study in Dostoevsky.* Translated by Norman Cameron. London: Harvill Press, 1952.

———. "Osnovnoi mif v romane *Besy.*" In *Borozdy i mezhi,* 61–72. Moscow: Musaget, 1916.

Jackson, Robert Louis. *The Art of Dostoevsky: Deliriums and Nocturnes.* Princeton: Princeton University Press, 1981.

———. *Dostoevsky's Quest for Form: A Study of His Philosophy of Art.* New Haven, Conn.: Yale University Press, 1966.

Jones, Malcolm V. "The Death and Resurrection of Orthodoxy in the Works of Dostoevskii." In *Cultural Discontinuity and Reconstruction: The Byzanto-Slav Heritage and the Creation of a Russian National Literature in the Nineteenth Century,* edited by Jostein Børtnes and Ingunne Lunde, 143–67. Oslo: Solum Forlag, 1997.

———. "Dostoevskii and Religion." In *The Cambridge Companion to Dostoevskii,* edited by W. J. Leatherbarrow, 148–74. Cambridge: Cambridge University Press, 2002.

———. *Dostoyevsky after Bakhtin: Readings in Dostoyevsky's Fantastic Realism.* Cambridge: Cambridge University Press, 1990.

Kelly, Catriona. *Petrushka: The Russian Carnival Puppet Theatre.* Cambridge: Cambridge University Press, 1990.

Kjetsaa, Geir. *Dostoevsky and His New Testament.* Atlantic Highlands, N.J.: Humanities Press, 1984.

———. *Fyodor Dostoyevsky: A Writer's Life.* London: Macmillan, 1988.

Knapp, Liza. *The Annihilation of Inertia: Dostoevsky and Metaphysics.* Studies in Russian Literature and Theory. Evanston, Ill.: Northwestern University Press, 1996.

Kraeger, Linda, and Joe Barnhart. *Dostoevsky on Evil and Atonement: The Ontology of Personalism in His Major Fiction.* Lewiston, N.Y.: Edwin Mellen Press, 1992.

Langton, Edward. *Essentials of Demonology: A Study of Jewish and Christian Doctrine, Its Origin and Development.* New York: AMS Press, 1981.

———. *Satan, a Portrait: A Study of the Character of Satan Through All the Ages.* London: Skeffington and Son, 1945.

Leatherbarrow, W. J. "Apocalyptic Imagery in *The Idiot* and *The Devils.*" *Dostoevsky Studies* 3 (1982): 43–52.

———, ed. *The Cambridge Companion to Dostoevskii.* Cambridge: Cambridge University Press, 2002.

———. "The Devils' Vaudeville: 'Decoding' the Demonic in Dostoevsky's *The Devils.*" In *Russian Literature and Its Demons,* edited by Pamela Davidson, 279–306. New York and Oxford: Berghahn, 2000.

———. *Dostoevsky:* The Brothers Karamazov. Cambridge: Cambridge University Press, 1992.

———. *Fedor Dostoevsky.* Boston: Twayne, 1981.

———. *Fedor Dostoevsky: A Reference Guide.* Boston: G. K. Hall, 1990.

Likhachev, D. S. *Chelovek v literature drevnei Rusi.* Moscow: Nauka, 1970.

———. *Smekhovoi mir drevnei Rusi.* Leningrad: Nauka, 1976.

Linnér, Sven. *Staretz Zosima in "The Brothers Karamazov": A Study in the Mimesis of Virtue.* Stockholm: Almqvist and Wiksell, 1975.

Loginovskaia, E. "Motiv demonizma v *Besakh* Dostoevskogo: Tekstovye i vnetekstovye koordinaty." *Scando-Slavica* 26 (1981): 33–52.

———. *Poema M. Iu. Lermontova "Demon."* Moscow: Khudozhestvennaia literatura, 1977.

Lord, Robert. "An Epileptic Mode of Being." In *Dostoevsky: Essays and Perspectives,* 81–101. London: Chatto and Windus, 1970.

Lossky, Vladimir. *Orthodox Theology: An Introduction.* Translated by Ian and Ihita Kesarcodi-Watson. Crestwood, N.Y.: St. Vladimir's Seminary Press, 1978.

Lotman, Iu., and B. A. Uspenskii. "The Role of Dual Models in the Dynamics of Russian Culture (to the End of the Eighteenth Century)." In Lotman, Iu., and B. A. Uspenskii, *The Semiotics of Russian Culture,* edited by Ann Shukman, 3–35. Ann Arbor: Department of Slavic Languages and Literature, University of Michigan, 1984.

———. "New Aspects in the Study of Early Russian Culture." In Lotman, Iu., and B. A. Uspenskii, *The Semiotics of Russian Culture,* edited by Ann Shukman, 36–52. Ann Arbor: Department of Slavic Languages and Literature, University of Michigan, 1984.

Lotman, L. M. "Romany Dostoevskogo i russkaia legenda." *Russkaia literatura* 15, no. 2 (1972): 129–41.

Maksimov, S. V. *Nechistaia, nevedomaia i krestnaia sila.* St Petersburg: Poliset, 1994.

Mann, Robert. "Elijah the Prophet in *Crime and Punishment.*" *Canadian Slavonic Papers* 23 (1981): 261–72.

———. "The Faustian Pattern in *The Devils.*" *Canadian Slavonic Papers* 24 (1982): 239–44.

Masing-Delic, Irene. "The Impotent Demon and Prurient Tamara: Parodies on Lermontov's 'Demon' in Dostoevskij's *Besy.*" *Russian Literature* 48 (2000): 263–88.

Matlaw, Ralph E. *The Brothers Karamazov: Novelistic Technique.* The Hague: Mouton, 1957.

———. "Recurrent Imagery in Dostoevskij." *Harvard Slavic Studies* 3 (1957): 201–25.

Merezhkovsky, Dmitry. "Gogol and the Devil." In *Gogol from the Twentieth Century: Eleven Essays,* edited by Robert A. McGuire, 55–102. Princeton: Princeton University Press, 1974.

Mikhniukhevich, V. A. *Russkii fol'klor v khudozhestvennoi sisteme Dostoevskogo.* Cheliabinsk: Cheliabinsk State University Press, 1994.

Miller, Robin Feuer. *Dostoevsky and "The Idiot": Author, Narrator, and Reader.* Cambridge, Mass.: Harvard University Press, 1981.

Mochulsky, Konstantin. *Dostoevsky: His Life and Work.* Translated by M. Minihan. Princeton: Princeton University Press, 1967.

Monas, Sidney. "Across the Threshold: *The Idiot* as a Petersburg Tale." In *New Essays on Dostoyevsky,* edited by Malcolm V. Jones and Garth M. Terry, 67–93. Cambridge: Cambridge University Press, 1983.

Morson, Gary Saul. *The Boundaries of Genre: Dostoevsky's "Diary of a Writer" and the Traditions of Literary Utopia.* Austin: University of Texas Press, 1981.

———. "Verbal Pollution in *The Brothers Karamazov.*" *PTL: A Journal for Descriptive Poetics and Theory of Literature* 3 (1978): 223–33.

Murav, Harriet. *Holy Foolishness: Dostoevsky's Novels and the Poetics of Cultural Critique.* Stanford: Stanford University Press, 1992.

Novichkova, T. A. *Russkii demonologicheskii slovar'.* St Petersburg: Peterburgskii pisatel', 1995.

Oates, Joyce Carol. "Tragic Rites in Dostoyevsky's *The Possessed.*" In *Contraries: Essays,* 17–50. New York: Oxford University Press, 1981.

Offord, Derek. "Dostoyevsky and Chernyshevsky." *Slavonic and East European Review* 57 (1979): 509–30.

Oinas, Felix J. *Essays on Russian Folklore and Mythology.* Columbus: Slavica, 1985.

———. "Heretics as Vampires and Demons in Russia." *Slavic and East European Journal* 22 (1978): 433–41.

Ollivier, Sophie. "L'Ambiguïté fantastique dans le chapitre des Frères Karamazov: 'Le Diable. Le Cauchemar d'Ivan Fedorovic.'" *Dostoevsky Studies* 8 (1987): 121–33.

Orlov, M. N. *Istoriia snoshenii cheloveka s d'iavolom.* Moscow: Barks, 1992.

Panichas, George A. "Dostoevsky and Satanism." *Journal of Religion* 45 (1965): 12–29.

Paperno, Irina. *Suicide as a Cultural Institution in Dostoevsky's Russia.* Ithaca: Cornell University Press, 1997.

Pattison, George, and Diane Oenning Thompson, eds. *Dostoevsky and the Christian Tradition.* Cambridge: Cambridge University Press, 2001.

Peace, Richard. *Dostoyevsky: An Examination of the Major Novels.* Cambridge: Cambridge University Press, 1971.

Perlina, Nina. *Varieties of Poetic Utterance: Quotation in "The Brothers Karamazov."* Lanham, N.Y.: University Press of America, 1985.

Perrie, Maureen. *Pretenders and Popular Monarchism in Early Modern Russia.* Cambridge: Cambridge University Press, 1995.

Piksanov, N. K. "Dostoevskii i fol'klor." *Sovetskaia etnografiia* 1–2 (1934): 152–80.

Pletnev, R. "O dukhakh zla i d'iavola u Dostoevskogo i Tolstogo." *Novyi zhurnal* 119 (1975): 92–100.

———. "O zhivotnykh v tvorchestve Dostoevskogo." *Novyi zhurnal* 106 (1972): 113–33.

———. "Zemlia." Vol. 1 of *O Dostoevskom: Sbornik statei,* edited by A.L. Bem, 153–62. Prague: Legiographic, 1929.

Pomerantseva, E. V. *Mifologicheskie personazhi v russkom fol'klore.* Moscow: Nauka, 1975.

Praz, Mario. *The Romantic Agony.* London: Oxford University Press, 1970.

Putney, Christopher. *Russian Devils and Diabolic Conditionality in Nikolai Gogol's "Evenings on a Farm near Dikanka."* Middlebury Studies in Russian Language and Literature, 15. New York: Peter Lang, 1999.

Rahv, Philip. "Dostoevsky in *Crime and Punishment.*" In *Dostoevsky: A Collection of Critical Essays,* edited by R. Wellek, 16–38. Englewood Cliffs, N.J.: Prentice Hall, 1962.

Riazanovskii, F. A. *Demonologiia v drevne-russkoi literature.* Moscow: n.p., 1915.

Rice, James L. *Dostoevsky and the Healing Art: An Essay in Literary and Medical History.* Ann Arbor: Ardis, 1985.

Rosen, Nathan. "Ivan Karamazov Confronts the Devil," *Dostoevsky Studies* 5 (2001): 117–28.

Rosenshield, Gary. "*The Bronze Horseman* and *The Double:* The Depoeticization of the Myth of Petersburg in the Young Dostoevskii." *Slavic Review* 55 (1996): 399–428.

————. *Crime and Punishment: The Techniques of the Omniscient Author.* Lisse: Peter de Ridder, 1978.

Rougemont, Denis de. *The Devil's Share: An Essay on the Diabolic in Modern Society.* Translated by H. Chevalier. New York: Meridian, 1956.

————. *Talk of the Devil (La Part du Diable).* Translated by Kathleen Raine. London: Eyre & Spottiswoode, 1945.

Rozanov, V. V. *Dostoevsky and the Legend of the Grand Inquisitor.* Translated by Spencer E. Roberts. Ithaca: Cornell University Press, 1972.

Russell, Jeffrey Burton. *The Devil: Perceptions of Evil from Antiquity to Primitive Christianity.* Ithaca: Cornell University Press, 1977.

————. *Lucifer: The Devil in the Middle Ages.* Ithaca: Cornell University Press, 1984.

————. *Mephistopheles: The Devil in the Modern World.* Ithaca: Cornell University Press, 1986.

————. *Satan: The Early Christian Tradition.* Ithaca: Cornell University Press, 1981.

Ryan, W. F. *The Bathhouse at Midnight: An Historical Survey of Magic and Divination in Russia.* University Park, Penn.: Pennsylvania State University Press, 1999.

Sandoz, Ellis. *Political Apocalypse: A Study of Dostoevsky's Grand Inquisitor.* Baton Rouge: Louisiana University Press, 1971.

Saraskina, Liudmila. *"Besy": Roman-preduprezhdenie.* Moscow: Sovetskii pisatel', 1990.

Scanlan, James P. *Dostoevsky the Thinker.* Ithaca: Cornell University Press, 2002.

Shneidman, N. *Dostoevsky and Suicide.* Oakville, Ontario, New York, and London: Mosaic, 1984.

Slattery, D. P. "Idols and Icons: Comic Transformation in Dostoevsky's *The Possessed.*" *Dostoevsky Studies* 6 (1985): 35–50.

Stenbock-Fermor, Elisabeth. "Lermontov and Dostoevskij's Novel *The Devils.*" *Slavic and East European Journal* 17 (1959): 215–30.

Struc, Roman S. "Petty Demons and Beauty: Gogol, Dostoevsky, Sologub." In *Essays on European Literature: In Honor of Liselotte Dieckmann,* edited by Peter Hohendal, et. al. St Louis: Washington University Press, 1972.

Sutherland, Stewart R. *Atheism and the Rejection of God: Contemporary Philosophy and "The Brothers Karamazov".* Oxford: Blackwell, 1977.

Terras, Victor. "The Art of Fiction as a Theme in *The Brothers Karamazov.*" In *Dostoevsky: New Perspectives,* edited by Robert Louis Jackson, 193–205. Englewood Cliffs, N.J.: Prentice Hall, 1984.

————. *A Karamazov Companion: Commentary on the Genesis, Language, and Style of Dostoevsky's Novel.* Madison: University of Wisconsin Press, 1981.

———. "On the Nature of Evil in *The Brothers Karamazov*." In *Text and Context: Essays to Honor Nils Åke Nilsson,* edited by P. A. Jensen, et. al., 58–64. Stockholm: Almqvist and Wiksell, 1987.

———. "Turgenev and the Devil in *The Brothers Karamazov*." *Canadian-American Slavic Studies* 6 (1972): 265–71.

Thompson, Diane Oenning. *"The Brothers Karamazov" and the Poetics of Memory.* Cambridge: Cambridge University Press, 1991.

———. "Dostoevskii and Science." In *The Cambridge Companion to Dostoevskii,* edited by W. J. Leatherbarrow, 191–211. Cambridge: Cambridge University Press, 2002.

Thompson, Ewa M. *Understanding Russia: The Holy Fool in Russian Culture.* Lanham: University Press of America, 1987.

Uspenskii, B. A. "Tsar and Pretender: *Samozvancestvo* or Royal Imposture in Russia as a Cultural-Historical Phenomenon." In Lotman, Iu., and B. A. Uspenskii, *The Semiotics of Russian Culture,* edited by Ann Shukman, 259–92. Ann Arbor: University of Michigan, 1984.

Vetlovskaia, V. A. "Literaturnye i fol'klornye istochniki *Brat'ev Karamazovykh:* Zhitie Alekseia cheloveka bozhiia i dukhovnye stikhi o nem." In *Dostoevskii i russkie pisateli: Traditsii, novatorstvo, masterstvo: Sbornik statei,* edited by V. Ia. Kirpotin, 325–54. Moscow: Sovetskii pisatel', 1971.

———. "Poeticheskaia deklaratsiia rannego Dostoevskogo: Simvolika povesti *Khoziaika.*" *Zbornik za slavistiku* 28 (1985): 91–104.

———. *Poetika romana "Brat'ia Karamazovy."* Leningrad: Nauka, 1977.

———. "Simvolika chisel v *Brat'iakh Karamazovykh.*" In *Drevnerusskaia literature i russkaia kul'tura XVIII-XIX vv,* 139–50. Leningrad: Nauka, 1971.

Vinogradova, L. N. "Kalendarnye perekhody nechistoi sily vo vremeni i prostranstve." In *Kontsept dvizheniia v iazyke i kul'ture,* edited by T. A. Agapkina. Moscow: Indrik, 1996.

Ward, Bruce K. *Dostoyevsky's Critique of the West: The Quest for Earthly Paradise.* Waterloo, Ontario: Wilfried Laurier University Press, 1986.

Warner, Elizabeth A. *The Russian Folk Theatre.* The Hague and Paris: Mouton, 1977.

Wasiolek, Edward. *Dostoevsky: The Major Fiction.* Cambridge, Mass.: MIT Press, 1964.

Weiner, Adam. *By Authors Possessed: The Demonic Novel in Russia.* Evanston, Ill.: Northwestern University Press, 1998.

Wigzell, Faith. "Dostoevskii and the Russian Folk Heritage." In *The Cambridge Companion to Dostoevskii,* edited by W. J. Leatherbarrow, 21–46. Cambridge: Cambridge University Press, 2002.

———. "The Russian Folk Devil and His Literary Reflections." In *Russian Literature and its Demons,* edited by Pamela Davidson, 59–86. New York and Oxford: Berghahn, 2000.

Wolfson, Boris. "C'est la faute à Rousseau: Possession as Device in *Demons.*" *Dostoevsky Studies* 5 (2001): 97–116.

Worobec, Christine D. *Possessed: Women, Witches, and Demons in Imperial Russia.* De Kalb, Ill.: Northern Illinois University Press, 2001.

Ziolkowski, Margaret. *Hagiography in Modern Russian Literature.* Princeton: Princeton University Press, 1988.

Index

Index

Ivanova, S. A., 103

Jackson, Robert Louis, 19–20, 22, 28–29, 30, 31, 35–36, 42, 43, 44, 45, 58–59, 61, 186, 187, 188, 189, 193, 194
Jones, Malcolm V., 52, 144, 145, 187, 188, 189, 190, 191, 194, 196
Joseph of Volokolamsk, 106
Josephians, 106

Karakozov, Dmitry, 118
Katkov, M. N., 68, 73, 87, 139
Keats, John, 20
Kelly, Catriona, 126, 127, 129, 193
kenoticism, 105–106
Kireevsky, I. V., 48, 188
Kirpotin, V. Ia., 90, 91, 191, 195
Kiukhelbeker, V. K., 17
Kjetsaa, Geir, 191, 194
Knapp, Liza, 58, 187, 188, 196
Kraeger, Linda, 187
Kukolnik, N. V., 130

Leatherbarrow, W. J., 183, 187, 188, 189, 191, 192, 193, 194, 195
Leighton, Lauren G., 185
Lermontov, M. Yu., 18–19, 47, 54, 60–61, 71–72, 135, 136, 147, 168, 186, 188, 189, 193; *The Demon*, 18–19, 60–61, 71, 135, 136; "A Fairy Tale for Children," 19; *A Hero of Our Time*, 18, 47, 72, 136, 147; *Masquerade*, 54
Linnér, Sven, 194
Liubimov, N. A., 169, 170
Loginovskaia, E. V., 135, 184, 193
Lord, Robert, 108–109, 192
Lotman, Yu. M., 4, 5, 10–11, 14, 85, 124, 183, 184, 185, 190, 193
Lunacharsky, A. V., 17

Maikov, A. N., 116, 137, 152
Matlaw, Ralph, 194
Mendeleev, D. I., 179
Miller, O. F., 186
Miller, Robin Feuer, 191
Milton, John, 4, 17–18, 135; *Paradise Lost*, 17
Mochulsky, Konstantin, 30, 45, 88, 171, 187, 188, 191, 196
Monas, Sidney, 78, 84–85, 190, 191

Morson, Gary Saul, 64–65, 136, 164, 172, 189, 194, 195, 196
Murav, Harriet, 118, 124, 129, 191, 192, 193

Natural School, 52
Nechaev, S. G., 116–17, 120
Nekrasov, N. A., 52
New Times (Novoe vremia), 56
Nicholas I, 31, 69
Nuttall, A. D., 49, 188

Offord, D., 185, 189
Oinas, Felix J., 6, 126, 184, 185, 192, 193
Otrepev, Grigory (Grishka), 5, 26, 82–83, 123, 129, 131, 133–34
Owen, Robert, 156

Pafnuty, Abbot, 105–106, 110
Paxton, Sir Joseph, 41
Peace, Richard, 21, 185, 186, 189, 191, 193, 195
Perlina, Nina, 194, 195
Perrie, Maureen, 190
Peter the Great, 24, 37, 38, 83, 85–86, 134
Petrashevsky circle, 27, 116
Petrushka: see puppet theater
Pike, Christopher, 64, 189
Piksanov, N. K., 183
Plato, 20
Pobedonostsev, K. P., 56, 169, 170, 172
Prévost, l'Abbé, 43
puppet theater, 2, 117, 125, 126–29
Pushkin, A. S., 12, 18, 26, 37, 42, 45, 47, 54, 59, 60, 82, 84, 85–86, 90, 104, 117, 118, 125, 135–36, 139, 149, 159, 189, 190; *Boris Godunov*, 26, 82, 149, 190; *The Bronze Horseman*, 84, 86; "The Demon," 18, 60, 135–36, 159; "The Devils," 45, 117, 118, 135–36; *The Miserly Knight*, 37, 42, 59; *The Queen of Spades*, 47, 82, 90; "The Shot," 54
Putney, Christopher, 107, 183, 185, 192, 195

Rabelais, François, 125
Radcliffe, Ann, 152, 173
Rahv, Philip, 66–67, 189
Rice, James L., 193

209

About the Author

W. J. Leatherbarrow is a professor of Russian at the University of Sheffield, where he also heads the School of Modern Languages and Linguistics. He is the author of *Dostoevsky's* The Devils: *A Critical Companion,* also published by Northwestern University Press.